Jean-Paul Sartre
Key Concepts

Key Concepts

Theodor Adorno: Key Concepts
Edited by Deborah Cook

Alain Badiou: Key Concepts
Edited by A. J. Bartlett and
Justin Clemens

Pierre Bourdieu: Key Concepts
Edited by Michael Grenfell

Gilles Deleuze: Key Concepts
Edited by Charles J. Stivale

Michel Foucault: Key Concepts
Edited by Dianna Taylor

Jürgen Habermas: Key Concepts
Edited by Barbara Fultner

Martin Heidegger: Key Concepts
Edited by Bret W. Davis

Immanuel Kant: Key Concepts
Edited by Will Dudley and
Kristina Engelhard

Merleau-Ponty: Key Concepts
Edited by Rosalyn Diprose and
Jack Reynolds

Jacques Rancière: Key Concepts
Edited by Jean-Philippe Deranty

Jean-Paul Sartre: Key Concepts
Edited by Steven Churchill and
Jack Reynolds

Wittgenstein: Key Concepts
Edited by Kelly Dean Jolley

Jean-Paul Sartre

Key Concepts

Edited by
Steven Churchill and Jack Reynolds

LONDON AND NEW YORK

First published in 2013 by Acumen

Published 2014 by Routledge
2 Park Square, Milton Park, Abingdon, Oxon OX14 4RN
711 Third Avenue, New York, NY 10017, USA

Routledge is an imprint of the Taylor & Francis Group, an informa business

Editorial matter and selection © Steven Churchill and Jack Reynolds, 2013.
Individual chapters © contributors, 2013

This book is copyright under the Berne Convention.
No reproduction without permission.

All rights reserved. No part of this book may be reprinted or reproduced or utilised in any form or by any electronic, mechanical, or other means, now known or hereafter invented, including photocopying and recording, or in any information storage or retrieval system, without permission in writing from the publishers.

Notices
Practitioners and researchers must always rely on their own experience and knowledge in evaluating and using any information, methods, compounds, or experiments described herein. In using such information or methods they should be mindful of their own safety and the safety of others, including parties for whom they have a professional responsibility.

To the fullest extent of the law, neither the Publisher nor the authors, contributors, or editors, assume any liability for any injury and/or damage to persons or property as a matter of products liability, negligence or otherwise, or from any use or operation of any methods, products, instructions, or ideas contained in the material herein.

ISBN: 978-1-84465-634-9 (hardcover)
ISBN: 978-1-84465-635-6 (paperback)

British Library Cataloguing-in-Publication Data
A catalogue record for this book is available from the British Library.

Typeset by JS Typesetting Ltd, Porthcawl, Mid Glamorgan.

Contents

Contributors	vii
Acknowledgements	xi
Note on abbreviations	xii

1. Introduction: Sartre *vivant*   1
   Steven Churchill and Jack Reynolds

2. Life and works   5
   Gary Cox

PART I: PSYCHOLOGY, PSYCHOANALYSIS AND LITERATURE

3. Sartre and Husserl's *Ideen*: phenomenology and imagination   12
   Beata Stawarska

4. Sartre's understanding of the self   32
   Christian Onof

5. Contingency and ego, intentionality and nausea   44
   Steven Churchill

6. Sartre: novelist and playwright   66
   Adrian van den Hoven

7. Psychoanalysis and existential psychoanalysis   76
   Betty Cannon

PART II: ONTOLOGY: FREEDOM, AUTHENTICITY AND SELF-CREATION

8.	Nothingness and negation *Sarah Richmond*	93
9.	The look *Søren Overgaard*	106
10.	Bad faith *David Detmer*	118
11.	Authenticity *Jonathan Webber*	131
12.	Knowledge *Anthony Hatzimoysis*	143
13.	The fundamental project *Paul Crittenden*	152
14.	Self-making and alienation: from bad faith to revolution *Thomas W. Busch*	163

PART III: ETHICS AND POLITICS

15.	Politics and the engaged intellectual *William L. McBride*	173
16.	Sartre's theory of groups *Peter Caws*	184
17.	Sartre's second or dialectical ethics *Thomas C. Anderson*	195
18.	Hope and affirmation: an ethics of reciprocity *Marguerite La Caze*	206
19.	Sartre's legacy *Steven Churchill and Jack Reynolds*	213
	Bibliography	229
	Index	241

Contributors

Thomas C. Anderson is a retired Professor Emeritus of Philosophy at Marquette University, Milwaukee, Wisconsin, where he also served as chair. He is the author of *The Foundation and Structure of Sartrean Ethics* (1979), *Sartre's Two Ethics: From Authenticity to Integral Humanity* (1993) and *A Commentary on Gabriel Marcel's "The Mystery of Being"* (2006), as well as many articles on Sartre, Marcel and Søren Kierkegaard. He is past president of the American Catholic Philosophical Association, and was the founder and first president of the Gabriel Marcel Society in North America.

Thomas W. Busch is Professor of Philosophy at Villanova University, and is a leading scholar in existentialism. Aside from numerous journal articles in the field, representative books include *Circulating Being: From Embodiment to Incorporation: Essays on Late Existentialism* (1999), *The Power of Consciousness and the Force of Circumstances in Sartre's Philosophy* (1990), and *Merleau-Ponty, Hermeneutics and Postmodernism* (edited with Shaun Gallagher, 1992).

Betty Cannon is Adjunct Professor at Naropa University and Professor Emerita of the Colorado School of Mines, where she taught literature and psychology for twenty years. She is the author of *Sartre and Psychoanalysis* (1991), and numerous chapters and articles on existential therapy. She is a member of the editorial boards for three professional journals: *Sartre Studies International*, *Review of Existential Psychology and Psychiatry*, and *Existential Analysis*.

CONTRIBUTORS

Peter Caws is University Professor Emeritus of Philosophy at The George Washington University in Washington, DC. His eight books and more than 150 articles include work on the philosophy of the natural sciences, on ethics and continental philosophy (Sartre and the structuralists), and more recently on psychoanalysis and the human sciences. His books include *Religious Upbringing and the Costs of Freedom: Personal and Philosophical Essays* (co-edited with Stefani Jones, 2010), *Structuralism: A Philosophy for the Human Sciences* (1997), and *Sartre* (1979, 1984).

Steven Churchill has lectured in the Melbourne School of Continental Philosophy, including on Jean-Paul Sartre's philosophy and literature. He has also served as tutor in Philosophy at La Trobe University, and is writing a PhD on Sartre and Flaubert.

Gary Cox is an honorary research fellow at the University of Birmingham, and the author of several books on Sartre, existentialism and general philosophy, including *The Sartre Dictionary* (2008), *How to Be an Existentialist* (2009) and *The God Confusion* (2013).

Paul Crittenden is an Emeritus Professor of Philosophy in the School of Philosophical and Historical Inquiry at the University of Sydney. He writes mainly on topics in ethics and epistemology, Greek philosophy, and modern European philosophy from Nietzsche to Sartre. Recent publications include *Sartre in Search of an Ethics* (2009) and *Reason, Emotion and Will* (2012).

David Detmer is a Professor of Philosophy at Purdue University Calumet. He is the author of *Sartre Explained* (2008), *Challenging Postmodernism: Philosophy and the Politics of Truth* (2003) and *Freedom as a Value* (1988). He is executive editor of *Sartre Studies International* and a past president of the North American Sartre Society.

Anthony Hatzimoysis is Associate Professor at the History and Philosophy of Science Department of the University of Athens. He is the author of *The Philosophy of Sartre* (Acumen, 2011), and editor of *Philosophy and the Emotions* (2003) and *Self-Knowledge* (2011).

Marguerite La Caze is Associate Professor in Philosophy at the University of Queensland. She has research interests and numerous publications in European and feminist philosophy. Her publications include *The Analytic Imaginary* (2002), *Integrity and the Fragile Self* (with

CONTRIBUTORS

Damian Cox and Michael Levine, 2003), *Wonder and Generosity: Their Role in Ethics and Politics* (forthcoming 2013) and articles in *Contemporary Political Theory*, *Derrida Today*, *Hypatia*, *Parrhesia*, *Philosophy and Social Criticism*, *Philosophy Today*, *Political Theory*, *Simone de Beauvoir Studies*, *Symposium* and other journals, and book collections, including on Jean-Paul Sartre, existentialism, Hannah Arendt, Simone de Beauvoir, Sigmund Freud and Michèle Le Dœuff.

William L. McBride is Arthur G. Hansen Distinguished Professor of Philosophy at Purdue University, and the president of the International Federation of Philosophical Societies (FISP), of which there 120 national and international member societies. He is also former president of the North American Society for Social Philosophy and co-founder and former director of the North American Sartre Society. He has authored, edited and co-edited nineteen books – among them *Sartre's Political Theory* (1991), *Social and Political Philosophy* (1994) and *Philosophical Reflections on the Changes in Eastern Europe* (1999) – and published well over 100 journal articles and book chapters.

Christian Onof is Honorary Research Fellow in Philosophy at Birkbeck College, University of London. He has published on Kant's ethics and metaphysics (*Kant Studien*, *Kant Yearbook*), on Heidegger and Sartre, as well as on the nature of consciousness (*Philosophy and Phenomenological Research*, *Journal of Mind and Behavior*). He is co-founder of the journal *Episteme*, and on the editorial board of *Kant Studies Online*. He is reader at the Faculty of Engineering, Imperial College London.

Søren Overgaard is Associate Professor of Philosophy at the University of Copenhagen. He is the author of *Husserl and Heidegger on Being in the World* (2004) and *Wittgenstein and Other Minds* (2007), co-author of *An Introduction to Metaphilosophy* (2013) and co-editor of *The Routledge Companion to Phenomenology* (2011).

Jack Reynolds is Associate Professor in Philosophy at La Trobe University and Deputy Dean of the Faculty of Humanities and Social Sciences. He is author of *Chronopathologies: Time and Politics in Deleuze, Derrida, Analytic Philosophy and Phenomenology* (2012), *Understanding Existentialism* (2006) and *Merleau-Ponty and Derrida: Intertwining Embodiment and Alterity* (2004). He is also co-author of *Analytic versus Continental: Arguments on the Methods and Value of Philosophy* (2010), and co-editor of *Continuum Companion to Existentialism* (2011) and *Merleau-Ponty: Key Concepts* (2008).

CONTRIBUTORS

Sarah Richmond is Senior Lecturer in Philosophy at University College, London. Her primary research interest has been in recent French philosophy, especially phenomenology, existentialism and deconstruction and she has published several articles on Sartre's early philosophy. Other interests include feminism and some questions within applied ethics. She is the co-editor of a collection of essays on the ethical implications of brain imaging, *I Know What You're Thinking* (with Geraint Rees and Sarah J. L. Edwards, 2012).

Beata Stawarska is Associate Professor of Philosophy at the University of Oregon. She has published numerous articles on Sartre's relation to phenomenology and psychology, and on the applicability of his concepts to developments in contemporary cognitive sciences. These essays have been published in *Phenomenology and the Cognitive Sciences*, *Sartre Studies International* and *International Journal for Interdisciplinary Studies*. She is also an author of *Between You and I: Dialogical Phenomenology* (2009) and *Saussure's Philosophy of Language* (forthcoming).

Adrian van den Hoven is Professor Emeritus at the University of Windsor, Ontario. He was a founding executive editor of *Sartre Studies International* and was twice elected president of the North American Sartre Society. He has translated Jean-Paul Sartre's *Truth and Existence* (1992) and Jean-Paul Sartre/Benny Lévy's *Hope Now: The 1980 Interviews* (1996) for the University of Chicago Press. He has also co-edited several publications on Sartre and Albert Camus and published articles on them, as well as on Simone de Beauvoir. Together with Ronald Aronson he has co-edited *Jean-Paul Sartre: We Have Only This Life to Live, Selected Essays: 1939–1975* (2013).

Jonathan Webber is Reader in Philosophy at Cardiff University. He is the author of *The Existentialism of Jean-Paul Sartre* (2009), editor of *Reading Sartre: on Phenomenology and Existentialism* (2011), and translator of Sartre's book *The Imaginary* (2004). He has published papers on moral psychology and virtue ethics in leading philosophy journals, including *European Journal of Philosophy*, *Journal of Moral Philosophy*, *Mind* and *Philosophical Quarterly*.

Acknowledgements

We would like to thank all those who assisted us in the planning, production and editing of this book. In particular, we owe a debt of gratitude to Jo Shiells for her assistance in preparing earlier drafts of the manuscript, and especially in compiling bibliographical references. Ricky Sebold assisted us greatly in compiling the index. We are extremely grateful to each of the contributing authors for their commitment to this book, many of whom have very significant teaching and research loads to contend with. We wish to thank everyone at Acumen Publishing involved in bringing this book to publication.

On a personal note, we would like to thank our families for their love and ongoing support.

Note on abbreviations

There are many different editions, with different pagination, of *Being and Nothingness* in English, notwithstanding that Hazel Barnes remains the only translator of the entirety of the text. We have standardized all references to refer to the pagination of the two most commonly circulated Routledge editions: the one published between 1969 and 2003 (abbreviation BN1), and the one published since 2003, when the pages were reset (BN2). The French pagination is also included where provided, indicated by EN. Other references to Sartre texts are made with the author–date system.

ONE

Introduction: Sartre *vivant*

Steven Churchill and Jack Reynolds

Most philosophers live and die in relative obscurity. If they are both insightful and fortunate, they sometimes achieve a measure of fame and posterity afterwards. Jean-Paul Sartre (1905–80) bucked this trend. Perhaps no other philosopher was as famous in his own time as Sartre, or so we would claim. Fame, of course, does not entail or denote value, whether it be philosophical value or otherwise. It can also be fleeting, as the posthumous life of Henri Bergson showed, at least for quite some years. Sartre also seemed "dead" in academic circles, perhaps twenty years ago, and much earlier in France. Sartre himself would no doubt have been unhappy to learn of this posthumous fate; after all, in his beautifully crafted autobiography, entitled *Words* (1964), he positioned his life's work as a writer as rooted in his desire to achieve a kind of immortality through his writings, which would survive him into posterity. It became fashionable to declare that we have "been there and done that", as far as the study of Sartre's life and works are concerned, and have long since moved on.

Yet those declaring that all there was to be known about Sartre had already been written (whether by Sartre himself or by others) were arguably doing so from a position of "bad faith", as Sartre might have said. Perhaps those dismissing Sartre as irrelevant had read and enjoyed some of Sartre's short stories, plays or novels, such as *Nausea* (*La Nausée*; Sartre 1938, 1965a). Maybe they had read Sartre's famous public lecture, *Existentialism and Humanism* (*L'Existentialisme est un humanisme*; Sartre 1946b, 1973), or even thumbed their way through parts of *Being and Nothingness* (*L'Être et le néant*; Sartre 1943a, 1958a). Few, though, would have examined Sartre's earlier, psychologically motivated philosophical works in any real depth, such as *Imagination* (*L'Imagination*; Sartre 1936, 1972a) or its sequel, *The Imaginary* (*L'Imaginaire*; Sartre 1940, 2004a); then there is *The Transcendence of the Ego* ("La Transcendance de l'ego"; Sartre 1936–7, 1957a) to be considered, not to mention his *Sketch for a Theory of the Emotions* (*Esquisse d'une théorie des emotions*; Sartre 1939a, 2002). Fewer still have attempted to grapple with Sartre's later works, including his massive two-volume *Critique of Dialectical Reason* (*Critique de la raison dialectique*; vol. 1: Sartre 1960b, 1960c; vol. 2: Sartre 1985b, 2006), or his multi-volume masterpiece, *The Family Idiot* (*L'Idiot de la famille*; Sartre 1971–2, 1981c, 1987, 1989a, 1991a, 1993c). Indeed, parts of Sartre's body of work – particularly those projects that he had started but simply never finished – only appeared quite some years after his death; the *Notebooks for an Ethics* (*Cahiers pour une morale*; written during 1947–8, but only published in 1983 in French, and in 1992 in English translation), which Sartre composed while initially trying to construct an ethical philosophy, provide an important example of the extent to which Sartre's body of work has continued to grow and develop, even in his absence. So, then, those claiming to have "exhausted" Sartre's body of work, thereby safely confining his intellectual figure to a halcyon period, had typically read and understood only a fraction of his vast, and *ongoing* contributions, made across multiple fields of inquiry.

Since Sartre's works have yet to be understood and appreciated in their full depth as the totality they represent, we would argue that Sartre is very much *alive*, particularly for those willing to resist these persistent claims of irrelevancy. Today, there are new biographies and scholarly interpretations that extend understanding of his thought into texts that simply never received the attention they deserved, there are reissues of his earlier works, and various books on Sartre and existentialism continue to appear. Recently, *Les Temps modernes* (*Modern Times*), the journal founded by Sartre and his life-long partner Simone de Beauvoir, published a special edition entitled *The Readers of Sartre*, intended to rebut the claim that Sartre is no longer read, either in France or elsewhere. The current editorial director of *Les Temps modernes*, famed documentary filmmaker Claude Lanzmann (himself a close friend to Sartre), asserted that "it is simply not true" that Sartre has faded into obscurity.

Despite these positive developments, much remains to be done in the field of Sartre scholarship. Perhaps the most important of these tasks is to try to grasp Sartre's works as the totality we have just now asserted they represent. While we do not claim in this concise volume to achieve anything approaching a totalizing perspective on Sartre's works, we do seek to make a small start toward this immense project, by attempting to make Sartre's broader body of work accessible to a wider audience. By bringing together a diverse group of philosophers working across multiple disciplines, we hope to introduce those new to Sartre to works of his beyond those that appear regularly in the public domain, such as the *Existentialism and Humanism* lecture or *Nausea*. At the same time, we hope to provide those familiar with Sartre's works with a range of perspectives which may serve to spur new insights and further research.

With these goals of achieving a balance of both breadth and depth in mind, we have sought to organize the essays in this volume thematically, rather than in terms of a strict chronology of Sartre's works. Nevertheless, the three parts may be loosely defined as representing Sartre's early philosophy (in Part I), Sartre's "middle period" as a mature thinker (in Part II) and, finally, Sartre's later thought (in Part III).

Part I, Psychology, Psychoanalysis and Literature, deals primarily with Sartre's efforts to give an account of the human condition in terms of a phenomenological psychology and existential psychoanalysis. This part encompasses Sartre's early perspectives on the imagination, selfhood, and the emotions and so on, as well as Sartre's dramatization of these themes in literary form in *Nausea*.

Part II, Ontology: Freedom, Authenticity and Self-Creation, deals with the development of Sartre's early phenomenology into a mature phenomenological ontology, particularly as it appears in *Being and Nothingness*. The conceptual terrain covered here includes Sartre's conceptualizations of "bad faith", authenticity and the fundamental project, along with Sartre's account of inter-social relations via his notion of "the look". Part II concludes with an account of Sartre's intellectual trajectory from a relatively apolitical writer to a politically engaged provocateur *par excellence*.

In Part III, Ethics and Politics, the overview of Sartre's political progression initially continues; particular attention paid to his post-war works, including *What Is Literature?* (*Qu'est-ce que la littérature?*; Sartre 1948a, 1988), *Anti-Semite and Jew* (*Réflexions sur la question juive*; Sartre 1946a, 1948b) and "Materialism and Revolution" ("Matérialisme et révolution"; Sartre 1946c, 1962a). Then, Sartre's theory of groups is considered, bringing to light Sartre's conceptualizations of revolutionary praxis and institutional power, particularly in the *Critique of Dialectical Reason*, but also in *The Family Idiot*. Sartre's attempt to produce an ethics guided by his view of Marxian dialectics then follows, in which Sartre's concepts of "need" and "scarcity" serve as the main elements in his vision for an ethical society, under socialism.

Part III concludes with a perspective on Sartre's final efforts towards an ethics, as chronicled in his final interviews in 1980. Sartre's concepts of "need" and "scarcity" that featured in his dialectical ethics are complemented in these interviews by his concept of "reciprocity" (alternatively described as an ethics of the "We"). Ethical action is driven here by the ideal that individuals may relate to each other in a way that positions the Other's interests and needs as continuous with one's own. In this "fraternal" mode of being-together, the objective of ending scarcity and lack would become goals shared in common by all of humanity, bringing about truly ethical relations between human beings.

Although the essays in this volume are organized according to a thematic and loosely chronological order as we have noted, the essays may also be read as self-contained articles, should readers so desire. Søren Overgaard's chapter on "the look", for example, provides context on the development of Sartre's ontology, such that the central concept of the look is sufficiently explained, without the need to refer to subsequent chapters. At the same time, though, each chapter is designed to build on the one that precedes it; suggested further readings at the end of each chapter are designed to both explore the ideas covered in a particular chapter, and to encourage further research and discovery.

In his moving obituary for his friend and colleague Maurice Merleau-Ponty (1908–61), entitled "Merleau-Ponty *vivant*" – that is, "Merleau-Ponty alive", or "Merleau-Ponty lives" – Sartre asserted that "Merleau is still too much alive for anyone to be able to describe him" (Sartre 1961). We assert that the same may be said of Sartre himself, even now, over three decades after his death. Even a volume many thousands of words longer than this collection would still leave something of Sartre fleeing beyond one's grasp, so to speak. Nevertheless, this posthumous elusiveness of Sartre is confirmation for us – and, no doubt, for the marvellous group of contributors appearing in this collection – of one thing: Jean-Paul Sartre *vivant*!

TWO

Life and works
Gary Cox

The keynote speaker at the 2011 UK Sartre Society Conference in London was Annie Cohen-Solal, Sartre's foremost biographer and author of the magnificent *Jean-Paul Sartre: A Life* (Cohen-Solal 2005). Her chosen theme was a series of public lectures Sartre gave in the early 1930s, during his time as a school teacher in Le Havre. Sartre's time in Le Havre has been characterized as his wilderness years – the brilliant student of the prestigious Parisian École Normale Supérieure exiled to the provinces, unappreciated, unpublished and unhappy. Yet they were also hugely formative and creative years for Sartre: a nine-month sabbatical in Berlin in 1933 to study the phenomenology of Edmund Husserl and the incessant revising of a work on contingency that eventually became the classic existentialist novel *Nausea* (Sartre 1938, 1965a).

Sartre's chosen theme for his public lectures was literature. Like his great friend and lifelong intellectual sparring partner, Simone de Beauvoir, Sartre was interested in contemporary English and American literature; in the novels of Virginia Woolf, James Joyce, Aldous Huxley, John Dos Passos and William Faulkner. Sartre's original lecture notes are lost, but fortunately Cohen-Solal possesses photocopies of several pages of them. She told an enthralled conference how she was summoned one morning by de Beauvoir, who appeared at the door of her Paris apartment in one of her famous turbans. She did not invite Cohen-Solal in, but handed her a sheaf of papers with strict instructions to have the material back by the end of the day. Cohen-Solal hastened to the nearest Xerox machine.

The photocopies, a sample of which Cohen-Solal passed around the audience, show de Beauvoir's neat, clear handwriting on the left, with Sartre's scribble on the right. De Beauvoir had clearly translated passages of the aforementioned novelists for Sartre to analyse. Sartre's lectures explore the techniques of these English and American novelists, particularly their use of "stream of consciousness" to reveal the depths of the unconscious mind. In his lectures Sartre philosophizes about literature and in so doing develops himself as a philosopher, novelist and literary critic. Not least, he sows the seeds of what later became his theory of existential psychoanalysis.

Sartre is famous for his wide and copious reading. He devoured thousands of texts in his lifetime, always looking to feed his own theories, and in his early days was capable of producing a new or modified theory on a daily or even thrice-daily basis. He had no respect for the constraints of the traditional divisions between philosophy, psychology and literature and tended to see each as somewhat retarded when isolated from the others. Always a supreme interdisciplinarian, he advocated a more philosophical psychology and a more literary philosophy. In his *Sketch for a Theory of the Emotions* (Sartre 1939a, 2002), for example, he argues that pure psychology will only make genuine progress when it takes on board the insights of philosophy, or, more specifically, phenomenology. Meanwhile, *Nausea* demonstrates that some of the most profound philosophical insights into the human condition can only be achieved through literature, or more specifically the novel form. Sartre was a philosopher in the broadest, truest and best sense of the word: a lover of wisdom wherever and however expressed.

Sartre succeeded in breaking down many traditional, stultifying barriers between intellectual subjects and in so doing opened up many new territories to intellectual enquiry. It is this that is perhaps the most impressive feature of his life's work. The longer one studies him, the more territories appear. Perhaps these territories cannot be enumerated because where Sartre did not explore a territory so thoroughly as to make it his own, he pointed the way towards it, either promising to reach it himself in due course or inviting others to investigate his sketchy insights.

In a sense, the number of Sartre territories there are seems now to depend on which of his myriad insights Sartre scholars wish to pursue. There is much work to be done, for example, in developing the ethical aspects of Sartre's theory of authenticity in light of the posthumous publication of his *Notebooks for an Ethics* (Sartre 1983b, 1992). This research cannot ignore Sartre the post-Kantian, Sartre the Marxist, or even Sartre the post-Aristotelian virtue theorist. And whatever emerges from this particular intellectual labour must surely influence our understanding of Sartre's existential psychoanalysis and therefore the practice of existential counselling. Today, to name just a few areas of enquiry, there are Sartre scholars exploring his ideas on ontology, consciousness, imagination, anti-Semitism, colonialism, revolution, biography, French literature, freedom and bad faith. One has only to consider the wide variety of themes explored in this present volume to be reminded of the extraordinary breadth of Sartre's thought.

As already suggested, Sartre's many territories are not best seen as separate areas that he chose to explore at one time or another during his long career. His territories must instead be seen as integrated regions of a single, extensive landscape. Or, to employ a slightly different (and hopefully more revealing) topographical metaphor, his extensive writings seek to comprehensively schematize the complex landscape of the human condition with all the accuracy, honesty and attention to detail of an Ordnance Survey map.

Sartre knew that the complex landscape of the human condition is best mapped out by writing in a variety of literary media. Straightforward philosophical writing may be best when it comes to pinning down the abstract fundamentals of a theory, but at other times only the novel, with its irony, its capacity for description, and its ability to capture ideas through atmosphere and action, is sufficiently subtle to do the job. Sometimes, a play or a film script may be more effective at saying what needs to be said than a novel, or a biography may serve better than a play and so on. Sartre was not a philosopher who happened to have a quirky sideline in short stories, novels, plays, biographies, diaries and film scripts. Each literary form makes a unique and indispensable contribution to the intricate and integrated whole that is his complex, multifaceted philosophy. If Sartre were alive today he would undoubtedly further enrich his oeuvre by blogging and tweeting.

Sartre's compelling need to understand, theorize, explain and provoke, in whatever literary media best served his purposes, was matched only by his compulsion to write. Contrary to popular myth, Sartre was not into drugs. He liked to drink alcohol and smoke tobacco, but he took a hallucinogenic drug only once in his life, in 1935, as part of a medically controlled experiment. He wanted to experience a genuine hallucination so that he could write about it in his book *The Imaginary* (Sartre 1940, 2004a). As for his famous penchant for speed, the ageing Sartre took far too many Corydrane tablets, a once legally available mixture of aspirin and amphetamine. His aim was not intoxication but warding off tiredness in order to maintain his prodigious literary output. It is doubtful that he could have written *Critique of Dialectical Reason* (Sartre 1960b, 1985b), his vast two-volume synthesis of existentialism and Marxism, without the tablets. So, Sartre was not addicted to drugs but to writing. As an existential psychoanalyst might argue, Sartre, like many a so-called drug addict, used drugs to fuel a far deeper addiction.

From childhood, he wrote for six hours a day most days of his life. As he writes in his 1964 autobiography *Words*, "My commandments have been sewn into my skin: if I go a day without writing, the scar burns me; and if I write too easily, it also burns me" (Sartre 2000a: 104). Sartre also says in *Words* that his books "reek of sweat and effort" (*ibid*.: 103), but the truth is that with the help of a little chemical stimulation as he grew older, he was more often than not possessed by a kind of total fluency that allowed him to write without pausing: the next idea, the next sentence, always ready to be set down on paper as required. Sartre was fond of arguing that genius is as genius does, and he is surely right that the genius of a great writer consists in his or her work. As he writes in *Existentialism and Humanism*, "The genius of Proust is the totality of the works of Proust; the genius of Racine is the series of his tragedies, outside of which there is nothing" (Sartre 1993a: 41–2). The creation of Sartre's genius in the form of his body of work, however, was surely facilitated to a considerable extent by his rare talent for total fluency. As they say, you've either got it or you haven't, and he had it in abundance.

Sartre might reluctantly accept that he had a *natural* ability as far as his fluency was concerned, but he would insist that it was what he chose to do with his ability that was all important, that brought it into reality. Without his choice and self-determination to write, his natural ability would have been nothing.

This is not to say that what Sartre churned out was not in need of extensive revision and editing. When he went blind in 1973 he said that he could no longer write because he could no longer undertake the necessary revisions he felt were necessary to convey certain ideas in a certain style. He was not satisfied with simply dictating his thoughts. The younger Sartre, with considerable help from de Beauvoir, was willing to rewrite and polish with the kind of attention to detail that produced *Nausea*, his stylistic masterpiece. As he grew older, busier and more directly involved in political campaigning around the world, however, much of his output was less well edited.

Another feature of the output of the older Sartre was the number of significant but nonetheless *unfinished* works that he produced. Always fond of working on more than one project at once, it was inevitable that not everything he started would be finished. Not least, an old theory would be eclipsed by a new one, while one French writer would suddenly seem a far more worthy subject for a biography than another. But as he grew older he was in danger of never finishing anything. This seems an unfair accusation, as his unfinished *Critique of Dialectical Reason*, for example, is two huge volumes long, while his unfinished *The Family Idiot* (Sartre 1971–2) – a biography of Gustave Flaubert – is three huge volumes long, 2,081 pages in all. Sartre had more and more to say as he got older, at least until the cataclysm of his blindness in 1973. He was a man in a hurry, a man obsessed with opening up new intellectual territories while he still had the brain power and eyesight to do so. Fine-tuning everything he produced would have required a wealth of time he simply did not possess.

Fortunately, not all the works of the later Sartre are unfinished and somewhat unpolished. *Words*, in particular, is finished, highly stylized and beautifully crafted; a work to rival *Nausea* or *Being and Nothingness* (Sartre 1943a, BN1, BN2). *Words* secured the offer of the 1964 Nobel Prize for Literature, which Sartre politely declined on the grounds that "The writer must refuse to let himself be transformed by institutions, even if these are of the most honourable kind" (Sartre press statement to Carl-Gustav Bjurström, 22 October 1964).

Words is not the vast autobiography that one would expect from a man whose life was so eventful and historic, spanning two world wars, and who was so in the habit of writing such immense tomes as *Being and Nothingness* and the Roads to Freedom trilogy (Sartre 1945a, 1945c, 1949a). A surprisingly slim volume, *Words* is nonetheless packed with concise and wittily expressed ideas, observations, ironies and sentiments. Like all of Sartre's biographies – *Baudelaire* (Sartre 1947b), *Saint Genet* (Sartre 1952, 1963) and *The Family Idiot* – it is an exercise in existential psychoanalysis. It is certainly the place to go to discover what, according to Sartre, really made Sartre tick.

Sartre was little over one year old when his father died. His mother and her father worshipped the child, viewing him as a being "meant to be". The child, however, was not fooled by the myth of his own necessity, and from a surprisingly early age felt that his existence was absurd and pointless. He dreamt he was travelling on life's train without a ticket, without justification or purpose. He soon realized that only he could give himself a purpose and he chose writing as his *raison d'être*. He adopted the ambition of becoming a great, dead French writer, although of course he knew he had to live a relatively long life first in order to achieve this goal. This was his *fundamental choice* of himself, an original choice of self that influenced all subsequent choices and so shaped his life.

The notion of fundamental choice as the basis of each person's fundamental life project is central to Sartre's existentialism: his philosophy and psychology of the human condition. His childhood sense that a person is nothing more than what he or she chooses to be was reinforced by his study of philosophy. He learnt from Kant, Hegel, Husserl, Bergson and Heidegger that consciousness is relational rather than an entity in its own right, that it exists only as a temporal consciousness of the world and is nothing beyond that. The central principles of Sartre's worldview unfold readily from this basic premise regarding the nothingness of consciousness.

As we are essentially nothing, whatever we are, we must choose to be it. We are burdened with the constant responsibility of having to choose, or, as Sartre puts it, we are "condemned to be free" (BN1: 439; BN2: 462). Of course, there are certain givens: our body, our immediate physical situation, our mortality. Sartre calls these givens *facticity*. Facticity does not limit freedom because freedom is not doing whatever one imagines but constantly having to choose in face of one's facticity: what to do with one's body, one's circumstances, one's limited life span; what meaning to give to it all. Constantly having to choose what we are by choosing what we do makes us anxious. We would like to be complete, a being at one with itself rather than a being constantly striving for completion in a future that is never reached. So most, if not all of us resort to some degree of bad faith, fooling ourselves that we are fixed entities that need not or cannot choose. We use our freedom to try and cancel out our freedom by choosing not to choose. But as Sartre points out, "Not to choose is, in fact, to choose not to choose" (BN1: 481; BN2: 503).

Bad faith cannot achieve its goal, and the person in bad faith lives their life in denial, refusing to positively affirm their freedom. The existentialist holy grail of authenticity involves a person overcoming their bad faith, recognizing that they are inalienably free and living their life accordingly. In practice, this involves living a life without regrets or excuses, throwing oneself into each situation and meeting its demands head on. As Sartre writes in his war diaries:

> To be authentic is to realize fully one's being-in-situation, whatever this situation may happen to be ... This presupposes a patient study of what the situation requires, and then a way of throwing oneself into it and determining oneself to "be-for" this situation.
> (Sartre 2000b: 54)

Sartre recognized that humans are very flawed and that the goal of authenticity is therefore very difficult to obtain. Indeed, he admitted his own failure to achieve it. "I am not authentic. I have halted on the threshold of the promised lands. But at least I point the way to them and others can go there" (*ibid*.: 62). Arguably, the holy grail of *sustained* authenticity is just too difficult for anyone to achieve, in that it must be maintained moment by moment in face of life's myriad temptations to slide back into bad faith. Just as one cannot *be* anything, only play at being it, one cannot simply *be* authentic. To believe that one *is* authentic, as a stone *is* a stone, is simply another form of bad faith. Nonetheless, authenticity is a goal worth striving for if one wants to live life to the full and draw near to achieving one's full potential.

Certainly, Sartre's life was that of a man constantly striving against bad faith in light of the nagging realization that he was inalienably free. From childhood, he knew that he was nothing more than what he chose to be, that he had no destiny other than the destiny he must create for himself. He wrote to construct an identity for himself out of nothing and the central purpose of his writing, beyond saving himself, was to remind people of their own essential nothingness and inalienable freedom; of the great and pressing need to respect freedom in themselves and in others. At the end of *Words* he writes, "I have never seen myself as the happy owner of a 'talent': my one concern was to save myself – nothing in my hands, nothing in my pockets – through work and faith" (Sartre 2000a: 158). These words echo a passage from his play *Kean* (1954, 1994). Like Sartre, like all of us, the great Shakespearean actor Edmund Kean was nothing beyond the parts he played. "I live from day to day in a fabulous imposture. Not a farthing, nothing in my hands, nothing in my pockets, but I need only snap my fingers to summon spirits of the air" (Sartre 1994: act 2, 31).

Further reading

Cox, G. 2009. *Sartre and Fiction*. London: Continuum.
Manser, A. 1981. *Sartre: A Philosophic Study*. Oxford: Greenwood Press.
Murdoch, I. 1968. *Sartre: Romantic Rationalist*. London: Fontana.
Webber, J. 2009. *The Existentialism of Jean-Paul Sartre*. London: Routledge.

THREE

Sartre and Husserl's *Ideen*: phenomenology and imagination
Beata Stawarska

> With [the] distinction [between noetic and noematic analysis] … there becomes salient a distinction between two realms of being which are radically opposed and yet essentially related to one another. (Husserl 1983: §128)

> Since the being of consciousness is radically different, its meaning … is opposed to the being-in-itself of the phenomenon.
> (BN1/BN2: Introduction)

Sartre's relation to Husserl may seem curious, if not downright paradoxical. An outspoken enthusiast of phenomenology, which would liberate philosophy of its idealist heritage and bring it back into the world, Sartre was simultaneously, and just as passionately, an uncompromising critic of the methodological and categorical apparatus the Husserl of *Ideen I* (first published 1913; translated as *Ideas Pertaining to a Pure Phenomenology and to a Phenomenological Philosophy*, Husserl 1983) put into the service of mapping out transcendental consciousness. One could dissolve this paradox by deeming Sartre faithful to the perceived spirit of Husserl's phenomenology, but not to its word. Yet such a settlement glosses over the fact that this paradox is not simply a result of a scholarly disagreement. Sartre holds philosophy accountable in the face of the world where suffering, hunger and the war are both a possibility and a daily reality – the philosophical task cannot therefore ever be confined to a narrowly epistemological problem, but must also be existential, ethical and political. Husserl's phenomenology was oriented towards the more classically academic task of ascertaining true knowledge and founding a rigorous philosophical science. Even though Husserl's phenomenology opened up a window out of the comfortable refuge of interiority celebrated in idealism and out onto the world, it took its role to be that of providing an alternative school of thought, hence lacking in the kind of engagement and commitment Sartre sought. Sartre's eventual alignment of phenomenology with idealism in the late 1930s testifies of his crisis of faith in a philosophy that was too attached to ideas and representations in its doctrine, but also, and more importantly, too attached to the comfortable refuge of the academia in its practice and way of life. The manifest tension in Sartre's relation to Husserl extends then beyond doctrinal and methodological disagreements, and touches on the problem, what are we, philosophers, to do?

This tension between differing philosophical aspirations sheds some light on the fact that Sartre, a self-professed Husserlian, could have been both transformed and animated by Husserl's vision of philosophy as phenomenology, and actively rebelling against its perceived traditionalism, especially the concessions made to a thinking that softens the bite of reality by turning it into a representation. Thus, while Sartre caught a glimpse of the liberating potential of the phenomenological method, he seemed just as eager to liberate the set of doctrines espoused by Husserl's phenomenology from its perceived *scholastism* (in the literal and not historical sense of the word). No furniture adopted from the older schools of thought, especially the idealism taught by Brunschwicg and dominating the philosophical climate at the École Normale Superieure during Sartre studies, should populate the cleared phenomenological field. Sartre is then an anti-scholastic thinker in seeking to take philosophy out of the school; this disposition clashes with Husserl's motivation to establish phenomenology as a recognized academic discipline, on a par with the sciences. The overt disagreements between Sartre and Husserl discussed below can only be deciphered, in my view, within this larger horizon of differing visions of the philosopher's tasks and responsibilities.

Sartre's introductions to Husserl

While Sartre's engagement with Husserl's *Ideen I* can be safely dated back to 1933–4, the time Sartre spent at the Maison Académique Française (the French Institute in Berlin), it is much harder to date his initial exposure and interest in Husserl's phenomenology, which precipitated him to read Husserl closely. Husserl's phenomenology was largely unknown in France at the time; Sartre did not attend Husserl's lectures at the Sorbonne on 23–6 February 1929 (Contat & Rybalka 1981: xlvi). His initial exposure would probably have been channelled via informal conversations within his circle of friends and acquaintances rather than through institutions.

The most oft-cited account of such a conversation is the one given by Simone de Beauvoir in the second book of her memoirs, *La Force de l'âge* (de Beauvoir 1989, first published in 1960). According to her testimony, Sartre's (and de Beauvoir's) interest in Husserl's *Ideen I* was inspired by the now famed conversation over apricot cocktails in a Parisian café with Raymond Aron in 1932. Excited by this exchange, Sartre reportedly dragged de Beauvoir around Paris on a search for a book dealing with Husserl's phenomenology. They found Levinas's *La Théorie de l'intuition dans la phénoménologie de Husserl* (Levinas [1930] 1963), and Sartre was "so eager to inform himself on the subject that he leafed through the volume as we walked along, without even having cut the pages" (de Beauvoir 1989: 157; de Beauvoir 2001: 135, 112). Sartre later himself recalls this conversation in a 1972 interview, although the beverage in question was, in his memory, a glass of beer (Sartre 1978: 26). Sartre concurs that his and de Beauvoir's discovery of Husserl took place during the conversation with Aron and emphasizes that Husserl's influence began "no earlier than 1933" (*ibid.*: 25). In the interview, Sartre notes the great promise Husserl's phenomenology held for describing the concrete reality of things. As he put it: "Well, I can tell you that knocked me out. I said to myself: 'now here at long last is a philosophy'. We thought a great deal about one thing: the concrete" (*ibid.*: 26). The necessity of moving towards the concrete was deeply felt by the young French intellectuals around that time, and expressed forcefully in Jean Wahl's influential monograph *Vers le concret* (Wahl 1932), which argued for a move away from a philosophy founded on idealism and theory towards a description of reality as encountered in everyday life.

A slightly earlier dating of Sartre's initial exposure to Husserl is given in a more recently published series of interviews, *Talking with Sartre: Conversations and Debates* by John Gerassi (2009). Questioned about his Berlin stay, Sartre responds:

> I got the same fellowship to go study [in Berlin in 1933] that Raymond Aron had the previous year. He helped me get that deal and so he also gets the credit for introducing me to phenomenology, but as you know it was your father [Fernando Gerassi] who did that. (*Ibid.*: 25)

Dismissing Aron as "another con man", Sartre states:

> your father [Fernando Gerassi] talked to me about Husserl for two years before Aron went to Germany. I even had read a book by Lévinas about it. No, what Aron made me want to do is go to Germany, all expenses paid, to have a good time. (*Ibid.*: 253)[1]

This testimony puts pressure on Aron's self-attributed credit for Sartre's initial interest in Husserl in general and *Ideen I* in particular. Since Sartre refers to "the book by Levinas" (i.e. Levinas [1930] 1963) in the context of his conversation about his introduction by Fernando Gerassi to Husserl, it is feasible that he read it before the conversation with Aron. Sartre seems to corroborate this inverse chronology in "Une vie pour la philosophie" (Rybalka 2000).

De Beauvoir herself may have played a more active role in introducing Sartre to phenomenology than her memoir suggests. According to Margaret Simons, de Beauvoir may have been introduced to Husserl's phenomenology via her Sorbonne professor Jean Baruzi in 1927 (de Beauvoir 2006). A student of Husserl's phenomenology, Baruzi gave a lecture in 1926 on Leibniz that referred to Husserl's phenomenology and the method of reduction; he completed a dissertation in 1924, published in 1931 as *Saint Jean de la Croix et le problème de l'expérience mystique*, which gives an existential description of religious anguish and the lived experience of the mystic (Baruzi 1931). Simons notes that even though de Beauvoir credits Sartre with introducing her to phenomenology in the 1930s, "given her close work with Baruzi in 1927, it is possible that she misrepresented the date of her introduction to phenomenology just as she did her early interest in philosophy" (de Beauvoir 2006: 49n). De Beauvoir, who actively deployed the phenomenological category of lived experience in her own work, would then likely have had some familiarity with Husserl's phenomenology when she met Sartre in 1929.

There is also evidence that Sartre was holding weekly conversations for two and a half months in 1928 with the Japanese philosopher Baron Shuzo Kuki, a student of Husserl in Freiburg and of Heidegger in Marburg, where the topic of German phenomenology was regularly brought up. Shuzo Kuki therefore deserves credit for steering Sartre towards phenomenology a number of years before Aron (Light 1987: 4).

In sum, Sartre's multiple introductions to Husserl in the 1920s were of an informal and conversational sort, and as such left limited traces in the published literature. Sartre was beyond doubt ripe to receive Husserl by the time he engaged the *Ideen* in Berlin – already his earliest writings demonstrate careful attention to descriptive detail, which earned him the title of a "savage" and "unconscious" phenomenologist (de Coorebyter 2003). The early essays include a 1924 piece "L'Apologie pour le cinema: defense et illustration d'un art international", where Sartre adopts the starting point of consciousness in describing the film, and equates the latter with consciousness itself due to their shared indivisible duration (Sartre 1990: 380). Sartre may then come across as a phenomenologist *sans le savoir*, who practises a return to the things themselves in his own writings well *avant la lettre* of classical phenomenology. The influence of Bergson is unmistakable there, before the influence of Husserl, and it will play out at length in the 1929 thesis on the image (discussed below). As a student of Bergson's philosophy at ENS, Sartre, together with other French intellectuals at the time, was favourably disposed towards a rigorous philosophy of consciousness developed by Husserl, and adopted it wholesale when he started reading the *Ideen* in Berlin.

Sartre, the Husserlian

Sartre obtained a grant to pursue research at the Maison Académique Française in 1933–4, where he replaced Aron. He divided his days between reading *Ideen I* in the mornings, and writing what he referred to as his "memo on contingency" (*"factum sur la contingence"*), published in 1938 as *La Nausée*, in the afternoons. It was during this time that Sartre drafted his early phenomenological essays, all of them engaged with aspects of Husserl's phenomenology from *Ideen I*, but also drawing on Husserl's other works. Sartre wrote "La Transcendance de l'ego" in 1934, first published in the avant-garde journal *Recherches Philosophiques* in 1936–7. A lesser-known but forceful expression of Sartre's allegiance to phenomenology is found in a brief article titled "Une idée fondamentale de la phénoménologie de Husserl: l'intentionalité", which was also drafted in 1934 in Berlin, but published only in 1939. The two monographs on the imagination, *L'Imagination* and *L'Imaginaire*, came out in 1936 and 1940, respectively. *Esquisse d'une théorie des émotions* was drafted in 1937, and first published in 1939. It is usual to regard the writings from the 1940s, such as "Conscience de soi et connaissance de soi" (Sartre 1948c) and the magnum opus *L'Être et le néant: essai d'ontologie phénoménologique* (Sartre 1943a), as breaking away with phenomenology, due to the uncompromisingly polemical stance adopted by Sartre in the critique of Husserl. However, this relation is complicated by Sartre's continued adherence to the stance of consciousness and intentionality in these later works. What changes most dramatically, in my reading, is the tone of Sartre's pronouncements; most of the criticisms and revisions are sketched out already in the expressly phenomenological phase.

Even though Sartre was to distance himself from Husserl's intellectual influence in favour of Heidegger, and then Marx, Husserl's role in Sartre's philosophical trajectory remains unique: it renewed his confidence in the value and relevance of philosophy to the quotidian and the mundane, and launched Sartre on the path of sustained philosophical writing. As he noted, "Husserl had gripped me. I saw everything through the perspectives of his philosophy ... I was 'Husserlian' and long to remain so" (Sartre 1985a: 225, 183). Husserl thus figures as an adopted philosophical master and mentor to the early Sartre; the latter expresses his philosophical provenance, however, in a decidedly contrary fashion. Sartre may come across as a parasitic reader of Husserl, who is leaching the available intellectual resources to the very bone and acknowledging the master's authority by repeatedly testing the validity of his claims. Hence, even though Sartre's early phenomenological pieces ("La Transcendance de l'ego", Sartre 1936–7; *L'Imaginaire*, Sartre 1940) were, on his own admission, written directly under Husserl's inspiration, they were just as much written "against" Husserl; yet such counter-writing was possible "just insofar as a disciple can write against his master" (Sartre 1985a: 184). The rebellious tone found in the early works is therefore an expression of inspired discipleship seeking to define its own distinctive philosophical voice while partially channelling another.

Sartre employs the phenomenological method adopted from Husserl to suspend the validity of the claims and concepts posited by Husserl; his loyalty is in the approach and not in the doctrine, and his goal is to purify the phenomenological field established by Husserl by clearing it of any mental furniture adopted from the philosophical tradition (the egological notion of consciousness, the representationalist view of the imagination, recourse to passive matter or *hyle* in descriptions of the activity of consciousness) – ultimately up to the point of equating consciousness with nothingness. Sartre makes Husserl taste his (Husserl's) own medicine by pointing the sharp end of the phenomenological razor back onto the field of the master's own philosophy; he thus uses the method borrowed from Husserl to suspend the validity of claims made by Husserl. As such Sartre may be positioned in the sphere separating what Husserl (in Sartre's view) says and what he effectively does with phenomenology, or what he promises and what he effectively accomplishes. The promise of phenomenology is revolutionary, the fruit overly saturated with the usual juices of academic thinking; Sartre's goal is then to liberate Husserl from himself. He claims to be (albeit he is rarely recognized as) consistently Husserlian throughout this process; henceforth, when engaged in his ontological project that posits a dialectical opposition between the realms of being and nothingness, Sartre makes this claim: "I'm coming back to dogmatism via phenomenology. I'm keeping all of Husserl, the being-in-the-world, and yet I'm reaching an absolute neo-realism" (Sartre 1993b: 43). The phenomenological method becomes in Sartre's hand a radical purifying solution that leaves nothing behind – or better, that attains nothingness as ultimate realization of consciousness itself; the world is restored in its density and transcendence unmediated by essences and ideas; the dialectic of being and nothingness is then a logical and necessary extension of phenomenology of consciousness.

This mixture of loyalty and rebellion resonates with the profound ambivalence in Sartre's relation to Husserl; in some testimonies, the relation is described by a series of unmistakably alimentary metaphors, as a kind of intellectual cannibalism, feasting on Husserl's corpus (a curious stance to adopt by a scholar overtly critical of any notion of alimentary philosophy!) – but ultimately destined to immortalize the spirit (if not the corpus) of phenomenology. Hence Sartre makes this observation about Husserl's impact on "La Transcendance de l'ego" in particular, and his thinking in general:

> I wrote it ... under the direct influence of Husserl; although I must admit that I take in it an anti-Husserl position. But that's because I am argumentative by nature ... I have to take [things] in and assimilate them completely until they become part of me ... And even when I do understand, it's always with arguments and reservations, since I have to pick everything apart, cut it into little pieces, remove the bones, etc. And after all that long process had taken place, I was absolutely pro-Husserl, at least in certain areas, that is, in the realm of the intentional consciousness, for example; there he really revealed something to me, and it was at that time in Berlin that I made the discovery. (Sartre 1978: 30)

If a patricide was committed while Sartre was reading Husserl's *Ideen I* in Berlin, the latter text still provided a nourishing ground for Sartre's philosophizing – up to a point of "exhaustion" of this ambivalent relation in the 1940s.

Intentionality against transcendental ego

The overt task of "La Transcendance de l'ego" (Sartre 1936–7, 1960a) is to adopt and improve on Husserl's phenomenology so as to free it of unnecessary encumbrances, turning Husserl's method back onto the field of his philosophy. Sartre adopts the method of phenomenological reduction to gain access to the field of pure consciousness, but he radicalizes it to the point of excluding the transcendental ego itself. Sartre therefore challenges the claims made by Husserl in *Ideen I* (Husserl 1983: §80), relative to the irreducibility of the pure ego-pole in consciousness. Contrary to Husserl, Sartre claims that the ego is not a necessary substrate of all the individual acts of the cogito; it would rather be an object engendered *après coup* by reflection which therefore distorts the originally non-thetic or non-positional character of (pre-reflective) consciousness, making it appear as an object, rather than as pure subjectivity. Against Husserl's claim that the ego "survives the annihilation of the world", Sartre contends that the ego is an element of the transcendent world and so "falls like the other existences at the stroke of the epoché" (Sartre 1960a: 104).

Sartre's argument expressly challenged Husserl's presumed "Kantianism", unresolved in *Ideen*; specifically, a move from a *de jure* claim that the "I think" *must* be able to accompany all my presentations to a *de facto* claim that "I think" *does* in fact accompany all my presentations. Sartre found no phenomenological support for turning the Kantian requirement that it be *possible* to identify any act of consciousness as mine into the claim that the *I* is an *existent* subject of any *cogito*. *Contra* Husserl, Sartre argues that the synthetic unity of apperception makes no existential claims concerning the *I*. Kant is interpreted to be saying that "I can always regard my thought or perception as mine: nothing more" (Sartre 1960a: 104). In Sartre's view, there is no phenomenological place for a pure ego. And even though he does not cite it, the following passage from *Ideen I* can help appreciate the possibility of Husserl converting the Kantian prerequisite of necessary unity in consciousness into a phenomenological datum:

> In every actional cogito the ego lives out its life in a special sense. But all mental processes in the background likewise belong to it; and it belongs to them. All of them, as belonging to the *one* stream of consciousness which is mine, *must* admit of being converted into actional cogitations as immanental constituents. In Kant's words, "The 'I *think*' *must be capable of accompanying all my presentations*". (Husserl 1983: §57)

This necessary conversion of mental processes into I-acts justifies, in Husserl's view, the postulate of the *I* as an irreducible subject of actional cogito.

Sartre argues that the unity of consciousness is safeguarded already by its intentional relatedness to an object:

> Now, it is certain that phenomenology does not need to appeal to any such unifying and individualizing *I*. Indeed, consciousness is defined by intentionality. By intentionality consciousness transcends itself. It unifies itself by escaping from itself ... The object is transcendent to the consciousnesses which grasp it, and it is in the object that the unity of the consciousnesses is found.
> (Sartre 1960a: 38)

This passage brings into focus what Sartre considered to be a *fundamental* idea of Husserl's phenomenology in the *Ideen*, and what he developed in the same year in an article bearing its name: intentionality. In Sartre's handwritten notes in the margins of his personal copy of the *Ideen* (cited in de Coorebyter 2003), intentionality constitutes one of the central and recurrent themes. In response to Husserl's emphasis that intentional relation is included *a priori* in the "pure essences" of eidetic phenomenology (Husserl 1983: §36), Sartre notes in the margin what this emphasis excludes, namely a "relation from the outside which would be contingent and reducible to an external relation" (*"liaison par le dehors qui serait contingente et se réduirait à un rapport externe"*). Husserl's claim (*ibid.*: §128) that "eidetic description of consciousness leads back to that of what is intended to in it, that the correlate of consciousness is inseparable from consciousness and yet is not really inherent in it" is underlined twice and emphasized by a triple vertical line in the margin. Similarly, Husserl's insistence that a material object, like "this sheet of paper given in the mental process of perception, is by essential necessity not a mental process but a being of a wholly different mode of being" (*ibid.*: §35) is underlined, as are similar passages in §23, where emphasis on the difference and transcendence of the *intentum* to the intentional consciousness is clearly stated.

This emphasis strongly resonates with the entire ontological vision of a dialectical tension between consciousness and being developed by Sartre in 1943, and can be found in passages like this: "In the case of the perception of the chair, there is a thesis – that is, the apprehension and affirmation of the chair as the in-itself which consciousness is not" (BN1: 140; BN2: 163). Sartre's handwritten notes and emphases in and around the text of the *Ideen* thus pick up the threads and then weave them into the cloth of his own ontology; the threads add up retroactively to an unexpected *fil rouge* which a more usual, transcendental reading would be unlikely to reveal. Sartre's atypical emphasis of the *otherness* of the noematic to the noetic in the *Ideen* thus awakens the reader to a previously unnoted strangeness stirred by the "different mode of being" within (and without) consciousness. It also lends credence to his self-ascription as a Husserlian – as Sartre is writing in the margins of *Ideen*, he is also writing a phenomenological ontology of *Being and Nothingness*, a project ambiguously situated within the body and on the margins of phenomenology itself.

Intentionality, this basic stance of consciousness, figures as a mark of consciousness's direct and unmediated contact with the transcendent world already in the 1930s. Sartre makes this claim with force in the 1934 essay:

> Against the digestive philosophy of empirico-criticism, of neo-Kantianism, against all "psychologism," Husserl persistently affirmed that one cannot dissolve things in consciousness. You see this tree, to be sure. But you see it just where it is: at the side of the road, in the midst of the dust, alone and writhing in the heat, eight miles from the Mediterranean coast. It could not enter into your consciousness, for it is not of the same nature as consciousness ... Consciousness and the world are given at one stroke: essentially external to consciousness, the world is nevertheless essentially relative to consciousness. (Sartre 1970: 4)

Sartre thus credits the intentionality thesis with two things: a delivery from the idealist worldview that populates the inner world with semblances of the outer, *and* from the realist worldview that turns the real into an absolute, which can be only subsequently encountered by consciousness. Husserl would have restored the real world of "artists and prophets ... with its havens of mercy and love" (*ibid.*: 5), and delivered us from the notions that "the spidery mind trapped things in its web. Covered them with a white spit and slowly swallowed them, reducing them to its own substance" (*ibid.*: 4). As such, intentionality would be, inescapably, an ontological thesis spelling out the being in the world of phenomenal consciousness, it would be a dialectical thesis bringing into light the conflict-within-the-contact of transcendental consciousness and the transcendent world, where ontological belonging can be experienced as horror and mortal danger.

Sartre's decidedly realist reading of intentionality does not mention that the meaning-endowing consciousness actively constitutes its object.

Or rather, he reads the constitution of the world as an imprisonment of transcendental consciousness in an empirical one (Sartre 1960a: 36), a tragic fall into brute contingency, as narrated in *Nausea* and then *Being and Nothingness*. The two parallel tracks of projects pursued in Berlin: reading *Ideen I* and writing a factum on contingency, effectively intersect in Sartre's early phenomenological essays, such that Sartre is still writing on contingency while reading (and writing about) Husserl. The interest in contingency of a world encountered as a brute factum informs his emphasis on transcendence as being both external *and* indissociable from consciousness. Intentionality is figured as externality, a bond of non-assimilable excess weighing down consciousness to the world.

Intentionality so redefined is then turned back onto its nourishing ground, and put in the service of arguments *contra* Husserl; it puts pressure on any need to locate transcendence within immanence, and to posit an ego as a transcendental substrate of experience (and then against the argument against a representationalist theory of the imagination and discussed below). The ego could only divide consciousness from itself like "an opaque blade", and thus constitute the "death of consciousness" (*ibid.*: 40); following the fundamental character of intentionality, (pre-reflective) consciousness is still granted *self*-consciousness but that does not suppose a self separable from consciousness: "consciousness is aware of itself *insofar as it is consciousness of a transcendent object*" (*ibid.*: 40). This constant contact with transcendence translates into absolute clarity and lucidity within immanence; later in *Being and Nothingness*, Sartre will make a similar point that consciousness (of) self should not be read in terms of a barrier separating a subject from an object.

While "La Transcendance de l'ego" is overtly a critique of the postulate of the transcendental ego, it is written as much "for" as it is "against" Husserl, and its engagement with Husserl's phenomenology transcends the narrow confines of this technical argument. The overtly critical tone can easily make the reader lose sight of Sartre's positive investment in the phenomenological project, and an intent to carry it further. First, intentionality reread with a determined focus on transcendence can answer the problem of whether or not distinct consciousnesses can be said to perceive one and the same world (Sartre 1985a: 184). Sartre is advancing the phenomenological project by actively countering the charge that each individual consciousness may be shown to constitute its own private world only. This concern is obviously tied to the charge of solipsism, and Sartre considers the problem of the being of the world on a par with the problem of knowing others. Ultimately, that is, by the time Sartre is developing his ontology, the latter problem will be grounded in such a realist notion of the common world. Yet Sartre is tackling this problem already in his phenomenological phase, and his argument "against" the transcendental ego is simultaneously an argument "for" the possibility of knowing others within phenomenology of consciousness. (It is obviously also "against" Husserl's own stated views, whose refutation of solipsism Sartre deems "inconclusive and weak" – see *ibid.*: 184). An ego-less construal of consciousness would dispel the threat of solipsism hovering over Husserl's phenomenology. Refigured as transcendent rather than transcendental, the ego is not locked in the interiority of the first person experience and can engage in relations with others. There is no longer anything "impenetrable" about the other nor about the self in this perspective (Sartre 1960a: 77, 96); the threat of *solus ipse* is rendered null and void.

There are other instances of "La Transcendance de l'ego" being written both "for" and "against" Husserl: for example, the notion of impersonal consciousness would provide the motivation for performing the phenomenological reduction. Sartre argues that "the epoché appears in the phenomenology of Husserl as a miracle", since no reasons or motives for suspending the otherwise coherent natural attitude are put forward (*ibid.*: 102). Reduction appears as an excessively intellectual method, an erudite procedure, capable of being performed only at the end of lengthy study, and as such gratuitous (*ibid.*: 103). Refigured as a spontaneity without a subjective centre, manifest in states of anxiety, insomnia or obsessional thinking, consciousness would be more prone, so to speak, to suspending and thematizing its quotidian beliefs even when it is not deployed by an academic philosopher; the *epoché* would emerge then as "both a pure event of transcendental origin and an ever possible accident of our daily life" (*ibid.*: 103) – rather than as a scholastic method. The *epoché* thus gets tied directly to a philosophy of existence, in its return to the concerns of the mundane and quotidian human condition, not limited to furnishing the toolbox of an *Erkenntnistheorie*. It is also brought into contact with empirical narratives documenting such instances of monstrous spontaneity within consciousness itself, notably the psychology of Pierre Janet (see Stawarska 2005).

An ego-less construal of consciousness can also help respond to the charges of the political left that phenomenology, like idealism, is a "philosophy without evil" that dissolves reality into a stream of representations (Sartre 1960a: 104–5). As such, non-egological consciousness can give full and concrete measure of human agonies, suffering – and rebellion. This expressly ethical and political interest is obviously closer to Sartre's own rather than Husserl's philosophical aspirations; using the yardstick of social relevance to assess the validity of transcendental claims brings a more engaged orientation to phenomenology, which distances Sartre from Husserl more radically than any specific theoretical disagreement in method and doctrine ever could. It confirms the need to situate their philosophical projects within the respective visions of the philosopher's responsibilities and commitments, or what a philosopher is to do.

Imagination

Sartre authored two monographs devoted to the imagination, and while both take up themes from *Ideen I*, they also extend his earlier thesis "L'Image dans la vie psychologique: role et nature", which Sartre presented to obtain the *diplôme d'études supérieures* at the École Normale Superieure in 1927. This unpublished thesis focuses on the role of the image in perception and conception, and draws on a number of authors, notably Alain and Bergson, but also Binet, Piaget, Taine, Delacroix (his thesis adviser), Descartes, Jaspers, Leibniz, Kant, Spinoza, Ribot, Freud and others. There is lack of clarity in the scholarship relative to when Husserl became an influence on Sartre's thinking about the imagination. According to one claim, Sartre referred to Piaget, Freud and Jaspers, and even Husserl, in his 1927 thesis (Moran 2000: 365). Left as is, this claim risks overstating the facts – especially considering lack of public access and extensive publications on the thesis. The actual text, transcribed from thesis into type by Michel Rybalka, is mainly concerned with the transition from Alain to Bergson. The new influence on Sartre in this work is Bergson, not Husserl. Of the two references to a "Hüsserl" (*sic*) in the thesis, the first is embedded in a citation (from Flach), the second invokes a logician, author of a cursorily rendered critique of psychologism. The existing references are therefore either secondhand (de Coorebyter 2003: 21) or unrelated to the topic of the imagination. Similarly to his writings on cinema from 1924, Sartre may well be developing a precocious phenomenology in his writing on the image, but the interlocutor on the subject of consciousness is Bergson.

Sartre's first published work on the imagination, *L'Imagination* (Sartre 1936, 1972a), does engage Husserl directly. While the bulk of the book is devoted to a critical survey of the existing theories of the imagination by Berkeley, Hume, Bergson and the psychologists Bühler, Titchener, Köhler, Wertheimer and Koffka, the final chapter takes up the phenomenology of Husserl as a much-needed alternative. Sartre praises Husserl for having "blazed the trail" for his own theory of the imagination, even though he regretted that the scattered and fragmentary character of Husserl's observations on imagination contained in *Ideen I* makes their exposition exceedingly difficult (Sartre 1972a: 143). To the principal merits of Husserl's phenomenological theory belong, in Sartre's view, first, explicating the intentional structure of conscious acts, including the imaginary acts of consciousness, and, secondly, laying the ground for the assimilation of pure fantasy with the consciousness of physical pictures (paintings, drawings, photographs). The latter contribution is especially important in that it provides the basis for Sartre's own unitary theory of imagination developed at length in *L'Imaginaire* (Sartre 1940, 2004a), which subsumes "mental" images and physical pictures in one extended "family" (*famille d'images*). While the first book on imagination proceeds by first critiquing existing empirical and experimental accounts as falling short of defining the essence of the psychological facts, and then opts for an eidetic reflection on the phenomenon under investigation, the second book starts off with the "certain" characteristics of imagining consciousness as yielded by phenomenological reflection.

In both books, Sartre deems intentionality to be key to understanding imagination. The principal merit of the intentionality thesis is that it provides the only means of preserving the transcendence of the object of a conscious act, whether perceptual or imaginary. Defining consciousness in terms of intentionality ultimately breaks with any form of immanentism where the object *of* consciousness gets identified with a content *in* consciousness, and so where its transcendent character with regard to consciousness is compromised. Sartre targets especially Berkeley's idealism for having reduced transcendent objects to their mode of appearance, and so reduced the objective world to subjective impressions. The intentionality thesis permits, Sartre contends, to restore the transcendent character to the world, because the intendum ceases to be the content of the subjective act. To be sure, the act of consciousness is still composed of impressional data, but these hyletic components of a subjective act are not to be confused with the *object* of a conscious act (Sartre 1972a: 132). More importantly still, the intentionality thesis provides the ultimate means of breaking away with a long and faulty tradition of theorizing imagination as a variant of perception. Sartre's critical studies of the dominant theories of imagination produced in the history of Western philosophy, from Descartes to Bergson, aim to dissipate the common illusion haunting these theories that the image is a sort of a lesser thing, a trace of the perceived object. This illusion gives rise to, what Sartre calls, the "naive ontology of the image" for which "the image is made into a copy of the thing, existing as a thing" (*ibid*.: 4). However, the procedure of locating images in the mind renders it effectively impossible to distinguish between perception and imagination – while we can easily tell them apart in experience; furthermore, it falls prey to the "illusion of immanence" which takes consciousness to be a receptacle for mental representations. The intentionality thesis permits to theorize imagination otherwise than as observation of perceptual traces left behind in consciousness with the mind's eye. The image ceases being an immanent psychic content.

Sartre refers to Husserl's example of imagining a "centaur playing the flute" from §23 of *Ideas I* to illustrate this point. Following Husserl, the centaur produced in this flight of fancy can be called a mental 'representation' only as long as it is understood that "we mean by "representation" what is represented" rather than "a psychic state". The centaur can thus be termed an intentional object of the imaginary consciousness even though it does not have an independent existence and is no more than a product of the mind. "It exists neither in the soul nor in consciousness nor anywhere. It does not exist at all, it is invention through and through" (Sartre 1972a: 133). Sartre thus credits Husserl for having "restored to the centaur, in the very heart of its 'unreality'," its transcendence" (*ibid*.: 134). The centaur can be regarded as a "transcendent nothing" (Ricoeur 1981: 170), irreducible to the mental act despite its non-existence.

Another important influence of *Ideen I* on Sartre's theory of the imagination can be found in the link established by Husserl between fantasy and picture consciousness. Even though the object of an imaginary act is a "nothing", Sartre does not deny that there is real content in the imaginary act. The question of what makes up this psychic content is discussed fully in *L'Imaginaire*; still, Sartre assimilates pure fantasy, such as imagining a "flute-playing centaur", with the consciousness of a physical picture, such as a painting, a drawing or a photograph due to impressional matter or "stuff" being found in both already in the earlier essay. He finds the "germ of this assimilation" in another passage from the *Ideen I*, where Husserl comments on Dürer's engraving "The Knight, Death and the Devil". Husserl distinguishes there between two ways in which the engraving can be apprehended: as an object of a "normal perception", where it is grasped as a physical thing, a sheet of printed paper, or as an object of aesthetic contemplation where the figures of the Knight, Death and the Devil get represented "in image" or where "we are directed to the 'imaged' realities (*abgebildet*), the knight in flesh and blood, etc". This passage leads Sartre to conclude that the consciousness of a physical picture, such as "The Knight, Death and the Devil" engraving, can be aligned with an act of pure fantasy, for example, imagining a flute-playing centaur, in that both acts consist of intentionally animating some content, which may be either physical or mental (Sartre 1972a: 135). The foundation for Sartre's own unitary theory of the imagination defined in *L'Imaginaire* as "an act [of consciousness] which aims at an absent or non-existent object as a body (*dans sa corporéité*), by means of a physical or mental content which is present only as an 'analogical *representative*' of the object aimed at" (Sartre 2004a: 20; 1940: 46) emerges thus in direct dialogue with relevant passages from *Ideen I*.

That is not to deny Sartre's overt disagreement with Husserl on the subject of the imagination, apparent especially in *L'Imaginaire*. The main disagreement concerns the relation between imagination and perception, and to the possibility of obtaining intuitive fulfilment in imagination. Thus, while Sartre adopts Husserl's bodily presence (*Leibhaftigkeit*) of the object of perception, he denies that such presence of what he calls the flesh (*la chair*), that is the intimate texture, can be found in the object of the imagination itself (Sartre 2004a: 16; 1940: 38). In imagining an object one has an immediate consciousness of its nothingness (2004a: 13; 1940: 33), and so absence or lack are the defining features of the imaginary, not a (possible or intended) presence. Sartre emphasizes therefore the negating power of consciousness (in reference to Heidegger), and deems the theory of fulfilment "outrageous": "We cannot allow that an image comes to fulfil a consciousness; it is itself a consciousness. It seems that Husserl was here the dupe of the illusion of immanence" (Sartre 2004a: 59). One could retort that Sartre's own theory of the imagination is at least ambiguous on the question of mental content, since it adheres both to the understanding of the imagination as intentional relation *and* posits the analogue as a necessary mediating term (whether physical or mental) between consciousness and its object (Stawarska 2001). Sartre's critique of Husserl's reliance on impressional data applies then to Sartre's own theory of imagination just as well, and may showcase the difficulty of ever attaining absolute purity and translucence within the phenomenal field. In any case, Sartre overtly chastizes Husserl for failing to rise to the standards of (Sartre's own) understanding of the intentionality of consciousness as being like a vortex expelling any content out into the world.

The rationale of Sartre's critique of Husserl can be found in his commitments to the creative force deployed by imaginary activity, as irreducible to simply re-presenting what is already there (or what was already realized in perception), and thus as direct expression of freedom. Sartre argues throughout *L'Imaginaire* that imagination and perception are the two irreducible attitudes of consciousness, the former deploying the free rein of creative activity unmotivated by any intuitively available contents. What is primary then is not perception but a duality of positive and negative acts – perception and imagination, with imagination having its object manifest in a *sui generis* fashion, and despite the greatest paucity of content. The presumed richness and vivacity of the imaginary world is illusory; rather than attribute quasi-perceptual presence to it, we should bring out the, at times, acutely experienced lack of the imaged object, as when I imagine a loved one who is away or maybe even dead. In such cases, imagination stages the non-being of its object in a dramatic fashion, and it is precisely the impossibility of attaining fulfilment that constitutes the drama of realizing that the loved one is *not* there, not in this photograph, painting, caricature, or mental vision. Imagination then has everything to do with the potential of consciousness to live and gain distance from the ensnaring presence of the perceptual world; it frees consciousness up from the usual entanglement in the brute being-there and opens up a space of non-being and negativity. Imagination provides the royal road to consciousness as a field where lack and absence are both possible (consciousness is a necessary and sufficient condition thereof) and acutely felt. Neither Husserl nor Heidegger would have given justice to this basic fact that the existential nature of consciousness is that of a *lack* (Sartre 1993b: 70).

Intentionality and the emotions

Esquisse d'une théorie des émotions (Sartre 1939a,1975) is an extract from a much larger treatise in phenomenological psychology, *La Psyché*. This planned "big book" of some four hundred pages, written "enthusiastically" in three months in the autumn of 1937 (Sartre 1985a: 184), has remained unpublished. Sartre discarded most of it as "pure Husserl": it expressed Husserl's ideas as assimilated and expressed by Sartre in a different style (de Beauvoir 1987: 231). Sartre regarded the salvaged sketch on the theory of the emotions, on the other hand, as original work (*ibid.*). The published book is similar in design and orientation to the first book on the imagination in that it critiques the empirical and experimental accounts (the classic theories of James, Janet and Wallon) as falling short of defining the essence of the psychological facts, and opts for an eidetic reflection on the phenomenon under investigation. Like the first book on the imagination, and in agreement with its title, the book offers a rough sketch and not a complete treatise in phenomenological psychology of the emotions.

Sartre contends that the emotion like any other act of consciousness must be intentionally oriented to an object – to hate someone is to find them hateful, to love is to find them loveable. Furthermore, emotions, together with all other conscious acts, involve a non-thetic or pre-reflective consciousness of self. As such, emotions possess and must be thematized according to their meaning or signification, rather than as sheer accidents or as mere sum totals of scientific facts. This signifying quality justifies resorting to the method of *phenomenological psychology* as an alternative and a foundation for the empirical approaches.

In addition to this adoption of Husserlian themes, one finds the usual Sartrean commitment to the freedom of consciousness in his sketch. The emotions are purposive, rather than being passive states or hidden treasures of the unconscious. The object of the emotion is not simply discovered in the pre-existent natural world, but consistently tied to the magical productivity of consciousness itself, and engendered in an effort to flee the world experienced as resistant or difficult. Like the imagination, the emotions deploy therefore the creative potential of consciousness and involve a measure of active distancing from the already available world. Furthermore, since pre-reflective consciousness of self is distinct from knowledge of self (see also the 1943 essay *Consciousness of Self and Knowledge of Self* on this distinction), the emotional consciousness involves a degree of captivity or bad faith, which can only be dispelled by purifying reflection.

Phenomenological ontology

All the consequences of Sartre's critique of Husserl developed in the earlier phenomenological essays can be found in the works published in the 1940s. In "Conscience de soi et connaissance de soi" (Sartre 1948c, 1967), Sartre notes:

> We have in Husserl a gradual elucidation and a remarkable description of the essential structures of consciousness ... but never the posing of the ontological problem, namely that of the being of consciousness. In the same way the problem of the being of the world remains in suspense ... we never return from the phenomenological epoché to the world.   (Sartre 1967: 55)

Transcendental phenomenology needs therefore to be expanded into ontology – it needs to raise the question of being as irreducible to appearance, but without dropping the descriptive method of phenomenology.

The 1943 opus *L'Etre et le néant*, subtitled "an essay in phenomenological ontology", seeks to accomplish just that: it develops an ontological system from the perspective of phenomenal consciousness. At the same time, Sartre has definitely arrived at the point of "exhaustion" in his relation to Husserl in the 1940s, and is uncompromising in his critique of the entire methodological and categorical apparatus. Husserl is charged with "infidelity" to his original conception of phenomenology, for the following reasons:

- for his Berkeleyan idealism in interpreting Being and transcendent objects of intentional consciousness as non-real (BN1: xxvi; BN2: 6);
- for not having escaped the thing-illusion (*illusion chosiste*) by introducing the passive *hyle* and being bound to the doctrine of sensation in his account of consciousness (BN1: xxxvi; BN2: 15–16);
- for remaining timidly on the level of purely functional description, which confines him to the level of appearances and forecloses the possibility of pursuing an existential dialectics;
- for being, "despite all his denials, a phenomenalist rather than a phenomenologist" (BN1: 73; BN2: 97), only able to surf the surface of the infinite myriad of appearances;
- for sketching a mere caricature of genuine transcendence that fails to pass beyond a consciousness into a world and beyond the present into the past and the future (BN1: 109; BN2: 132);
- for being unable to escape solipsism any more than Kant, particularly by the useless and fateful hypothesis of the transcendental subject (BN1: 233–4; BN2: 257–8);
- for not taking sufficient account of the refractoriness (*coefficient d'adversité*) in our immediate experience (BN1: 328); and
- for assuming that an eidetic phenomenology of essences can lay hold of freedom, which Sartre identified with consciousness and regarded as the prior ground of any elucidation of human essences (BN1: 439; BN2: 461) – the last challenge ultimately entailing a shift from a phenomenological to an existentialist orientation.

This long litany of accusations adds surprisingly little to our knowledge of Sartre's relation to Husserl documented by the writings from the 1930s – many of the now overtly stated concerns were heard in the earlier phenomenological essays, the new ontological directions expressly followed were explored already within a perspective now deemed too phenomenal. The concerns stated and new directions followed may then have implicitly oriented the entire trajectory of Sartre's engagement with Husserl's phenomenology, and have only been brought into sharp focus in the 1940s. The professed break with Husserl appears then more as a blurred line; a phenomenology of an unequivocally classical kind continues to provide the frame of reference for the ontological Sartre. The unwillingness to abandon the perspective of consciousness, which sets him apart from both Merleau-Ponty and Heidegger, is evidence enough of Sartre's continued adherence to classical phenomenology. Even though Sartre's critical stance towards Husserl is more articulate and more radicalized in the 1940s, what changes the most is the tone – we no longer hear a trailing disciple refer to a master but an author speak on behalf of his own opus magnum, in his own voice. The question of break and/or continuity is therefore as complex in Sartre's *oeuvre* as it is the philosophy of Merleau-Ponty and Heidegger; Sartre's *provocateur* tone may amplify the tension of writing simultaneously from within and on the margins of phenomenology, for and against Husserl, up to the point of exhaustion and a turn to politics.

Note

1. I'd like to thank Matthew R. Lexow for pointing out Fernando Gerassi's role in Sartre's introduction to Husserl's phenomenology interviews to me, and Dennis Gilbert for providing information about Sartre's unpublished thesis on the imagination.

Further reading

Brann, E. 1991. *The World of the Imagination: Sum and Substance.* Lanham, MD: Rowman & Littlefield.
Moran, D. 2000. *Introduction to Phenomenology.* London: Routledge.
Roeckelein, J. 2004. *Imagery in Psychology: A Reference Guide.* Westport, CT: Praeger.
Sepp, H. R. & L. E. Embree (eds) 2010. *Handbook of Phenomenological Aesthetics.* Dordrecht: Springer.

FOUR

Sartre's understanding of the self
Christian Onof

Sartre's metaphysics are borne out of phenomenological investigations into the emotions, the imagination, and particular phenomena that are revelatory of ontological truths, such as the famous experience of *La Nausée* (Sartre 1938, 1965a) in which the novel's protagonist, Roquentin, experiences the fundamental difference characterizing the way of being of things from what it is to be a conscious being (Sartre 1965a: 182–3). This chapter aims to present how, from this basic insight and the theory of consciousness that accompanies it, Sartre develops an understanding of the self. In the first part of the chapter I will focus largely upon *The Transcendence of the Ego* (Sartre 1936–7, 2004c). In the second part I examine how *Being and Nothingness* contributes to this task. Although largely expository, the chapter will make some critical comments, because identifying the weaknesses of a theory is a precondition for properly grasping its strengths.

Sartre's early theory of the ego

The phenomenological investigations that are illustrated so powerfully in Sartre's novels, and *La Nausée* in particular, provide building blocks for a theory of consciousness that has direct implications for the understanding of the self who is conscious. With Roquentin's experience, Sartre is clearly drawing attention to the fact that consciousness cannot be viewed as a way of being that is comparable to that which we are, in normal circumstances, familiar with in our environment. This sets the foundation for what Sartre will distinguish in *Being and Nothingness* as the being of the for-itself, in opposition to that of the in-itself. For our purposes, what is first fundamental about this distinction is that the in-itself "is" in a self-contained way, while the for-itself's existence can only be understood in relation to the in-itself. Second, this relatedness defines a fundamental characteristic of consciousness for Sartre: it is always to be understood as consciousness of something: consciousness is fundamentally intentional.

This different way of being of consciousness implies that any notion of self cannot be a notion of a self as substance in the sense that being in-itself is the type of being of substances. And not being substantial means two interrelated things for Sartre: first, it means that there is no substratum for this type of being, which is pure appearance; second, it means that this kind of being is not its own foundation.

Consciousness before Being and Nothingness

Focusing now on the claim of intentionality, let us note that there is a long history to the conception of intentionality, or directedness towards an object, and much of it is marked by the introduction of a notion of representation, which explains how the intended object constitutes mental content. To have a certain representation, on this account, is to be intentionally directed towards an object, *and* the object defines, in some sense, the content of the representation.

Some such representational theories identify a role of intermediary for the representation in accounting for the epistemology of the perception of an object: to see an object is just to have a representation that is related in the right way to the object (for example, causally). Such an understanding of the role of mental representations is rejected by Sartre in his early work on the imagination (*L'Imagination*, Sartre 1936, 1972a; *L'Imaginaire*, Sartre 1940, 2004a). There are no such things as mental images inside consciousness, and which account for our relation to objects (Moran 2000: 380). Sartre wants to avoid the opacity that is introduced into consciousness by means of such a mediation: Sartre is a direct realist. If one can indeed talk of the appearances of an object, and thus differentiate the object from any single or finite number of appearances for a perceiver (the object would then correspond to an infinity of possible appearances, as Husserl or phenomenalism would have it; *ibid*.: 115, 160; Gardner 2009: 53), this is not to give these appearances any separate status as mental entities. Indeed, it is a fundamental feature of Sartre's understanding of consciousness, that it is a pure transparency directed to the object. Consciousness is not therefore understood in terms of the usual notion of mental content for Sartre.

This has an important implication for the understanding of the self. Namely, there is no locus for something like an ego to be found in consciousness. For Sartre, any such notion of ego would negate the diaphanous nature of consciousness, as "The Transcendence of the Ego" shows (Barnes 1992: 29). Here, in particular, any notion of ego that would be the ground of all the subject's intentional relations is excluded. By making this claim, Sartre is directly targeting Husserl's notion of transcendental ego. Husserl (1983: 132–3) claims that such an ego can be identified as that which does not change throughout our experience. That is, once one has carried out the phenomenological reduction he calls *epoché*, through which the world is reduced to its way of appearing, one grasps this world as it is constituted by a transcendental ego (Husserl 1980: §12). Sartre replies, however, that once the world and empirical subjectivity have been excluded through the *epoché*, there is no such residual ego to be found (Moran 2000: 377); indeed, any transcendence should, for Sartre, fall under the *epoché*, and thus be understood as not constitutive of consciousness (Sartre 2004c: 14). Moreover, to claim that there is a transcendental ego would amount to "slicing through each consciousness like an opaque blade" (*ibid.*: 7), in so far as it would destroy the transparency of consciousness.

Sartre diagnoses Husserl's error as stemming from a misinterpretation of the meaning of Kant's transcendental unity of apperception (TUA). Sartre correctly points out that the TUA arises in the context of the *de jure* question of the possibility of objective knowledge. Husserl's transposition of this notion into the context of phenomenology belongs to a "dangerous tendency in contemporary philosophy ... of turning the conditions of possibility determined by critique into a *reality*" (*ibid.*: 2). Sartre thus accuses Husserl of borrowing a *de jure* notion and using it to make a *de facto* claim.

Let us note here that, while Sartre is right to uphold Kant's distinction between *de jure* and *de facto* issues (Kant 2003: A84–5/B116–7), his realism implies that he does not assign the TUA the constitutive function it has for Kant. Rather, Sartre has it that the "I" is the result of a synthetic unity of representations: "it is this pre-existing unity which, on the contrary, makes it possible" (Sartre 2004c: 5). It is arguable that had he embraced Kantian idealism, Sartre's views on the "I" would have been altered. Leaving this issue aside, Sartre's theory of the ego in *The Transcendence of the Ego* involves more than these negative statements about a transcendental ego: this critique concerned unreflective first-order consciousness, directed onto the world, but there is more to Sartre's understanding of the ego in *The Transcendence of the Ego* than the absence of the "I" from any such unreflective consciousness.

Reflective consciousness in The Transcendence of the Ego

Aside from non-reflective positional consciousness, Sartre explains that there is a form of *reflective* consciousness in which an "I" appears. Husserl had already observed that the psychological ego is the result of a constitution by the subject (Moran 2000: 169–71). Sartre now claims that the same applies to Husserl's transcendental ego, and that this constitution occurs through reflection (Sartre 2004c: 28). This is what is encountered in the "I think": what the kind of reflection involved in Descartes's cogito achieves is not the discovery of an "I", but the creation of one (*ibid.*: 42).

In the second part of *The Transcendence of the Ego*, Sartre provides an account of what is entailed in the constitution of a transcendent ego in reflection. Psychological entities that transcend consciousness, such as states, qualities and actions, are unified by being brought under a "transcendent pole of synthetic unity" (*ibid.*: 21).

Moreover, in the conclusion to *The Transcendence of the Ego*, Sartre brings out the practical dimension of the natural attitude (where the world is considered as it appears naturally, without any phenomenological reduction) in which the ego appears alongside pure consciousness. For Sartre (*ibid.*: 48), the natural attitude masks consciousness's spontaneity, a spontaneity that is anguish-inducing. This pre-empts a theme that Sartre develops at length in BN, namely that of bad faith: by interpreting oneself as having some apparent identity in the ego, the subject can conceal the fact that it is in fact a pure spontaneity that bears full responsibility for its choices (*ibid.*: 48). Indeed, for Sartre, the distinction between voluntary and involuntary spontaneity is only possible if "all activity is given as emanating from a passivity that it transcends" (*ibid.*), whereas the pure spontaneity of consciousness is such that such a distinction is not possible. This practical dimension of the constitution of the ego is further developed by Sartre in the *Sketch for a Theory of the Emotions*, where he explains how emotions present the world in a different light, which serves the purpose of relieving us of the burden of acting to alter it (Sartre 1939a: 43–4).

Self-consciousness

A type of consciousness that is obviously of utmost importance for the understanding of the self, is self-consciousness. Sartre makes the important claim that all consciousness must involve self-consciousness: this is described by Sartre as a form of "non-positional" consciousness (Sartre 2004c: 7–8), and distinguished from reflection: "a consciousness has no need of a reflective consciousness in order to be conscious of itself" (*ibid.*: 11). This account has the advantage of avoiding an infinite regress of consciousnesses that take other consciousnesses as their object. The claim is that consciousness is transparent, and in particular transparent to itself; hence it must be the case that all consciousness is conscious of itself. What is rather unclear, however, is where this leaves the "self", and indeed it appears that Sartre somewhat skirts this problem in *The Transcendence of the Ego* by referring to "consciousness of itself" rather than "self-consciousness". We shall see below that the danger of another type of infinite regress of self-consciousness leads Sartre to developing his theory of self-consciousness in BN in a way that will provide the foundation for a more developed theory of the self.

Sartre's minimalist metaphysics of *The Transcendence of the Ego* do indeed raise two sets of questions that crystallize the concerns implicit in this worry, as Gardner (2009: 14–15) points out. These are related to fundamental phenomenological features of what it is to be a self. Namely:

- Consciousness is personal. There is nothing in the above to suggest how any notion of personal individuality of the field of consciousness can arise from the impersonal description that it amounts to.
- Reflective consciousness has not been properly analysed: Sartre only made negative observations as to its not being sufficient to account for the immediacy of self-consciousness. But in reflection, the subject is related to herself in a way that is distinct from the relation of the subject to the world. An analysis of reflection is therefore required to account for the familiarity of the subject with herself as object that is encountered in reflection.

These issues are interrelated, as we shall see, and one of the achievements of BN will indeed be to fill in the metaphysics of the self in such a way as to meet these two concerns.

The self in *Being and Nothingness*

Pre-reflective consciousness

From the outset, a key feature of Sartre's analysis of consciousness in BN is the introduction of a pre-reflective level of consciousness. This move in effect recognizes a problem that has historically plagued many theories of self-consciousness found in the philosophical tradition. If self-consciousness were knowledge, how would the subject consciousness know directly and infallibly that the object consciousness is identical to it (BN1: xxviii)? As Frank (1991: 161) notes, following Henrich (1967), the notion of reflection does nothing to eliminate this problem (BN1: xxix), but rather crystallizes it: a third term that knows the identity of the reflecting subject and the reflected one is always required, if reflection is to explain the immediate acquaintance characteristic of self-consciousness, which leads to an infinite regress that traditional reflective theories of self-consciousness are open to. More directly, Sartre argues that I can only make sense of the act of counting my cigarettes if I am aware of my consciousness of each individual cigarette, thus enabling me to be conscious that I now have counted up to twelve. Else, I would have to count my non-self-conscious consciousnesses of cigarettes (Gardner 2009: 46–7). This means that self-consciousness is a non-positional consciousness that is pre-reflective.

What does this mean for the self? This new analysis of self-consciousness brings out an intimacy of self-consciousness prior to any reflective activity. This provides the necessary grounding for the development of a theory of the self, a task that Sartre does indeed address in part 2 of *Being and Nothingness*.

He describes the guiding thread of the investigation by claiming that the pre-reflective cogito is "homologous with the reflective cogito since it appears as the first necessity for non-reflective consciousness to be seen by itself" (BN1: 74; BN2: 98). This is a new take on the nature of pre-reflective consciousness, and it is a move that is well suited to addressing the two issues raised by Sartre's analysis of *The Transcendence of the Ego* mentioned above. That is, by bringing reflective and pre-reflective consciousness closer together, it will be possible to explain how reflection has an immediate familiarity with its object, and to use reflective structures to identify the individuating characteristics of a for-itself. What is the justification for this move? Sartre tells us that it follows from the fact that "the cogito includes the nullifying characteristic of existing for a witness" (BN1: 74; BN2: 98). We shall return to this claim later in the chapter.

Aside from the introduction of this new take on the pre-reflective cogito, the phenomenon that Sartre uses to illustrate this approach is one of thetic consciousness, rather than positional consciousness. Sartre distinguishes consciousness of an object O (positional consciousness) from consciousness that p (thetic consciousness). In both cases, such consciousness is transparent to itself and there is therefore a pre-reflective consciousness that Sartre calls non-positional (no object or proposition is thereby posited), and which is non-thetic (BN1: xxix; BN2: 9–10). To characterize this, Sartre uses parentheses. So, I am pre-reflectively conscious (of) any positional or thetic consciousness. In the case of the belief that p, this leads to the claim that I am conscious that I believe that p.

In this pre-reflective consciousness lies an instability that Sartre takes as characteristic of the instability of the for-itself. That is, since there is total transparency (Sartre 2004c: 7–8), it must be the case for Sartre that the pre-reflective consciousness (of) a belief just is the belief. This necessary unity is, however, not that of the identity of being in-itself: "the subject and the attribute are radically different though still within the indissoluble unity of one and the same being" (BN1: 75; BN2: 99). The instability which characterizes the being of the consciousness (of) belief is such that "as soon as we wish to grasp this being, it slips between our fingers" (BN1: 75; BN2: 99): there is thus no straightforward identity between belief and the consciousness (of) belief. As Sartre explains (*ibid.*), to avoid this conclusion by claiming rather that the identity statement should be spelt out at the level of consciousnesses (of), so that there is a non-problematic identity (as that characterizing the in-itself) between the consciousness (of) belief and the consciousness (of) belief, would amount to misunderstanding the role of the parentheses and turning the pre-reflective relation into a reflective one.

The pre-reflective self-consciousness of belief therefore involves our being "faced with a pattern of duality, a game of reflections" (BN1: 75, BN2: 100). Here, Sartre has not overstepped the well-defined divide between the pre-reflective and the reflective. Sartre is here referring to "reflection" in the sense of mirroring, rather than thinking, which the French text distinguishes as "*refléter*" and "*réfléchir*" respectively.

The persuasiveness of any such investigation into the pre-reflective domain is, of course, necessarily limited by what can be grasped through philosophical reflection, so that an analogical grasp of "*refléter*" through "*réfléchir*" is not necessarily misleading. And Sartre's understanding of consciousness as transparent to itself clearly requires that consciousness and self-consciousness define a unity. But the proximity of the two words "*refléter*" and "*réfléchir*" which lies in their common Latin root should not be overlooked. It is arguable that much of what Sartre claims about the pre-reflective cogito in the passages that follow the introduction of this notion of "*refléter*" gains its phenomenological persuasiveness from our experience of reflection as thinking, and the use of "grasp" in the passage quoted above confirms this. When Sartre talks of grasping ourselves as consciousness of belief, this may be striking a chord only in so far as we think of the reflective grasping that always fails to be identical with its target; and the choice of the example belief rather than any positional consciousness gives more plausibility to the notion of its thus being "troubled" (BN1: 75; BN2: 99).

Leaving this concern aside for now, with his understanding of pre-reflective consciousness, the problem that Sartre has identified through his claim of the inherent instability at the heart of consciousness is the need to account for the fact that, in the case of belief for instance, there is both unity and a duality of belief and the consciousness (of) belief. Sartre examines and rejects different options for resolving this problem (BN1: 76–7; BN2: 100–1). First, we have Hegel's account of it as a "return upon itself" (BN1: 76; BN2: 100), which reveals the presence of infinity at the heart of the phenomenon; for Sartre, this ultimately amounts to reducing the for-itself to the in-itself. Second, Spinoza's distinction "*idea–ideae*" only leads to reducing this pre-reflective self-consciousness to a duality, and thus "misses the pre-reflective phenomenon" (BN1: 76; BN2: 100).

No philosophical solution appears to be able to resolve the key problem that Sartre claims to have identified in terms of the pithy observation that "presence is an immediate deterioration of coincidence" (BN1: 77; BN2: 101). And what separates the consciousness from the belief it is consciousness (of) is exactly nothing. This is the nothingness that lies at the heart of the for-itself. If the duality and unity of belief and the consciousness (of) it are to remain irreducible to one another, Sartre has an interesting way of describing their relation which introduces teleology at the heart of the for-itself (thus justifying the use of the word "for-itself"). Namely, the consciousness (of) belief exists "in order to perform the act of faith" (BN1: 75; BN2: 99). This teleological dimension echoes directly the claim noted above that is made at the very beginning of this analysis, namely that "existing for a witness" is a key feature of the for-itself (BN1: 74; BN2: 98). And it explains how nothingness can be said by Sartre to be "made-to-be" (BN1: 78; BN2: 102): the for-itself is essentially a nihilation. A key manifestation of this teleological dimension is the phenomenon of lack, of which Sartre provides a detailed analysis.

Before examining this notion of lack, let us take stock of the progress made by Sartre's analysis of the for-itself in *Being and Nothingness* compared with *The Transcendence of the Ego*. In *Being and Nothingness* (BN1: 103–4; BN2: 128–9), Sartre explains in what ways he has altered his original account in *Transcendence of the Ego*. As we saw above, the account of consciousness in *The Transcendence of the Ego* stressed the error of assuming that an "I" can be found at the heart of the cogito. In so doing, however, it left unaddressed the issue of the individuality of the cogito. Each cogito is a personal one, but this was not explained by Sartre's account of consciousness as a transparency with no interior. The account in BN does remedy this lacuna through the notion of presence to oneself. In so far as I am present to myself, I am individuated as this person rather than another. So, without having to postulate some ego at the heart of consciousness, Sartre's account is able to account for the personal dimension of the for-itself.

It may, however, be objected that this is a fairly minimal account. All it achieves is that it individuates one consciousness from another, thereby essentially characterizing the sense in which I am not another. Sartre seems aware of this and reveals a more substantial notion of personality that arises from his notion of "selfness", of which Sartre says that "selfness represents a degree of nihilation carried further than the pure presence to itself of the pre-reflective cogito" (BN1: 103; BN2: 128). At the heart of the notion of selfness lies the Sartrean understanding of the for-itself as a lack.

The for-itself as lack and the notion of selfness

In the introduction to *Being and Nothingness*, Sartre had presented the for-itself as a degenerate form of being, one which, as the analysis of the notion of presence to itself has shown, contains nothingness at its heart. This form of being was contrasted with the plenitude of the in-itself which just is what it is (BN1: xli). Unlike the in-itself, the for-itself does not coincide with itself. In his analysis of the for-itself in part 2, Sartre reformulates the relation of the for-itself to the in-itself in terms of a dependence: the for-itself "can establish itself only in terms of the in-itself and against the in-itself" (BN1: 85; BN2:109). That means that the for-itself establishes itself as a lack of in-itself, and Sartre uses examples of desire to illustrate the phenomenology of lack (BN1: 87; BN2: 111). What the for-itself lacks is called the for-itself *possibilities*.

This lack is, moreover, the origin of transcendence for Sartre. "Human reality ... surpasses itself toward the particular being which it would be if it were what it is" (BN1: 89; BN2: 114). The being which thus haunts the for-itself is not just pure in-itself, for this would correspond to an annihilation of consciousness. Rather, it is the impossible synthesis of the for-itself and the in-itself (BN1: 90; BN2: 114). Sartre adds: "that being would be exactly the self which we have shown can exist only as a perpetually evanescent relation" (BN1: 90; BN2: 114). We thus have a notion of self "as the individual completion of the self which haunts itself" (BN: 91; BN2: 115).

This defines the teleological dimension of the for-itself as a lack, which Sartre later describes as the "second aspect of the person" (BN1: 104; BN2: 128), in contrast to the pure presence to itself analysed above, which is the first aspect. In so doing, he concurs with Heidegger that this notion of "selfness" essentially involves the world. Sartre takes the example of a satisfied thirst (what is lacked) haunting my actual thirst. This "causes itself to be transcended towards the glass" of which this thirst is conscious (BN1: 104; BN2: 128). The glass (which is an in-itself) is then constituted by the for-itself as a "glass to be drunk from" (*ibid.*). This constitutes a world beyond which lies the self "which I am in the form of 'having to be it'" (*ibid.*) in so far as this self is the impossible for-itself (-in-itself) which has satisfied its thirst. So, the lack defines a desire directed to the world; this amounts to making mine some in-itself by interpreting it as instrumental to the satisfaction of my desire (this is my possibility). This in turn identifies my selfness as the result of this circuit that connects my desiring consciousness to a satisfied one. This defines the self in terms of what Sartre calls a *circuit of ipseity* (*ibid.*).

We thus have a richer notion of the personal dimension of the self (here characterized in terms of the notion of lack and the correlative notion of possibility) than the mere appeal to presence to itself characterizing the pre-reflective cogito. And we also have a phenomenological characterization of the sense in which the for-itself is having to be itself, one which Sartre has in effect transposed (as we saw above) into the very analysis of the for-itself as presence to itself.

Reflection

Drawing upon the phenomenology of reflection to inform his understanding of pre-reflective consciousness is a strategy that has another advantage for Sartre with respect to the relative paucity of the interpretation of the nature of reflective consciousness in *The Transcendence of the Ego*. For this relating of the pre-reflective and the reflective works both ways, so that it provides a more plausible account of why consciousness reflects upon itself. In discussing reflection, Sartre (BN1: 150–58; EN: 196–205) criticizes traditional theories for which reflection amounts to a way of knowing one's mental states: self-knowledge is pre-reflective, and in any case, a phenomenon like reflection cannot be explained for Sartre by reference to epistemological relations.

Sartre's account builds upon the failure of the for-itself to coincide with itself in the pre-reflective structure of mirroring. The for-itself has, in effect, "lost itself outside itself" (BN1: 153; EN: 200). As that which is "having to be itself", the for-itself therefore seeks to recover its being by taking itself to be a unity which it apprehends as though it were a being in-itself, that is, a self-contained totality. But this attempt fails: in taking its possibilities as object of reflection, the for-itself distinguishes itself from them; and this negation defines a distance from the for-itself's possibilities (BN1: 175). This lack of identity takes on a temporal form: I am always beyond that which I reflect upon (BN1: 154; EN: 200). As a result, the psychological object, which is thus projected in reflection, fails to provide an adequate representation of the self.

This projection of a psychological object in reflection is a key component of Sartre's account of bad faith. For in so far as the for-itself flees from the abyss of its unlimited freedom (BN1: 464–5), and fails to recognize its nature as both facticity and freedom, it clings to an understanding of itself in terms of determinate psychological characteristics (Sartre 2004c: 46–8; BN1: 63, 66, 473). That is, it deceives itself that, rather than being a for-itself who is condemned to constantly having to choose for himself while recognizing his groundlessness, his is a grounded being which has the solidity of the in-itself (BN1: 57; BN2: 80).

And this has immediate moral consequences: claiming that the psychological object which I wrongly claim to be has certain determinations amounts to diminishing my responsibility as an agent (BN1: 57). But for Sartre, there are no pre-determinations to my choices (BN1: 448–9, 459): it is all up to me, and as a result, I have to face the full responsibility for my acts (BN1: 553–4; BN2: 574–5).

Conclusion

Sartre's account of the nothingness that lies at the heart of the cogito has the advantage of setting up the framework for his analysis of the human condition as defined by a pre-reflective presence to itself, which, as an instable unity/duality, reveals a teleological dimension manifested in the notion of lack, which in turn enables the for-itself to be viewed as a project. Ultimately, the justification for this account, as noted at the outset, lies rather in Sartre's claim that consciousness has "the nullifying characteristic of existing for a witness" (BN1: 74; BN2: 98). What grounds are there for such a claim? It would seem that these must lie in Sartre's anthropogenetic story about the origin of the for-itself. Namely, the for-itself arises from an original nihilation of the in-itself (BN1: 617; BN2: 637). As Gardner (2009: 69) points out, the status of this account is however uncertain. Is it a mere metaphysical fiction, as it would seem to be from the allusions to the Fall of Man? It would seem, however, that it has to be more if it is to provide the underpinning for the later claims made about the for-itself's nullifying characteristic. In other words, if this nullifying feature is at the heart of the for-itself, we are owed an account of why that is, and the notion of a nihilation of the in-itself would appear to play this role. But of course, this leads directly to the question of why the in-itself gives rise to such a nihilation: since the in-itself is the inert plenitude of being, there would appear to be no ground in it for the "upheaval" (BN1: 617–18; BN2: 637–8) from which the for-itself is born. This metaphysical problem is acknowledged by Sartre (BN1: 619; BN2: 639), and although he discusses it, it is noteworthy that he provides no solution to it.

However, even if some of the claims that are made along the way can be questioned, Sartre's analysis of consciousness provides a coherent picture of the for-itself's mode of being from which an illuminating understanding of the self can emerge, an understanding which has crucial moral implications.

Further reading

Busch, T. W. 1990. *The Power of Consciousness and the Force of Circumstances in Sartre's Philosophy*. Bloomington, IN: Indiana University Press.

Priest, S. 2000. *The Subject in Question: Sartre's Critique of Husserl in The Transcendence of the Ego*. New York: Routledge.

Webber, J. 2009. *The Existentialism of Jean-Paul Sartre*. London: Routledge.

Zheng, Y. 2005. *Ontology and Ethics in Sartre's Early Philosophy*. Oxford: Lexington Books.

FIVE

Contingency and ego, intentionality and nausea
Steven Churchill

> The first procedure of a philosophy ought to be to expel things from consciousness and to re-establish its true connection with the world. (BN1: xxvii; BN2: 7)

> Being is without reason, without cause, and without necessity; the very definition of being releases to us its original contingency. (BN1: 619; BN2: 639)

A man alone, *tête-à-tête* with the world

The early period of Jean-Paul Sartre's career is often characterized in terms of his devotion to the pursuit of his literary art, along with the development of his nascent philosophy. The typical imagery associated with the young Sartre of the early 1930s, up until the outbreak of the Second World War, is therefore that of a relatively solitary writer; we might well picture him busily filling the sheets of paper in front of him with the prose flowing swiftly from his pen in a café or a bar, largely oblivious to the goings-on around him. Indeed, Sartre arguably cemented this view of himself, by describing his self-image during this period as that of "a man alone" (Sartre 1977a: 45).

By contrast, the post-war imagery commonly associated with Sartre is that of the "engaged writer", using his words as a means of commenting on – and indeed actively fighting for – the social and political causes of his day. Accordingly, Sartre's life and works are often divided in half, with literature trumping politics on one side of the pre-war/

post-war divide, and literature serving as a vehicle for political engagement on the other.

Rightly, this rather simplistic division has increasingly come under scrutiny from Sartre scholars, particularly in the years following Sartre's death. It remains open to us to reposition the notions of "engagement" or "commitment" as it applies to Sartre's works. Rather than referring exclusively to Sartre's later, explicitly political writings, we might also employ these notions in referring to Sartre's foundational desire for philosophy to address itself directly to worldly experience. From this vantage-point, Sartre's view of his younger self as "a man alone" may be reinterpreted; although Sartre's general attitude towards the role of the writer in society might well be said to have favoured aloofness over direct political action, his philosophical perspective consistently resembled that of a man seeking to shape up to the world, as a fighter would to his opponent. In this sense, we may reasonably regard Sartre early on in his career as a man seeking constantly to engage with the world head-to-head, so to speak, in both philosophical and literary terms.

Realism

Sartre's drive toward engagement with the very stuff of existence began with his decision, from his earliest studies in philosophy, "in favour of Realism" (de Beauvoir 1988: 157). Sartre recounted in a 1974 interview with Simone de Beauvoir:

> I turned thoroughly against Idealism when I was taught it. I had two good years of philosophy before going to École Normale [in 1924], and there I had only one idea – that any theory that did not state that consciousness perceived exterior objects as they were, was doomed to failure. (*Ibid.*)

Sartre understood his perceptual realism as necessarily having socio-political implications. If one sees things as they really are, then one is able to critique the lives of those blinded to reality by their own moral and intellectual hypocrisy; for Sartre, those living in bourgeois society represented the very epitome of such hypocrisy. From Sartre's perspective, those immersed in bourgeois ideology carried on with tawdry affairs, all the while preaching the virtues of chastity and monogamy; they exploited those in their employ, all the while preaching the virtues of charity and kindness. In other words, the bourgeoisie lived mired in self-deception, on Sartre's view; he would later famously describe the phenomenon of self-deception at length, in his first great philosophical work *Being and Nothingness: An Essay in Phenomenological Ontology* (Sartre 1943a, 1958a), in terms of "bad faith" – the refusal to recognize the true extent of one's freedom, and to assume the full weight of the responsibility it entails. Sartre described this brash brand of perceptual and political realism as his "opposition aesthetics". He developed this view in the midst of an informal discussion group at the elite École Normale Supérieure in Paris. Meeting sporadically throughout Sartre's time at École Normale from 1924 through to 1929, the group consisted intermittently of Sartre himself, his life-long companion Simone de Beauvoir (from 1929), and friends including Raymond Aron, Paul Nizan and others; they referred to themselves as *les petits camarades* – classmates, peers, comrades. De Beauvoir describes her perspective on the group in these terms:

> [They] set out to prove that men were not rarefied spirits but bodies of flesh and bone, racked by physical needs and crudely engaged in a brutal adventure that was life … all they asked of me was that I should dare to do what I had always longed to do: look reality in the face. (de Beauvoir 1963: 336–7)

Although Realism proved crucial to the early intellectual development of both Sartre and de Beauvoir, each of their comrades ultimately came to walk their own intellectual path. Nizan, for example, wrote against Marxist Realism long before Sartre's own turn toward Marxism.

Radical contingency (*contra* Nietzsche's early romanticism)

Sartre's interpretation of realism, meanwhile, led him to grapple intensively with the contingency of existence, such that contingency became the defining "big idea" of the early part of his career. To say that existence is contingent, is to hold that there is no guiding hand of necessity that governs existence. The world does not *have* to be as it is, such that things *could* be otherwise; indeed, nothing *need* be, at all. At this point, the full extent of the radicalism associated with Sartre's idea of contingency begins to become clear; to say that anything is possible in a contingent world, means just that. Simone de Beauvoir writes of Sartre's early view of contingency in terms of a deliberately *dangerous* attitude on his part. De Beauvoir recounts that, in debates with Raymond Aron regarding contingency:

> Sartre went to unheard of extremes in his total rejection of universals. To him, general laws and concepts and all such abstractions were nothing but hot air: people, he maintained, all agreed to accept them because they effectively masked a reality which men found alarming. He, on the other hand, wanted to grapple with this living reality. (de Beauvoir 1983: 31)

The practical implications of Sartre's early radicalism with regard to contingency are nothing short of dramatic; on Sartre's account, one would have to countenance the possibility that a dropped glass would not fall to the ground and smash, but would instead remain floating in mid-air, or sprout wings and fly about, or do any number of other things besides. In other words, the whole of reality would have to be understood as underpinned by an increasingly flimsy consensus, as opposed to a firm series of evidentially verifiable laws. Physics, mathematics and indeed the pure sciences generally, would all have to be drastically re-evaluated (if not tossed aside altogether), were Sartre's view to be taken to its logical conclusion. Sartre's "theory of contingency", as he called it, thereby coincided with his realist thirst after personal and political authenticity; a view of existence as contingent, after all, is conceived entirely in opposition to the notion that there is (or ought to be) a necessary order of things, serving as the ultimate justification for maintaining the status quo.

In seeking to come to grips with the philosophical foundations of Sartre's view of apparently "necessary" laws, principles and so on as concealing the underlying contingency of existence, we might examine Sartre's relation to Friedrich Nietzsche's philosophy. In setting out to examine the Nietzsche–Sartre relation, it must be noted that Sartre himself tended to minimize the extent of Nietzsche's influence upon his philosophy. When questioned on the matter in a 1975 interview, Sartre claimed that he remembered "giving a seminar paper on Nietzsche in my third year at École Normale" (i.e. in 1927), and that Nietzsche "interested me like many others" (i.e. like many other philosophers); Sartre asserted, though, that ultimately Nietzsche "never stood for anything in particular in my eyes" (Sartre 1981b: 9). This ambivalent attitude towards the influence of Nietzsche's philosophy upon him later in life, would appear to sit convincingly alongside Sartre's youthful aggression toward Nietzscheans at École Normale; Sartre threw waterballoons on them, shouting "Thus pissed Zarathustra!", in a mocking reference to Nietzsche's masterpiece, *Thus Spake Zarathustra* (*ibid.*).

Despite Sartre's seeming reticence toward Nietzsche, however, there is genuine evidence to suggest that Nietzsche's perspective influenced the development of Sartre's view of contingency. The third-year seminar paper that Sartre referred to, for instance, was framed by the topic "Was Nietzsche a philosopher?". In responding to the topic, Sartre argued for a view of Nietzsche as a non-philosopher, who had revealed the extent to which all value-concepts were ultimately contingent, in the sense that they were not immanent, or otherwise "of the world"; rather, value-concepts were imposed by individuals upon the objects around them. On closer inspection, Sartre held, these apparently "necessary" structures of truth and meaning supposedly underpinning our existence, reveal themselves as fickle, transient and, indeed, absurd. The view of Nietzsche as a non-philosopher who was nonetheless engaged in revaluing foundational notions of truth and meaning, would appear to coincide with views Sartre had held regarding Nietzsche for some time – prior even to 1927. For instance, in 1924 (at around the age of nineteen) Sartre recorded his view of Nietzsche in one of his notebooks, as follows: "*Nietzsche*. He is a poet who had the misfortune of having been taken for a philosopher … he will always have success with those who prefer the form of ideas to their exchange" (Sartre 1990: 471).

In addition to Sartre's seminar paper and his assertions as a young man regarding Nietzsche, there is Sartre's creative work from the mid- to late 1920s to be considered. In 1926, at around the age of twenty-one, Sartre mentioned "writing about contingency" (Sartre 1974a: 5–6) in his correspondence with Simone Jollivet (also known as Simone Camille-Sans), his first "serious" love, prior to Simone de Beauvoir. Jollivet was a talented actress, starring on the French stage and screen, before ultimately declining into depression and alcoholism later in life. Now, during their brief romance (frustrated as it was by Sartre's inability to travel to Toulouse regularly to visit Jollivet), she revealed to Sartre her fascination with Nietzsche's philosophy. In response, Sartre wrote a semi-autobiographical novel over 1927–8, intended as a modern-day retelling of Nietzsche's relationships with both Richard Wagner and his wife Cosima – the so-called Tribschen triangle (Sartre 1990: 189–286). *A Defeat* does not see Sartre explicitly assert that existence is contingent (at least, not in the extant *Empedocles* section). Arguably, the novel was intended by Sartre to serve primarily as a kind of literary confessional for personal revelations regarding his personal relationships at the time (both with Jollivet and others), rather than as an explicitly philosophical allegory. Yet Sartre positions the figure of the philosopher – through the character of Fréderic, and therefore himself – as an individual who is able to conceive of the possibilities (but also the fundamental constraints) which arise in a world where we are free to interpret our situation in varied ways, in the absence of "necessary" states of affairs. Despite its role in the development of Sartre's ideas and also his literary technique, *A Defeat* was rejected for publication by Gallimard.

Around the same time (1927–8), Sartre worked on another Nietzschean novel project, *Er the Armenian*. Sartre intended this reworking of Plato's myth of Er, which appears at the conclusion of the *Republic*, as an examination of the theme of contingency in relation to moral value-concepts. In Plato's version of the myth, a man named Er (son of Armenios) dies in battle. Er's body remains undecomposed. Two days later he revives on his funeral pyre and tells others of his journey in the afterlife. The myth thereby introduces the idea that moral people are rewarded and immoral people punished after death.

In Sartre's rendering of the myth, however, Good and Evil are absent from the world itself, which is shown to be morally innocent. Sartre has Prometheus (the mythical Titan responsible for creating humans from clay, and punished by the gods for stealing fire for humankind's use) state that the situation of humankind would be bettered if the gods were vanquished. Prometheus asserts that "When the gods will be vanquished, there will be no more Evil on earth" (Sartre 1990: 322). This sentiment is broadly akin to the one Nietzsche expresses in an aphorism entitled "From paradise" in *The Gay Science* (Nietzsche 2001: §259). The classic biblical role of the snake as the tempter who brought about Adam and Eve's fall from grace is re-valued by Nietzsche, with the snake now positioned as the bringer of an anti-objectivist conception of morality, that paints moral absolutism as a form of divinely sanctioned bigotry. Nietzsche has the snake say: "Good and Evil are the prejudices of God" (*ibid.*: 150).

Sartre's early attempts to express his intuitions regarding contingency through his experimentations with Nietzschean ideas may well be viewed as lacking philosophical depth; indeed, in the case of his attempt to step into Nietzsche's shoes in *A Defeat*, Sartre's literary effort may seem pretentious, rather than a genuine homage. Yet, if we take together Sartre's earliest intuitions regarding realism with his radical view of contingency, then we are left with the view that the apparently "necessary" state of things serves, in fact, to conceal a reality where there are no guarantees. We are not just sent "down the rabbit-hole", so to speak, but *hurtling* down it, with no end in sight; a seemingly bottomless void. This is a view that can be examined via Nietzsche's early metaphysics of tragedy, in particular.

In *The Birth of Tragedy*, Nietzsche (1993) asserts that civilization is an illusion, constituted on the surface of the striving power that constitutes the whole of existence. Nietzsche refers to this striving power as the will (in a nod to Arthur Schopenhauer's philosophy). The will was represented in ancient Greek tragedy, on Nietzsche's interpretation, by the satyr chorus. Nietzsche asserts that the ancient Greeks were able to affirm their existence to themselves by casting-off the veil of civilization that cast them in the role of individuated subjects or persons, and returning to their original state of nature in primordial unity as satyrs, as pure will. In this way, Nietzsche argues, the Greeks were able to achieve a deep-going "metaphysical consolation" (*ibid.*: 39), in spite of their existential sufferings; the will, after all, is shown to be "indestructibly powerful and pleasurable", on Nietzsche's view (*ibid.*: 39). This supreme life-affirmation, though, could only be achieved through the Greeks' drive to grapple with the existential consequences of their realization of the illusion of civilization; in realizing the absurdity of existence, according to Nietzsche, we are "repulsed" (*ibid.*: 40). It was *in spite* of this repulsive absurdity, Nietzsche argues, that the Greeks found their respite, indeed their salvation, in their art, in their tragedies. The dialogic portion of ancient tragedy, according to Nietzsche, was governed by the art-impulse associated with the Greek god of light, learning and dream-seeing, Apollo. Meanwhile, the orchestral, musically driven aspect of tragedy was governed by the art-impulse associated with the god of ecstatic excess, Dionysus. By allowing these two oppositional art-impulses to come together in a titanic struggle, Nietzsche holds, the Greeks created a supreme art-form (*ibid.*: 32–40).

Now, the young Nietzsche's view of the absurdity of existence as "repulsive", is one that ought to resonate strongly with Sartre scholars, despite the fact that Nietzsche did not imbue the experience with the precise psychological character that Sartre attributes to it.

In Sartre's first published novel, entitled *Nausea* (Sartre 1938, 2007), the narrator, thirty-year-old dejected historian Antoine Roquentin, is repeatedly struck by nauseating qualms, which he records along with other day-to-day happenings and musings, initially on loose pages and then in a notebook. After years of travel, Roquentin has settled in the fictional seaport town of Bouville (roughly translated from French, Bouville means "mud-town"), to concentrate on his historical research focused on the life and times of a fictional eighteenth-century political figure, the Marquis de Rollebon.

In the winter of 1932, however, Roquentin first tastes the "sweetish sickness" (Sartre 2007: 11) he comes to call "the nausea" (*ibid.*: 18). From then on, this curious sensation of fearful, overwhelming disgust slowly seeps into every aspect of his existence (including his historical research, his sexual life, and his relationships with other people in general), driving him seemingly beyond the limits of his sanity. At first, Roquentin ascribes his malaise to the failure of a central project in his life. The subject of his historical research, the Marquis, will no longer "come alive" for him, so to speak. The Marquis's dying "for the second time", in this sense, thereby robs Roquentin of a justification for his work, and indeed, for his very existence (*ibid.*: 96). Roquentin also attempts to take refuge in his past, with a French-speaking Englishwoman named Anny with whom he was once intimate; it soon becomes clear, though, that Roquentin's recollections of Anny no longer match with the woman now before him. Indeed, the reader is left wondering whether Roquentin's view of Anny ever had any real substance, to begin with (*ibid.*: 135). Roquentin's feelings of repulsion and disgust ("the nausea"), are eventually revealed for him as having its source not in any one project, event or relationship, but rather in the sheer fact of Being, in the sheer fact of existence *itself*. The fact of existence is thereby unveiled not as an abstract epistemological designation bestowed upon things by academicians, but as a real and immediate *presence* in the world.

Roquentin is struck by the appearance of a chestnut tree root nearby the bench where he is sitting in a park, and it proves quite literally to be the "root" of the whole drama that has been unfolding up to this point. He realizes it has lost its significance for him, its essence *as* a chestnut tree, an essence he had thought of as stable, permanent, even eternal. Ultimately, this stripping-away of essences that were, in fact, accumulated by a fragile consensus in the first place, comes to apply to *everything* for Roquentin. Sartre has Roquentin say:

> I couldn't remember it [that is, the chestnut tree root] was a root any more. The words had vanished and with them the significance of things, their methods of use, and the feeble points of reference which men have traced on their surface. I was sitting, stooping forward, head bowed, alone in front of this black, knotty mass, entirely beastly, which frightened me. Then I had this vision. It left me breathless. Never, until these last few days, had I understood the meaning of "existence". I was like the others, like the ones walking along the seashore, all dressed in their spring finery. I said, like them, "The ocean is green; that white speck up there is a seagull," but I didn't feel that it existed or that the seagull was an "existing seagull"; usually existence hides itself. It is there, around us, in us, it is us, you can't say two words without mentioning it, but you can never touch it.   (*Ibid.*: 127)

Sartre soon has Roquentin make the transition from this experience with the tree root that *implies* the idea of contingency, to a more formalized conception of contingency that makes clear the weight of responsibility associated with the radical freedom that it entails. This time, he has Roquentin state:

> The essential thing is contingency. I mean that one cannot define existence as necessity. To exist is simply *to be there*; those who exist let themselves be encountered, but you can never deduce anything from them. I believe there are people who have understood this. Only they tried to overcome this contingency by inventing a necessary, causal being. But no necessary being can explain existence: contingency is not a delusion, a probability which can be dissipated; it is the absolute, consequently, the perfect free gift. All is free, this park, this city and myself. When you realize that, it turns your heart upside down and everything begins to float ... Here is Nausea; here there is what those bastards ... try to hide from themselves with their idea of their rights. But what a poor lie: no one has any rights; they are entirely free, like other men, they cannot succeed in not feeling superfluous. And in themselves, secretly, they are *superfluous*, that is to say, amorphous, vague, and sad. (*Ibid.*: 131)

Despite the prescient similarities we have considered regarding Sartre and Nietzsche's early views regarding the illusion of apparently "necessary" states of affairs concealing the absurdity of the underlying contingency of existence, Roquentin is no Dionysian disciple in the mould of the young Nietzsche; he does not find respite from his nausea (let alone ecstatic life-affirmation) in supreme artistic struggle and expression, even after his revelation in the park. It is true that Roquentin sees a slim hope of re-inventing himself at the conclusion of his diary, intimating that he might give up writing history and write fiction instead, after seeing a potential niche in existence for himself while listening to his favourite record, "Some of These Days". He asserts that this hypothetical fiction would have to be: "A story, for example, something that could never happen, an adventure. It would have to be beautiful and hard as steel and make people ashamed of their existence" (*ibid.*: 178).

This faint outline of a possible fictional plot comes after Roquentin's assertion earlier on, that he would "be better off writing a novel on the Marquis de Rollebon" (*ibid.*: 58). In other words, semi-biographical fiction is swapped for fiction proper by Roquentin, as a possible means of fundamentally reinvigorating himself. We might read Sartre here as asserting, through Roquentin, that fiction actually brings us *closer* to the "truth of things" than non-fiction, such as historical biography. Rather than trying to resurrect an historical existence and treat it as if it were real in the present, as Roquentin had tried and failed to do with his study of the Marquis, one can accept the fundamental *unreality* of fiction as capable of penetrating the very depths of existence. We have seen that this is possible with regard to Sartre's – and therefore Roquentin's – idea of contingency. Indeed, we might read *Nausea* as Roquentin's hypothetical novel, incorporating biographical elements with intrigues worthy of an adventure. Roquentin's hope for personal revitalization through creativity, though, is expressed as a tentative sort of hope, and nothing like the kind of powerful life-affirmation Nietzsche envisages. Whereas Nietzsche offered a vision of communal salvation from contingency in the form of therapeutic art, then, Sartre held that contingency could not be overcome, or even placated, by an affirmative force (whether artistic or otherwise), because such a power was simply *absent* from a truly contingent world.

In 1929, the year he graduated from École Normale, Sartre submitted his philosophical intuitions to a literary journal (*Les Nouvelles littéraires*) seeking submissions from students. In his piece, Sartre wrote (in part) to underscore the anti-Romantic, anti-vitalistic view of contingency he had been developing in contrast to the young Nietzsche. Sartre argues that there can be "no such thing" as an indestructibly powerful and pleasurable Will underlying all things; this is plainly evidenced, on Sartre's account, by the general frailty and feebleness of existence. Sartre argues that "Everything is too weak" to have ever been underpinned by such a well-spring of lively energy. Indeed, Sartre opposes Nietzsche's life-affirming Romanticism further still, in explicitly ascribing a feel of morbidity to this weakness; Sartre writes that "all things carry the seeds of their own death" (de Beauvoir 1963: 342–3). Sartre appears later to draw on this early critique of Nietzsche's Romantic vitalism in *Nausea*, when he has Roquentin say:

> There were those idiots who came to tell you about will-power and struggle for life. Hadn't they ever seen a beast or a tree? This plane-tree with its scaling bark, this half-rotten oak, they wanted me to take them for rugged youthful endeavour surging towards the sky. And that root? I would have undoubtedly had to represent it as a voracious claw tearing at the earth, devouring its food. (Sartre 2007: 133)

For Sartre, then, a view of all things as underpinned by a vitality nurtured by ongoing struggle requires too great an embellishment of the real state of things, as he understands it. Things are understood by him in terms of a mortal apathy, a pervasive *listlessness*.

Phenomenology: a way forward

Sartre's fundamental desire to maintain his radicalism while formalizing his ideas was eventually realized through his engagement with Edmund Husserl's phenomenology. The term phenomenology is derived from two ancient Greek words: *phainómenon* (that which appears) and *lógos* (study). Phenomenology, then, is a philosophical methodology for the study of the phenomena that appear in acts of consciousness; phenomenology's central aim therefore lies in revealing nature of consciousness and its objects, through the methodical and meticulous description of appearances in experience. Husserl asserts that the object is always given to a subject, and the subject is always directed towards an object; in other words, Husserl deftly succeeds in abolishing the subject/object divide between consciousness and the world.

From around 1933 onwards, Sartre read little else in philosophy except Husserl, with this period of intense study eventually concluding around 1939, only to give way to his close reading of Martin Heidegger's philosophy. By taking up the study of Husserl's works with such single-minded passion, Sartre had certainly left behind the brash intuitive simplicity of his earlier realism. Indeed, it may be thought that Sartre had retreated from his uncompromising initial assertion: namely, that philosophy ought to be founded on the claim that consciousness perceives things purely and simply as they are. Rather than abandoning his earlier realist intuitions, though, Sartre saw himself as realizing their rightful fruition, by grasping the real just as it is, through phenomenological description. Although Sartre did not interpret Husserl himself as advancing a philosophy of Realism *per se*, then, he nevertheless regarded his general goal of engaging directly with the world as it really is, as one he shared with Husserl. Sartre was now convinced that philosophy could address itself to the world as he saw and touched things, as he loved and fought with others, as he drank and smoked in bars; everything was now up for philosophical discussion.

Of course, Sartre also faced certain challenges in becoming a phenomenologist. Perhaps the most pressing of these was to integrate his realist sensibilities and his accompanying intuitions regarding existential contingency into a phenomenological framework; Husserl's account of the structures of consciousness and conscious experience would have to be purified of any elements that stood in the way of Sartre's radical worldview of contingency.

Fortunately, Sartre was presented with a timely opportunity to work through the philosophical underpinnings of his existential phenomenology. Taking leave from his first academic post as a high-school philosophy professor at Le Havre in provincial France, Sartre travelled to Berlin over the course of 1933–4 in order to study Husserl's writings intensively at the Maison Académique Francaise, the French institute in Berlin; meanwhile, Raymond Aron swapped places with Sartre at Le Havre. During this period, Sartre completed two philosophical texts that both drew upon, and deviated in crucial respects, from Husserl's philosophy; a long essay entitled *The Transcendence of the Ego* (Sartre 1957a) and a short text entitled "Intentionality: a Fundamental Idea of Husserl's Phenomenology" (Sartre 1970). In addition to these philosophical texts, Sartre also worked on drafting his *Factum on Contingency*, a forerunner to *Nausea*. We have already seen that it is possible (indeed, desirable) to interpret Sartre's early view of contingency in relation to Sartre's dramatization of Roquentin's discovery of contingency in *Nausea*. Given that Sartre wrote his philosophical texts in Berlin alongside his drafting of the *Factum*, it would seem reasonable to interpret *Transcendence* and Intentionality in relation to *Nausea*, as well.

Ego

In *The Transcendence of the Ego*, Sartre argues that Husserl's conception of the ego as transcendental, in the sense of its being included in consciousness, is inconsistent with his earlier views. In his *Logical Investigations*, published in 1900–1901, Husserl raises the tentative possibility that the ego might not, in fact, inhabit consciousness; he suggests that the ego may be an inert object *for* consciousness (Husserl 2001a: 202–4). In the first volume of his 1913 work *Ideas Pertaining to a Pure Phenomenology and to a Phenomenological Philosophy* (Husserl 1983), however, Husserl claims that such a perspective would involve a strange sort of transcendence for the ego. He describes this transcendence as one that is not constituted – a transcendence within immanence.

This was a philosophically peculiar position to hold in Husserl's view, and he was no longer prepared to entertain it as a possibility as his philosophy developed (*ibid.*: 133). Sartre argues that Husserl's change of heart with regard to the ego is philosophically inconsistent with his view of consciousness as intentional; one might even say that Sartre accuses Husserl of being in "bad faith" in this regard. Sartre reasons that if consciousness is fundamentally consciousness "of" something in the world, as Husserl claims it is, then *no* psychical object, least of all a transcendental ego, should continue to be included in consciousness. Accordingly, Sartre wrenches the ego out from its supposed hiding-place somewhere "behind" consciousness, and leaves it exposed to the travails of existence. In his introductory paragraph, Sartre succinctly describes his philosophical perspective, as well as his aims, in the following terms:

> For most philosophers the ego is an "inhabitant" of consciousness. Some affirm its formal presence at the heart of *Erlebnisse* [Husserl's term for "acts" or "states" of consciousness] as an empty principle of unification. Others – psychologists for the most part – claim to discover its material presence, as the centre of desires and acts, in each moment of our psychic life. I should like to show here that the ego is neither formally nor materially in consciousness: it is outside, in the world. It is a being of the world, like the ego of another. (Sartre 2004c: 1)

Consciousness, then, becomes quite literally self-less for Sartre, a totally transparent *nothing*. Consciousness purified of a transcendental Ego is constantly in the process of overflowing itself, of reaching out into the world in free pursuit of its possibilities. Sartre's view of self-creation here is understood in terms of a spontaneous, moment-to-moment process, that is never entirely "finished" in its becoming. Here, then, is a nascent formulation of Sartre's famous maxim, "existence precedes essence" (Sartre 2001: 28).

Sartre's choice of title is instructive here in its double meaning. The "transcendence of the ego" may initially be understood to refer simply to the subject of Sartre's inquiry, in that Sartre wants to show that the ego is transcendent, in so far as it is not an inhabitant of consciousness on, in his view. At the same time, though, the title can also be taken to refer to an active exhortation from Sartre to his reader, to transcend the culturally and intellectually pervasive conception of the ego as "transcendental", in the sense of its being included in consciousness, which is invoked by Husserl. In other words, Sartre's chosen title may be understood as capturing both the conception of the ego he is advocating, as well as the one from Husserl that he is opposing. At base, Sartre regards this view of selfhood and self-creation as the optimal foundation for an ethics and a politics that is outward-looking, worldly, and above all, positive.

Having now outlined the arguments put forward by Sartre in contrast to Husserl in *Transcendence*, we might now examine them closely.

Sartre gratefully acknowledges that Husserl's phenomenological method places him, as a philosopher, right in the midst of the objects of his experience. Yet Sartre seeks to show that Husserl needlessly *doubles* his conception of selfhood; Husserl identifies both a worldly psycho-physical self that is readily referred to by ourselves and by others as we go about living in the natural attitude, and a transcendental ego, that survives the *epoché* as an aspect of the fundamental structure of consciousness. Sartre refers to Husserl's transcendental ego as the "I", and to the empirical, worldly ego as the "Me". On Sartre's view, the very terms provided by Husserl's *own* methodology, ought to rule out the existence of an "I" that sits "behind" the "Me"; the *epoché*, Sartre reasons, is supposed to involve a suspension of any such fundamental existential assumptions and prejudices (Sartre 2004c: 5).

Sartre's critique of Husserl's holding-on to a transcendental Ego is not only based in his claim that Husserl's implementation of phenomenology (and in particular the *epochē*) lacks philosophical conscientiousness and rigour; Sartre also claims that Husserl's conception of the transcendental Ego would result in an explicit act of *violence* being perpetrated upon consciousness. Sartre conceives of Husserl's transcendental Ego as "slicing through" each moment of conscious activity like "an opaque blade", which would lead to the "death" of consciousness (*ibid*.: 7). A transcendental Ego would act to govern, and therefore weigh down consciousness, on Sartre's view, and he claims consciousness cannot be limited "except by itself" (*ibid*.: 7). Sartre acknowledges that one might argue that a transcendental Ego is the *source* of consciousness, without holding that a transcendental Ego is the *master* of consciousness. However, Sartre claims, nothing can be the source of consciousness, except consciousness itself.

On Sartre's account, consciousness is purified of a weighty transcendental Ego, leaving only a worldly "me". He then seeks to account for our experience of an "I" as sitting, in some sense, "behind", or "underneath" our immediate experience. According to Sartre, Descartes was not being misled when his methodical, introspective method of doubt revealed the *cogito*, or the "I think"; nor was Husserl being deceived when he discerned a transcendental Ego undisturbed the *epoché* (*ibid*.: 9). Where Descartes and Husserl both went wrong, though, on Sartre's account, was to presume that they were encountering an "I" that had been there *all along*. Sartre argues that what was actually occurring for Descartes and Husserl (as well as for anyone undertaking similar introspection) was the discovery of personalized consciousness, instantaneously created *through* reflection. In other words, Sartre holds that introspection does not *reveal* an "I", but instead *creates* one, at the very moment introspection takes place (*ibid.*: 11).

On this basis, Sartre asserts that we ought to approach with extreme caution the idea that it is possible to derive a solid ground for knowledge through introspective reflection, since it is in fact a seductive psychological mirage of sorts, which is often dubious, if not downright dishonest, in terms of the information it purports to provide us. Indeed, in the concluding section of *The Transcendence of the Ego*, Sartre asserts that all of the dramas people typically associate with their "inner life", including doubts, remorse and various emotional crises of the kind that people tend to record in diaries, are not features of our "inner selves" that are laid bare through introspection; rather, Sartre argues, these forms of inward-looking subject matter are "mere representations", that materialize along with the "I", upon introspection (*ibid.*: 43). Sartre is *not* claiming, it must be said, that our "inner lives" are of no consequence for us in terms of our attitude toward existence; rather, his claim is that we tend to treat what he regards as essentially transient and ephemeral thoughts, feelings and so on, as if they were immutable features of our self-hood, as it were, that cannot be grappled with, much less overcome.

It is especially interesting that in *Transcendence* Sartre invokes diary-writing as an example of what he regards as the inherent folly in self-scrutiny. After all, it is precisely this diary format that is employed to great literary effect by Sartre in *Nausea*. If Sartre's claims regarding self-exposés in *Transcendence* are anything to go by, then we must at the very least entertain the possibility that Sartre intends Roquentin's diary entries to be understood as a fundamentally futile exercise, revealing little more than red herrings and half-truths. These accounts, after all, are proffered by a poor witness: Roquentin's introspective "I" (Sartre 2007: 3). On the other hand, we might also interpret Sartre as asserting that one *can* overcome the illusion crafted by the introspective "I" (even if only momentarily) by attending closely to the objects of our worldly experience (*ibid.*: 2).

Having claimed that a transcendental ego is absent from consciousness, but also that the *appearance* of an "I" is created when we undertake introspective reflection, Sartre then makes a much brasher assertion; namely, that an "I" is absent from *unreflective* consciousness. Initially, this phenomenon seems impossible to describe, given that unreflective consciousness is, by definition, resistant to its being reflected-upon, let alone to its being phenomenologically described. It falls to Sartre to demonstrate how we might give expression to the absence of the "I" in un-reflective consciousness, in a way that does not defeat the very purpose of the exercise, by invoking personalized reflection. Sartre argues that unreflective consciousness can be demonstrated with recourse to memory; by carefully retrieving an experience in which we did not enter into reflection, Sartre argues, we may describe this situation without "disturbing" its unreflective quality. Sartre gives some substance to the role he envisages here for memory, through the experience of reading a particularly engrossing book.

Suppose I attempt to recreate the moment in which I was completely "involved", so to speak, in reading a book, such that I was no longer reflecting on the very fact of my reading as a personalized act, such that I was no longer reflecting on the fact that it was "I" who was reading. This moment was the precise moment in which an un-reflected consciousness, in Sartre's phrase, appeared. When I attempt to re-create that precise moment, I realize that although I am conscious "of" the book, conscious "of" the characters, the plot and so on, I am also aware that there is no "I" present in this experience. It is, therefore, not a case of describing an experience in which "I" am reading about a detective tracking down a murderer; there is only the detective's gruff demeanour, his penchant for cigarettes and whisky, his mistress's voluptuous figure, the murderer's sadistic cruelty, and so on. Everything is *happening*, but there is no sense of anything happening for *me* (Sartre 2004c: 12). In this way, the absence of an "I" in unreflective consciousness is demonstrated, without recourse *to* reflection (or at least, without recourse to the kind of reflection that would undermine Sartre's point). Although Sartre acknowledges that this demonstration of un-reflective consciousness lacks the *apodictic* certainty typically associated with phenomenological description due to the fallibility of memory, he nonetheless regards this method as the only suitable one for demonstrating the absence of the "I" in unreflective consciousness.

Following Sartre's demonstration to his satisfaction that a transcendental ego is absent from consciousness (even *un*reflective consciousness), he offers an account of how the one and only ego he *does* accept – the psycho-physical, worldly "me" – is constituted.

Sartre asserts that his conception of the ego is constituted of states, qualities and actions, with the ego serving to unify each of these entities as they are constituted in relation to consciousness. Having made a distinction between the various entities comprising the ego as they are constituted in relation to consciousness (*ibid.*: 21), Sartre then makes a rather startling claim: namely, that this relation between the "me" with its various entities and consciousness must be described in entirely *magical* terms (*ibid.*: 26). According to Sartre, this "magical" thinking is necessary because the lived spontaneity of conscious subjectivity cannot be grasped by a standard phenomenological framework that is concerned primarily with physical, rather than psychical, objects. Sartre asserts that, whereas physical objects are inert and reciprocally limited and defined by their relation to other such objects, consciousness is absolute and spontaneous. To demonstrate how this "magical" relation between the "me" and consciousness functions in practice, Sartre invokes a concrete emotional example, that of disgust. In everyday terms, we typically think of feelings of disgust towards someone as the *effect* of a state of hatred. Yet the spontaneity of consciousness that Sartre envisages means that such absolute causal links between a state (in this case, hatred) and an episode of consciousness (in this case, feelings of disgust toward someone in the world) are invalidated. Sartre argues that in the absence of a firm causal relation between psychical states and episodes of consciousness, we must rely on the "magical" notion of *emanation*, whereby a state does not "cause" a particular outcome or effect in an absolute sense, but instead, an effect *proceeds* from a state (*ibid.*: 25).

Sartre's use of the term "emanation" here is deliberately evocative of theology and the doctrine of the Holy Trinity, in particular. Just as the Son and the Holy Spirit "proceed" from God the father by emanation rather than by any kind of standard causal relation, Sartre holds that a similar idea can be applied to his example of the episode of consciousness involving disgust. The conscious episode of disgust, Sartre asserts, is not an *effect* of hatred, but its *emanation*. Whatever one might make of Sartre's claim here, the central thesis he advances in relation to the constitution of the ego is clear enough; the ego acts to bind together its own component-parts (states, qualities and actions), but the absolute spontaneity of consciousness means that the relation between consciousness and the "me" cannot be rendered in a typical phenomenological fashion. Sartre's conception of the ego, then, emphasizes the extent to which any attempt to "contain" or delineate consciousness in its pure spontaneity, particularly in terms of its relationship to the "me", is bound to slip through one's fingers, so to speak; "magical" notions therefore represent our only real hope of describing the interrelation between psychical states on the one hand, and episodes of consciousness on the other (*ibid.*: 26).

Sartre devotes the concluding portion of *Transcendence* to remarks on what he regards as having been the main achievements of his essay.

Sartre claims that his conception of the ego as "out there", in the world, just like the ego of another, overcomes two great philosophical conundrums, both of which also confronted Husserl: the problem of other minds, and the problem of solipsism. As far as Sartre is concerned, his conception of the ego's transcendence allows us to move from theorizing consciousness as secluded in the privacy of individual minds, to understanding it as an inherently worldly (and therefore *public*) phenomenon (*ibid.*: 43).

More than this, Sartre's perspective demonstrates an inherently *existential* motivation for the Husserlian *epoché*. Sartre holds that our primary motivation for eschewing the natural attitude should not be simply because of concerns over the internal coherence of Husserl's claims regarding a transcendental ego, though these concerns are of course pertinent to Sartre's project of purifying consciousness. Rather, Sartre asserts, the *epoché* attains its proper function by demonstrating the extent to which living in the natural attitude "masks from consciousness its own spontaneity". On Sartre's view, then, living immersed in the natural attitude allows us to avoid the anguish that would follow from recognizing the full extent of the freedom that this spontaneity entails. Indeed, Sartre claims that this realization of consciousness's spontaneity serves to explain the origins of certain forms of mental illness, in opposition to the predominant psychoanalytic explanations in vogue at the time (*ibid.*: 47).

A comparison with *Nausea* here again proves instructive. Roquentin's discovery of the contingency of existence occurs in the context of what appears to be a deep psychological disturbance. He experiences various hallucinations, troubled sleep punctuated by nightmares, paranoia and severe depression, among other symptoms. Indeed, he demonstrates an early insight into his condition when he decides he will have to undertake his own "psychological analysis", and he worries that his training as an historian will only allow him to describe his psychological state in the broadest terms (Sartre 2007: 4). Given Sartre's claim in *Transcendence* that a "vertigo of possibility" (Sartre 2004c: 47) may in fact be the true underlying cause of psychological suffering in many cases, it seems reasonable to understand Roquentin's predicament in terms of this "vertigo".

The *epoché*, in any case, is no longer motivated by rationality alone, but by a passionate grasp of the experience of anguish, and the desire to grapple with it. In his final remark, Sartre considers the political and ethical implications of his perspective. Interestingly, Sartre's targets here are theoreticians on the "extreme Left" who understand phenomenology as an Idealist philosophy (*ibid.*: 50). In certain respects, Sartre's position here appears commensurate with the classical view of him at this early point in his career as politically disengaged in comparison with his later philosophy, the political aspect of which was certainly aligned with the radical Left.

On the other hand, though, we might interpret Sartre's chastisement of the Left in relation to phenomenology as simply asserting that those on the Left who hold that phenomenology represents a form of Idealism, are actually doing their cause a *disservice*; after all, these critics, it may be argued, are failing to appreciate, and to harness phenomenology's power to describe our political situation, and to assist politically committed philosophers in bringing about concrete change. Sartre's bold claim here is that "nothing further is needed" (*ibid.*: 52) for an outward-looking, positive approach to ethics and politics, once his conception of a worldly Ego is accepted.

Intentionality

We have so far examined the arguments put forward by Sartre in the longer of the two philosophical texts he wrote in Berlin, namely *The Transcendence of the Ego*. We might now move to a consideration of the shorter text: "Intentionality: A Fundamental Idea of Husserl's Phenomenology". In this essay, Sartre forcefully restates his conviction – in concurrence with Husserl – that consciousness is fundamentally intentional, fundamentally consciousness "of" something. More than this, though, Sartre also argues that consciousness exhausts itself completely in its object. According to Sartre, consciousness is nothing other than its escaping itself in its Other – its object. In this way, Sartre gives expression to his view that consciousness is not a process that can be formally observed or grasped as such; consciousness is *pure* intentionality alone, in Sartre's view. In undertaking to purify consciousness of everything but its intentionality, its directedness toward its object, Sartre uses phenomenology's descriptive prose. According to Sartre:

> Consciousness is purified; it is clear as a strong wind. There is nothing in it but a movement of fleeing itself, a sliding beyond itself. If, impossible though it may be, you could enter "into" a consciousness, you would be seized by a whirlwind and thrown back outside, in the thick of the dust ... for consciousness has no "inside." Precisely this being-beyond-itself, this absolute flight, this refusal to be a substance, is what makes it be a consciousness.
> (Sartre 1970: 4)

At the same time, Sartre uses similarly descriptive prose to formally attack the subjective Idealism he had been educated in. Sartre writes evocatively (and indeed provocatively) of subjective Idealism as "digestive philosophy". On Sartre's account, subjective Idealism in France has been guided by the credo that "to know is to eat". Sartre laments that:

> We have all believed that this spidery Mind trapped things in its web, covered them with a white spit, and slowly swallowed them, reducing them to its own substance. What is a table ...? A certain assemblage of "contents of consciousness" ... O digestive philosophy! (*Ibid.*)

By casting the subjective Idealist view of the Mind in the role of a spider consuming its prey, and the subject as entrapped in the "moist gastric intimacy" (*ibid.*: 4) of this metaphoric digestive process, Sartre had given a vivid clarity to his central criticism of subjective Idealism: The object experienced is not the thing in itself; the subject experiences "contents of consciousness" constituted by its own mediating processes. Subjects therefore experience only *themselves*.

As was the case with *Transcendence*, the views Sartre expresses in "Intentionality" can be understood in relation to *Nausea*. Roquentin provides us early on with an account of the experience of being conscious of objects, in light of his particular project to dine using a fork, or smoke a pipe. He is aware of the fact that when he attempts to pick up and use either of them that he is projecting that intention onto the object, and this manifests itself in the feeling that something has changed "in [his] hands" (Sartre 2007: 4) when he attempts to do so. He is confused as to whether his fork, for instance, "now has a certain way of getting itself picked up", or it is he who is doing the picking up (*ibid.*). What we have here, then, is an undecided perspective on the intentional order of things, so to speak, but an awareness, nevertheless, of the concept of intentionality as fundamental to a view of consciousness as put forward by Sartre. That is to say, Roquentin shifts seemingly naturally from a consciousness of his being-conscious, to a "spreading" of this understanding onto objects of his experience. In short, he is conscious of his being-conscious "of" the objects of his experience.

The literary aspect of "Intentionality" that is arguably most pertinent in relation to *Nausea*, though, is its imagery of digestion. By conceiving of Roquentin's experience of contingency in terms of nauseating qualms, Sartre gives expression to the notion that Roquentin's discovery of contingency is too much for him to swallow, too much for him to digest. At the same time, Sartre may be read as expanding further on the critique of subjective Idealism developed in "Intentionality". Given that Roquentin cannot digest the fact of contingency, his "indigestion", so to speak, could be read as a negative parody of the stomach-like role Sartre claims is taken on by the Mind under a subjective Idealist worldview. Roquentin cannot assimilate the world into "contents of consciousness", left to slowly dissolve in the "moist gastric intimacy" (Sartre 1970: 4) of his mental interiority. Instead, everything he attempts to get hold of, to take in, simply throws him back out into the world, into the midst of the Nausea.

Conclusion

We began our exploration of Sartre's early philosophy guided by the intuition that it is possible to view the young Sartre not as an insular philosopher who subsequently came to be engaged with the world, but as a man actively engaged from the very beginning of his career in a fight to tear down all barriers that prevented him from grappling with life. To that end, we traced Sartre's initial raw realist intuitions through to his intuitions regarding the radical contingency of existence. I suggested that a reading of Sartre's early view of contingency as an anti-romantic, anti-vitalistic reaction to Nietzsche's early philosophy in particular, provides a useful way of interpreting the conceptual underpinnings of this aspect of Sartre's nascent philosophy. We then addressed the impasse posed for Sartre's realism and his view of contingency by subjective idealism, with phenomenology offering Sartre a way forward from this impasse. Given the life-changing importance of existential phenomenology for Sartre, we considered a reading of two of Sartre's early philosophical works (*The Transcendence of the Ego* and "Intentionality: A Fundamental Idea of Husserl's Phenomenology") that positions them as bound by their concern to position consciousness, and therefore the conscious experience of existence, as constantly "going beyond" itself, constantly tending outwards towards the world. Throughout our discussion of these early texts, we considered the relationship between Sartre's early philosophy in its essayistic form, and its literary dramatization in *Nausea*. This view of *Transcendence*, "Intentionality" and *Nausea* as an interrelated "set" of texts, allows for Sartre's initial conceptual intuitions to be understood not simply as psychologically insular insights that were superseded or overtaken by his "engaged", politically driven post-war philosophy. Rather, Sartre's early philosophy may rightly be regarded as underpinned by a conceptual framework that is inherently "engaged" with the world in its own right.

Further reading

Barnes, H. E. 1959. *Humanistic Existentialism: The Literature of Possibility*. Lincoln, NE: University of Nebraska Press.

Brombert, V. H. 1961. *The Intellectual Hero: Studies in the French Novel 1880–1955*. London: Faber & Faber.

Kaufman, W. 1975. *Existentialism from Dostoevsky to Sartre*. New York: New American Library.

Rolls, A. & E. Rechniewski (eds) 2006. *Nausea: Text, Context, Intertext*. Amsterdam: Rodopi.

SIX
Sartre: novelist and playwright
Adrian van den Hoven

Sartre the novelist

Sartre began his career as a novelist in 1938 with *Nausea*, and ended it with the third volume of the Roads to Freedom series (Sartre 1949a), as well as fragments of a fourth volume (posthumously published as *The Last Chance*; Sartre 1981a, 2009). In 1940, as a prisoner-of-war in Trier, Germany, Sartre wrote (and performed in) his first play, a Christmas mystery called *Bariona, or the Son of Thunder* (Sartre 1962b); he ended his playwriting career in 1965 with his adaptation of Euripides's *The Trojan Women*.

Nausea is a perfect illustration of Fernandez's conception of the novel "as unfolding in the present, as does life itself" (Sartre 1947a: 15). Events in this diary unfold in a discontinuous, haphazard manner, and Roquentin, the solitary narrator, adopts it "in order to see more clearly" (Sartre 1981a: 5). Its core passage "In the Public Park" illustrates Roquentin's experience of contingency, and, since it takes place towards the end of the novel, it requires that one keep this revelation constantly in mind if one wishes to arrive at a proper interpretation. Roquentin discovers that the "essential is contingency", that it is "the absolute … or the absurd", and that the universe is "perfectly gratuitous" (*ibid.*: 153–5). As a result, he views most human endeavours as pathetic attempts to disguise reality and to obscure, or embellish and prettify man's real position in the world. This applies to such arts as novel-writing, sculpture, architecture, theatre. The ragtime "Some of These Days" and geometrical figures escape from this stricture because as intangible non-existents they inspire in Roquentin the hope that perhaps he can save himself retrospectively by writing "an adventure that couldn't not have happened ... and that would allow people to guess at something that didn't exist, be beyond existence ... and make people ashamed of theirs" (*ibid.*: 210).

Nausea represents a quest for a lucid understanding of man's place in the universe. Therefore Roquentin satirizes the Autodidact's attempt to embrace the world's knowledge by reading the library's holdings in alphabetical order; he also realizes that novels rearrange events in order to suit the ending and abandons his biography of Rollebon because he appears to be resuscitating himself rather than his subject. In turn, Anny, his ex-mistress, rejects him. This actress had viewed life in theatrical terms as "privileged situations" that required the creation of "perfect moments" (Sartre 1981a: 169). She has given up that belief but is not willing to reconcile with him notwithstanding his recounting his epiphany in the Public Park. He also loses the Self-Taught Man. The humanist turns out to be a pederast and is caught fondling boys in the public library. After being punched in the face by the librarian, he disappears. After this series of abandonments, losses and painful discoveries, Roquentin is ready to return to Paris, live as a *rentier* and vegetate. Now his second epiphany occurs while he is listening to the ragtime "Some of These Days" a final time. Since neither geometrical figures nor music exist, he projects music as a possible solution to his dilemma. It does not add to the superabundance of existents and permits one to posit the creation of a purely imaginative work.

Roquentin's first experience with nausea is revelatory. At the beach he attempts to emulate young boys who are skimming stones. He picks up a pebble but stops before he can throw it: "the pebble feels flat and dry, especially on one side, damp and muddy on the other. I held it by the edges with my fingers wide open so as not to get them dirty" (*ibid.*: 6). The pebble's admixture of certain basic elements – mineral, water and mud – as well as the pseudo-homosexual encounter with the young boys relate this experience of absurdity to his epiphany in the Public Park and the Autodidact's fateful encounter in the library. Next Roquentin attempts to describe a cardboard container; it is "a parallelepiped rectangle" (*ibid.*: 5) but then gives up. Perspective, introduced by Dührer, and since then used to provide a stable viewpoint on the world is failing him. However, once he feels again "quite at home in the world" he is able to describe the world outside his window from a stable vantage point: "Here is my room facing north-east. Below the Street of the War Amputees and the construction site of the new station. I see the red and white flame of the 'Railroad Workers' Rendezvous' at the corner of Boulevard Victor-Noir" (*ibid.*: 6). But this stable perspective is illusory; when he brings his face close to the mirror, he remarks:

> what I see is well below the monkey, on the fringe of the vegetable world, at the level of jellyfish … The eyes are glassy, soft, blind, red-rimmed, they look like fish scales … A silky white down covers great slopes of the cheeks, two hairs protrude from the nostrils: it is a geologically embossed map. And, in spite of everything, this lunar landscape is familiar to me.   (*Ibid.*: 23)

As a human he has descended to the aquatic, the vegetable and the mineral realm. The traditional hierarchal view of man has collapsed; its substitute is a phantasmagorical conception of man in which all the universe's elements are intertwined. This lucid awareness of himself as a composite creation provokes him to reject the bourgeoisie in scathing terms: the "worthy citizens who did their duty and have rights" (*ibid.*: 98–113) and whose portraits hang in Bouville's ("Mudville" or "Cowtown") museum. They look down on Roquentin, this solitary individual "without social importance" (*ibid.*: 1) but he considers them "a bunch of bastards" (*ibid.*: 113). This satirical, parodical and critical work clears the air. It forces us to see beyond the distorting and illusionary veils that art, culture and philosophy (humanism) have imposed on us and recognize reality in all its overwhelmingly raw, and non-human manifestations. *Nausea* represents a comprehensive confrontation with the absurdity of mankind's existence and, paradoxically, it is also a valiant attempt to see beyond it and create a "human" space for us.

The collection of stories in *The Wall* (Sartre 1939c, 1969a) conform to Fernandez's conception of the *récit* in which "the action takes place in the past; it explains and the chronological order barely disguises the underlying causal framework" (Sartre 1947a: 16). "The Wall", set in the Spanish Civil War, deals with Tom, Juan and Pablo, who have been condemned to death. It succeeds admirably in depicting the psychological anguish of the condemned men who are sharing the knowledge that these are the last days. However, Pablo, the narrator, is set free after he accidentally betrays his leader Juan Gris in an attempt to make the enemy look ridiculous. Upon discovering that, Pablo bursts out in "laughter" (Sartre 1981a: 233). He now finds himself with his back to the wall rather than staring at it but his attempted farce has turned tragic.

"The Room" tells the story of Mr and Mrs Darbédat, their daughter Eve and her husband Pierre, who appears to be going mad. Mr Darbédat is the picture of rugged health, his wife is a hypersensitive homebody and Eve is colluding with Pierre in his plunge into the world of madness.

This story views madness as a flight into an imaginary universe that "common sense" people find impossible to penetrate.

In "Erostratus", the modern counterpart of the eponymous mythical "hero" fails pathetically to gain fame posthumously. In the surrealist manner he takes a loaded revolver into the street, pulls the trigger three times but mistakenly goes down the wrong street only to find himself in the midst of a crowd. He pulls the trigger two more times and hides in a washroom. Instead of using the sixth bullet for himself, he opens the door at the last moment. The ultimate surrealist's gesture has resulted in a pointless tragedy.

"Intimacy" satirizes modern romances as found in women's magazines. Lulu lives with her "impotent" husband Henri (*ibid.*: 280) but imagines a romantic getaway with her lover Pierre. Rirette, Lulu's girlfriend, eagerly attempts to have Lulu leave her husband and move to the Midi with Pierre. But Pierre turns out to be a mother's boy and Lulu soon returns to her impotent husband because in fact she prefers his helplessness to Pierre's ostensibly masculine ways. Another failure: Lulu prefers dramatic "gestures" to real change.

"The Childhood of a Leader," inspired to a degree by Sartre's own childhood, is first an attempt to satirize the bourgeoisie's pretentions to "duty", "responsibility" and to its deserving a "dominant role" in French society. Lucien is anything but a leader; he experiments with homosexuality, surrealism, women and right-wing fascist politics yet finally follows in his father's footsteps. He may well think that he has undergone a "metamorphosis" and become a "leader" but a look in the mirror reveals his "childish appearance". At that moment he decides "to grow a moustache" to appear "more terrible" (*ibid.*: 388). These dexterous verbal exercises illustrate Sartre's perfect mastery of the genre and clearly demonstrate his ability to pinpoint people's flights into bad faith and the imaginary.

Unlike *Nausea*, the Roads to Freedom series paints a much broader social and political canvas. Sartre's discovery of John Dos Passos's *Nineteen Nineteen* leads him to attempt to incorporate the most intimately personal and most social and public aspects of human existence in a novel. Hence, the series takes the form of a chronicle that deals with the lives of a philosophy professor Mathieu Delarue, his pregnant mistress Marcelle, the younger Ivich and others as these lives unfold in the late 1930s. The series begins with *The Age of Reason* (Sartre 1945a, 1947e). The second volume is the most successful. In *The Reprieve* (Sartre 1945c, 1947f), Sartre adapts Dos Passos's and others' technique of multiple perspectives to deal with the signing of the Munich Accord, which brought temporary peace to Western Europe but was disastrous for Czechoslovakia. It illustrates perfectly Sartre's eclectic talents as a novelist as it succeeds admirably in recreating the period's anguish, confusion and false relief that was the result of the politics of appeasement. *Iron in the Soul* (Sartre 1949a, 1950b) concludes with the apparently last moments of Mathieu shooting at the advancing Germans from a tower. He "blazes away" at all his past "failures" for "fifteen minutes" (Sartre 1981a: 1344); but is not killed. In *The Last Chance* (included in Sartre 1981a), the incomplete fourth volume, we encounter Mathieu and others in a POW camp. Ultimately, Sartre had hoped to demonstrate the "conversion" of his main characters into committed persons. But their highly dramatized metamorphoses would also have revealed the limits of Sartre's project. His very realistically drawn "types" could hardly have been expected to have become "genuinely" existential heroes or villains.

Sartre the playwright

Sartre's first play *Bariona* (Sartre 1962b; also included in Sartre 2005a, as are all Sartre's other plays discussed below) mixes elements of his own philosophy with biblical and literary sources and demonstrates his conception of the theatre as a world apart and distinct from ours in which speech, gestures and objects operate in a synecdochic relationship with the spectators' psyche and thereby allow a complete grasp of the underlying message. Bariona accepts the Romans' demand for an excessive tax increase but then imposes enforced celibacy on his people so that that the tribe will die off. He even insists that his wife abort. However, when the people hear about the Saviour, they disobey his commands and rush to Bethlehem. Bariona follows them and when he looks into Joseph's eyes he is instantly converted and decides to take on the Roman army to save the life of the Saviour. The "look" will play a significant role in Sartre's *Being and Nothingness*, published in 1943. Bariona's act of defiance prefigures Orestes's defiant refusal to bow to Jupiter's authority and Hugo's quixotic refusal to accept the Party's latest change of direction.

Sartre's second play *The Flies* performed during the Occupation is a reformulation of the Orestes story. He returns to Argos to find his roots but instead discovers that the city is living under a curse. The city stands for the Vichy regime. Like Pétain, Jupiter has imposed a fake hierarchy of values and the king and queen are colluding with him and imposing a sense of guilt on their citizens. His sister Electra begs Orestes to murder his mother Clytemnestra and her new husband

Egisthus, who are responsible for their father's murder. He does so, but, overcome with guilt, Electra decides to stay and Orestes declares himself free, abandons the city and accepts full responsibility for his murderous act. Orestes's decision has often been criticized; he should have stayed and assumed the throne. But by refusing it and rejecting Jupiter's fake value system, he ends up playing an exemplary role and telling Parisians they don't have to accept the Vichy's fake value system either because they too are free!

Sartre's play *No Exit* is deservedly his best-known drama. It fits his criterion that action should be set in a distant place: hell, and hence it becomes pure theatre. Since Garcin, Inès and Estelle are dead, all their acts are reduced to mere gestures. Sartre's hell turns the traditional depiction upside down, there is neither fire nor brimstone nor instruments of torture; these characters are tortured by their past and those still alive, they torture each other in the present and will forever continue to do so. This impossible trio composed of Garcin, the cowardly but macho womanizer, Inès, the hard-nosed lesbian and sado-masochist, and Estelle, the frivolous society woman and child killer, become each other's mirrors and judges. They can no longer undo their past and they must "live" forever fully aware of what they have become. As in *Bariona*, the look is crucial; the "multiple eyes" staring at him make Garcin realize that "Hell is other people" (Sartre 2005a: 127–8). None will ever escape the others' accusing glare and they will forever be trapped on their infernal merry-go-round.

The Victors and the farce *Nekrassov* deviate from Sartre's rule that dramatic action should be situated far away in time and space but in a sense the extravagant farce creates its own space and time. *The Victors*, similar in many ways to "The Wall", is set in the Vercors and deals with the French *milice* and the *maquis* but unlike in "The Wall" where the men's suffering is psychological, the *maquisards* are tortured on stage and, consequently, Sartre sins against a capital rule of neo-classical French theatre that excluded violence. Given Sartre's bourgeois audience the reaction was predictable and the play was a failure. When in "The Wall" Pablo accidentally betrays his leader, he is set free but that is not the case with the *maquisards*. They too will send the *miliciens* on a wild goose chase and they succeed in their ruse because Jean, their leader, is set free but in spite of the *miliciens*' promise, the *maquisards* are executed anyway. On the other hand, their torture is pointless because up until Jean is introduced into their midst they do not know his whereabouts.

The Respectful Prostitute resulted in Sartre being accused of anti-Americanism. Sartre had visited the USA in 1945 and written about racism in *Le Figaro* and subsequently he became a well-known advocate for the Third World; however, this play is as much an illustration of the Deep South's fraught race relations as it is a denunciation of that hierarchical society's value system. Sartre had read about the Scottsboro Boys trial and knew his Faulkner and the result is a play where the dominant whites get away with murder as they terrorize blacks and subjugate "white trash". Lizzie is a New York prostitute who is travelling South on a train hoping to settle down and be provided for by some rich elderly gentlemen. This improbable scenario is complicated by the fact that in the segregated South she shares her compartment with two blacks. When a group of white men enter a fight breaks out, one of the blacks is shot and one escapes. Lizzie is picked up in a nightclub by Fred, the murderer's cousin, and they spend the night together in Lizzie's newfound apartment. Next morning the escaped black man knocks on her door and begs her to testify in his favour in court. The honest Lizzie agrees but she had not counted on Fred, the puritanical, lustful racist. He has left two ten-dollar bills on the table to entrap her so that when the police arrive, who are in collusion with Fred, there is proof that she is a prostitute. Lizzie also has a sentimental and socially upward mobile side to her and when Fred's father, the senator, pleads the case of the murderer's mother he succeeds in forcing Lizzie to sign and declare her son Thomas the innocent victim. In the meantime the lustful Fred shoots at another black who is being lynched and sees Lizzie's face in the flames. If his father had made much of the superiority of whites over blacks, Fred in turn sings the praises of the white elite over such social outcasts as prostitutes. When Lizzie agrees to become his kept woman, Fred proclaims that everything is back in order. When Sartre became a fellow traveller of the Communist Party, he allowed to have the ending changed and at the last moment Lizzie and the black man escape in a waiting police car. Given that the police had been shown colluding with the white elite, that ending appears improbable. Yet the play is a good indication of Sartre's thinking about the pervasive power the elite exercise over groups they consider social outcasts.

Dirty Hands is rightly considered a masterpiece, but its seemingly anti-communist conclusion caused great embarrassment to Sartre, the fellow traveller. It conforms to Sartre's conception of theatre: it is set in a far-away country and presents us with a universe where the standard laws of space and time are suspended. We move from Olga's house to Hoederer's office and back to Olga's. In three hours we move from the present to the past during which most of the action is played out in a sort of suspended present. It pits the young idealist Hugo against the realist politician Hoederer but what makes it interesting is the extended flashback that recreates the period that Hugo spent as Hoederer's secretary and designated assassin. But Hugo ends up killing Hoederer not for political reasons but because he sees his wife in this "father figure's" arms. When, at the last moment he discovers that the Party has rehabilitated Hoederer, he rejects this latest political twist and defiantly allows himself to be eliminated to justify his own beliefs and Hoederer's tactics. The play leaves us suspended between his youthful idealism and the exigencies of realpolitik. "To lie or not to lie" has become the ultimate question (Noudelmann & Gilles 2004: 297–9).

The Devil and the Good Lord, once again set in a faraway place and time, plays on the paradox of good and evil and illustrates that Goetz, by alternatively playing both roles, is only fooling himself and that it is not the ultimate act of defiance that he thought it was. It is only when he accepts to do what he can do best, lead the army, that he realizes his true role. Ironically, he tells Nasty that he is not "born to command" but wants to "obey", which results in Nasty ordering him to assume leadership "of the army" and thus "to obey" (Sartre 2005a: 499). When next he kills a chief who would rather "die" than "obey" him, he proclaims: "I take the command against my own will; but I won't give it up. Believe me, if there is a possibility of winning this war, I will win it … There, the reign of man has begun". And finally: "I will remain alone with this empty sky above my head because I have no other way of being with you. We have to fight this war and I will fight it" (*ibid*.: 501). Once again, a series of empty gestures conclude with a definitive final act but it also brings out the forlornness of the modern hero who must act without the divine guidance he had previously sought in vain.

Sartre's adaptation of Dumas's *Kean* shows his marvellous grasp of the importance of gestures and acts and "theatricality" in general. Kean is admired as a genius on stage but despised as a lowly actor. This bastard is full of resentment against the aristocracy but it is only when he transgresses the rules, steps out of his role and orders the aristocrats to "keep quiet" because "on stage he reigns supreme" (*ibid*.: 638) that he regains his dignity. It represents the victory of meritocracy over the aristocracy and Kean confirms it by marrying Anna who will be his manager during the day and his lover at night.

Nekrassov satirizes not only the French right-wing press but also his own philosophy. It is a marvellous *tour de force* but it fails to convince us that all defectors from the Soviet Union are impostors. Sartre's dislike of the bourgeoisie was a well-known fact but this play shows the limits of his "fellow-travelling". If one can ignore the obviously fallacious message, it can be seen as a masterful display of his grasp of the spoofing done by the Keystone cops and others.

Unlike *The Victors*, *The Condemned of Altona* is a much subtler attempt to denounce torture as practised by the French army in Algeria. Set in Germany, it embraces a vast period from Luther and the rise of capitalism to the post World War II German *Wirtschaftwunder*. Hence it can also be viewed as a biting commentary on the collusion between leading industrial figures and whatever government is in power. Since Sartre was at the same time working on the *Freud Scenario*, it illustrates again, as did *Dirty Hands*, the fateful father-son relationship in which, in this case, the son, unable to loosen the bonds that bind them, becomes the "Butcher of Smolensk" and, hence, Sartre succeeds in "demystify[ing] military heroism by showing its link to unconditional violence" (*ibid.*: 1015). In this theatrical masterpiece Sartre exploits all the media resources, from cinema, to radio and the tape recorder, and illustrates the tenets of existential psychology in which the flashbacks and prolepses ultimately force Frantz to admit to his own war crimes. As in *No Exit*, the action takes place on two levels. Frantz's deliberate sequestration and feigned madness are desperate attempts to justify Germany's defeat as a disaster because he needs to deny Germany's evident economic rebirth and hide from his own failure. Father and son commit suicide together; their blindness to the horrific reality they have created leaves them no other way out. Yet, to the extent that we identify with Frantz, we recognize our own "complicity in that horrific universe's creation" (*ibid.*: 1028). It was Sartre's hope that the French public would "recognize that they are like the Germans portrayed" and that 'the theatrical mirage would disappear to leave room for the truth that hides behind the mirage" (*ibid.*: 1016).

Let us conclude with Sartre's remarks about his adaptation of the *Trojan Women*, which was a box-office failure and ended his career as a dramatist. This denunciation of war: "ends on a note of total nihilism ... In it the Gods die as well as the humans, and that death is the moral of the tragedy" (*ibid.*: 1051). Ultimately, Sartre's vision of a world without God thrives always on dramatic moments: both in his prose and his theatre it is the transforming act that makes man and ... makes all the difference.

Acknowledgement

I would like to thank Walter Skakoon for his insightful suggestions.

Further reading

Howells, C. 1988. *The Necessity of Freedom*. Cambridge: Cambridge University Press.
O'Donohoe, B. 2005. *Sartre's Theatre: Acts for Life*. Bern: Peter Lang.
Sartre Studies International 2012. "A Symposium on Sartre's Theater". *Sartre Studies International* 18(2): 49–126.

SEVEN

Psychoanalysis and existential psychoanalysis
Betty Cannon

Throughout his work Sartre has demonstrated a deep and continuing interest both in psychological theory in general and psychoanalysis in particular. His writing on psychological themes began with his thesis at the École Normale Supérieure in 1927, which was later published in revised form as the first part of *Imagination* (Sartre 1936, 1972a). This was followed by two classical philosophical/psychological treatises, *The Emotions: Outline of a Theory* (Sartre 1939a, 1975) and *The Imaginary: A Phenomenological Psychology of the Imagination* (Sartre 1940, 2004a). Sartre's first major philosophical work, *The Transcendence of the Ego* (Sartre 1936–7, 1957a), is at least as significant psychologically as it is philosophically. Of course, Sartre devotes a section of his philosophical masterpiece, *Being and Nothingness* (Sartre 1943a, BN1, BN2), to the development of premises for an existential psychoanalysis.

Sartre's interest in psychoanalysis took a new turn in 1956 when he did extensive research and reading based on a request from producer John Huston to write a screenplay on Freud's life. Posthumously edited and published by Sartre's friend and colleague, the eminent French psychoanalyst J.-B. Pontalis, *The Freud Scenario* (Sartre 1986a) is surprisingly vivid, favourable to Freud, and faithful to the Freud/Jones account of the birth of psychoanalysis (Jones [1953] 1961). A careful reading reveals that most of the evidence for the unconscious that Freud discovers can be interpreted in two ways – according to Freud's theory of the unconscious and Sartre's theory of bad faith. Sartre's rereading of Freud at this time may have influenced his account of Flaubert's hysterico-epilepsy in *The Family Idiot* (Sartre 1971–2, 1981c, 1987, 1989a, 1991a, 1993c). At the same time, Sartre's account of Flaubert's difficulties demonstrates a deepening of his own theory of bad faith to explain more fully the role of the body in the creation of symptoms. It may also be that when Sartre remarks in *Search for a Method* that only psychoanalysis "allows us to discover the whole man in the adult; that is, not only his present determinations but the weight of his history" (Sartre 1968: 60), he was thinking of his recent encounter with Freud in writing the screenplay.

Pontalis thought that one day the history of Sartre's deeply "ambiguous relationship" with psychoanalysis "will have to be written and perhaps his work reinterpreted in the light of it" (Sartre 1979: 220). The truth is that Sartre gave Freud an enormous amount of credit while disagreeing with him on many crucial issues. Sartre is aware that existential psychoanalysis could not have existed without the prior invention of Freudian psychoanalysis. He understands that his version of existential psychoanalysis is only a set of principles and that it provides nothing like the application to work with patients that fills out the literature of psychoanalysis. Sartre's psychobiographies provide examples, but they are not clinical examples. Existential psychoanalysis, Sartre says, has "not yet found its Freud" (EN: 734). Instead the "final discoveries" of ontology must become "the first principles of [existential] psychoanalysis" (EN: 735). Those principles are Sartrean, although Sartre has learned much from Freud. Later Sartre welcomed R. D. Laing's work, which is deeply influenced by Sartre, as exemplifying a psychoanalytic perspective compatible with his own (Laing & Cooper [1964] 1971: 6; Sartre 1979: 204).

This chapter will compare and contrast existential with Freudian psychoanalysis, concluding with a brief consideration of how Sartre might be useful to psychoanalysis today.

Freud's theory and method: the appeal to natural science

Freud, like many psychologists from various perspectives, from his time to ours, attempted to ground his approach in the natural science of his day. His position is fundamentally deterministic and materialist. He says that the intent of his early "Project for a Scientific Psychology", which is part of his posthumously published correspondence with his friend Wilhelm Fleiss, is "to furnish us with a psychology which shall be a natural science; its aim, that is, is to represent psychological processes as quantitatively determined states of specifiable material particles and so make them plain and void of contradictions" (Freud [1950] 1953–74: 355). In other words, Freud's aim is to reduce psychology to neurophysiology, an aim that is sometimes voiced by psychologists today.

Freud did not publish the Project during his lifetime because he realized that the science simply was not there. Yet he did not abandon the attempt to ground psychoanalysis in natural science explanations and metaphors, as some post-Freudian theorists have claimed. He never followed his own precept that psychoanalysis should cleanse itself of everything but "psychological auxiliary ideas" (Freud [1916–17] 1953–74: 21). The four major hypotheses of his psychological metatheory are all scientistic postulates in the sense that they use natural science metaphors to try to establish the validity of psychoanalysis. The most experience-distant of these, the drive theory of the economic hypothesis, is based on energy flow, inhibition and displacement – metaphors derived from charge and discharge theories borrowed from physics, hydraulic metaphors adapted from the discovery of the steam engine, and Freud's study with his mentors, Brucke and Meynert, in neurophysiology.

The flow of energy in the organism is first conceived in terms of psychobiological forces – libidinal and aggressive drives in the early Freud and, in his later work, life and death instincts, Eros and Thanatos. Freud believed that instinctual energy can neither be created nor destroyed, that it is at least theoretically measurable, that it can be condensed or displaced from its original objects to others (as in transference), that it can be "converted" from one form to another (as in hysterical blindness), and that it can be withdrawn from the external world towards the ego or a lost object (as in narcissism or mourning).

"Cathexis" is a concept implying the amount of energy attached to an object, an idea or ideas, or a body part. Before cathecting the mother and the breast, the infant is enveloped in primary objectless narcissism. Secondary narcissism involves investing in the ego rather than the object. A certain amount of narcissism is normal. Being in unrequited love drains energy away from the lover's ego, and thus leads to impoverishment. The ultimate aim of the organism, according to Freud, is the return to zero energy charge. The pleasure principle is a mechanical principle involving the physical reduction of quantities of energy in the organism. As Freud says, it "follows from the principle of constancy" (Freud [1920] 1953–74: 9).

Although many current psychoanalysts dismiss or minimize drive theory, it is actually the engine that makes the Freudian machine go. The dynamic (conflictual forces in the psyche), topographic (consciousness, preconscious and unconscious) and structural (ego, superego and id) hypotheses all require it. The repository of the drives is the id, and the source of reality orientation is the ego, where drive energy is neutralized or sublimated or displaced or defended against. The internalization of prohibitions against drive satisfaction combined with castration anxiety leads to the development of the superego, which may get some of its virulence from aggressive drives originating in the id. Because they do not have castration anxiety, women do not develop adequate superegos (Freud [1930] 1953–74).

The neurosis develops when drives press for gratification and are met with resistance from the outside world and/or the superego. Substitute satisfactions in the form of symptoms result since energy cannot be destroyed but only displaced in the psyche. For example, compulsive hand-washing substitutes for the desire to handle faeces or other "dirty" activities. Or Freud's patient Dora (Freud [1905] 1953–74) develops a hysterical cough as a substitute for her desire for oral sex. In psychosis, the ego may be overwhelmed by the drives and hence lose touch with reality.

In neurosis, defence mechanisms and resistance, as posed by the dynamic hypothesis, prevent the ego from seeing the disowned wishes (deriving from the drives) that are at the root of its troubles. The complex develops when intrapsychic conflicts and their substitute solutions are pushed into the unconscious and zealously guarded by the censor who stands sentinel between consciousness and the unconscious. Later Freud removed the repressive force from the censor to the superego and still later to the ego defences. Anxiety results when the disowned repressed material threatens to break through into consciousness.

On Freud's view, the way in which the methodology of psychoanalysis works can be explained in terms of these hypotheses – indeed Freud would say that he developed the hypotheses as a way of explaining the clinical material. The aim of therapy is to trace the development of the person, explained by dynamics based on the above theory, from earliest childhood to the present. Fixations at various psychosexual stages (oral, anal, phallic and genital) and substitute gratifications leading to the development of symptoms are primary data to be analysed. In the course of therapy, defences must be analysed and resistances to unconscious material (often manifesting as resistance to the therapy) must be overcome. The Oedipus complex, castration anxiety, psychosexual fixations, and resulting fantasies and symptoms must be confronted. Symbols appearing in dreams and other material are often of a universal nature, resulting from their roots in the drives and fixations in psychosexual development, and can be interpreted accordingly in the course of analysis. Analysis of the transference of energy from early libidinal fixations onto the analyst becomes a primary avenue for cure.

Freud's method involves asking the analysand to commit to a process in which she says everything that comes to mind. This is called the "fundamental rule". The analyst listens with an attitude of "evenly suspended attention" so as to allow the unconscious material to emerge without interference or preference. Usually this is done with the analysand lying on a couch with the analyst behind her in order to encourage the material to flow more spontaneously and uninhibitedly. The analyst interprets the unconscious material that emerges in the form of transference, resistance, defences, symptoms, symbols, fantasies, dreams, repetitive patterns and "acting out" so that it may become conscious. As Freud famously says, it is this making of unconscious material conscious that leads to cure: "Where id was, there ego shall be". The flow has been restored by removing the blocks to consciousness and if possible finding realistic outlets or sublimations for the repressed drive energy. Because civilization is full of "discontents" in the form of blocks to instinctual gratification (Freud [1930] 1953–74), the cure may mean nothing more, as Freud says, than allowing the analysand to move from neurotic symptomatology to "common unhappiness" (Freud [1895] 1953–74: 305).

Sartre's approach: phenomenological inquiry and the fundamental project of being

Although Sartre was always appreciative of Freud's great discoveries (the impact of childhood on adult development, the pervasiveness of self-deception, and the use of the current relationship between analyst and patient to explore the depths of the analysand's difficulties), he at the same time seriously objected to Freud's metapsychology. His objections are rooted in existential phenomenology, which rejects the premises of positivistic science as applied to human beings. Phenomenology is first and foremost an answer to Cartesian dualism: it does away with the division between mind and body, self and world, of seventeenth-century French philosopher René Descartes – a perspective that has deeply influenced the development of modern science. The founder of phenomenology, Edmund Husserl, poses a view of consciousness as intrinsically intentional and world-related. There is no self without the world, no world (in the sense of specified thises) without the self. By intentionality Husserl is not suggesting that consciousness has motives or intentions hidden away in the psyche, as in the ordinary use of the word "intention". Rather he means that consciousness is always consciousness of some real or imagined object. The intention exists not behind the act of grasping the world in this way or that, but rather in that very act.

Sartre takes Husserl's phenomenology a step further. Following Heidegger, who along with Husserl had a great impact on his philosophy, Sartre objects even to the "transcendental ego" of Husserl, which constitutes the world of meaning and objects. For Sartre and Heidegger, there is no transcendental ego. There is only consciousness (*Dasein*, or "being there", in Heidegger's philosophy) experiencing the world in this way or that. It is from the perspective of existential phenomenology that Sartre rejects Freud's four fundamental hypotheses. From this perspective, there is no such thing as a psyche with substance and structure. There is no ego, superego and id, no consciousness, preconscious and unconscious, no psychobiological drives behind intentional acts, no internal dynamics that are separated from the world in which a person lives. There is only bodily lived consciousness grasping the world in this way or that.

Hence when Sartre says that existential psychoanalysis attempts to grasp an individual's fundamental project of being, he is not simply talking about the Freudian complex in other language. As Sartre says, both the complex and the project are totalities rather than a collection of random responses, and both refer to an "infinity of polyvalent meanings" (BN1: 570; BN2: 591). Yet the complex is a pattern of emotions, memories, perceptions and wishes in the personal unconscious organized around a common theme and powered by drives. The project is instead an original gut-level bodily lived conscious choice of a way of being in the world. The complex is determined. The fundamental project is freely chosen, though that choice is always situated – that is, it is always a combination of what the world brings and what I make of what the world brings.

Both the complex and the original project are organized around desires, but the word desire means something different in each form of psychoanalysis. For Freud, desire refers to the sexual instinct and its objects, modulated through the psychosexual stages. For Sartre, desire refers to the fundamental lack of Being (nothingness or *no thingness*) that consciousness is. Sexuality is only one of its manifestations. My desire does not derive from a generalized drive that lies behind experience. It manifests in my experience as I relate to the objects of that experience in a variety of ways. It is motivated by the desire to fill the fundamental lack. It is the desire to use objects and other people to create a substantialized self.

The fundamental project, unlike the Freudian complex, is not fixed in childhood. It is less a totality in the static sense than a totalization, a continuous way of making sense of self and world that is always moving and changing. Its current meaning, though permeated by its childhood origins, is not reducible to those origins. As Sartre says in *Search for a Method*, a life develops in "spirals"; it "passes again and again by the same points but at different levels of integration and complexity" (Sartre1968: 106). We may even find abrupt breaks and "radical conversions" to a different way of being in the world. This happens, for example, when Genet, in Sartre's biography *Saint Genet* (Sartre 1952, 1963) turns from the life of crime for which he seemed destined to make himself a writer – or when a person changes radically in the course of analysis.

The fundamental project, like the complex, has its origins in the past, which Sartre says is the "background-depth of all my thoughts and all my feelings" (BN1: 141; BN2: 164). Sartre even agrees with Freud that both forms of psychoanalysis must explore "the crucial event of infancy [or early childhood] and the psychic crystallization around this event" (BN1: 569; BN2: 590). The project is not, however, like the Freudian complex, determined by those childhood events. Rather the child chose (on the level of non-reflective basic intentionality) to live them in a certain way and hence developed the project. The child Genet, for example, chose to "be the thief they said I was" (Sartre 1963). Obviously, the choice is not always (and in the case of mental illness it may never be) a viable choice. But it is a choice. It is I who live my circumstances in this way or rather respond mechanically to them.

The reason present symptoms may seem determined by past circumstances is that we remember the circumstances vividly and see no other way that we could have lived them. This is partially so because we did choose to live them in this way and not in another. Interestingly Freud himself recognizes in a rather remarkable passage that determinism only works backwards. When one attempts to move from the present neurosis to the childhood origins, all seems inevitable. But when one gets to the original circumstances, one becomes aware that there could have been a different outcome and that this might have been just as understandable. Hence, as Freud says: "The synthesis is not nearly so satisfactory as the analysis; in other words, from a knowledge of the premises we could not have foretold the nature of the results" (Freud [1920] 1953–74: 267). Freud thinks that this failure to predict happens because we can never know all of the etiological factors in a neurosis. Sartre thinks it happens because we are free.

The fundamental project is not just past-oriented. It is present and future-oriented as well. The present moment is, of course, where we live and where change takes place. Sartre describes the present simply as "presence to being" (BN1: 121–2; BN2: 145). Any therapy that is going to be effective must be profoundly present to this presence – and must encourage those undergoing therapy to be increasingly present (rather than trying to escape into the past or the future). Yet the present is not a static something. The fundamental project is moving through time – actually, to be more precise, it is temporalizing. It is a *pro-ject*, or throwing myself forward out of the past toward the future. While the past is its ground, the future is its meaning. Hence Sartre says that existential psychoanalysis must be "completely flexible" and adapt itself to "the slightest changes in the subject"– recognizing that different approaches may be suitable for different analysands or for the same analysand at a different time in therapy (BN1: 573; BN2: 594). It must also be a deeply relational and collaborative venture – a joint undertaking in which "each person takes his chances and assumes his responsibilities" rather than a hierarchical process (Sartre 1979: 201). Ultimately, it is the "final intuition of the subject," rather than the interpretations of the analyst, that is "decisive" in existential psychoanalysis (BN1: 574; BN2: 594).

In *Search for a Method* (Sartre 1968) and the *Critique of Dialectical Reason* (Sartre 1960c), Sartre proposes a methodology for the social sciences in general that he names the progressive-regressive method. The regressive moment is the usual method of social science inquiry. It analyses and attempts to bring to light all those seemingly objective conditions of a person's (or group's) situation, including historical and socio-material circumstances, even language and culture. The progressive moment instead uses comprehension, putting myself as a human being into the shoes of the other in order to understand the human meaning of a past event or action. This "pre-ontological comprehension that man has of the human person" (BN1: 568; BN2: 589) is also the beginning point of existential psychoanalysis. In looking at the past, this means not so much attempting to find causes and conditions as looking for motives and meanings. It means discovering the past as choice rather than as conditioning. This frees the future as well: If I was free, I am free. Often the future-directed dimension of a person's project can be elicited by asking the question: "What does (or did) it do for you to do/feel/think/respond [in this particular way]?"

The fundamental project is always an attempt to try to solve the problem of being, rather than a merely mechanical response to internal forces or external conditions. This is the problem of needing to create a substantial self while yet remaining free – to be somebody or something, as we say colloquially. Sartre says that the meaning of this desire is "ultimately the project of being God" – the *ens causa sui* of

Scholastic philosophy (BN1: 567; BN2: 587). Because it is impossible for a human being to be free and a substantial something at the same time, Sartre makes his famous statement: "Man is a useless passion" (BN1: 615; BN2: 636). Nonetheless, all our various ways of doing, being and having (with doing and having ultimately collapsing into being) are attempts to solve the problem of being – to create meaning down there in the future by bringing into existence a substantialized self as value.

All our ways of relating to self and others are attempts to solve the problem of being. All our ways of temporalizing, spatialializing and relating to objects in the world, all our ways of inserting (or failing or refusing to insert) ourselves into language and culture, all our actions, mannerisms, tastes and gestures are ways of attempting to solve the problem of being. Sartre says, "there is not a taste, a mannerism, or a human act which is not revealing". Our gestures, facial expressions, body stance, and all the various ways of living our bodies are attempts to solve the problem of being. As Sartre says, "A gesture refers to a *Weltanschauung* and we sense it" (BN1: 457; BN2: 479). It is the task of existential psychoanalysis to decipher that *Weltanschauung*.

In attempting to elucidate the analysand's solution to the problem of being, however, the existential psychoanalyst is not looking for a solution that is first invented and then lived. The fundamental project is not rational but "prelogical" (BN1: 570; BN2: 591), and it can never be known in its entirety exactly as it is since it is no different from our gut-level non-reflective way of living our lives in the world. It can, however, be known well enough to allow us to look at what we are doing and to shift and change. Hence the existential psychoanalyst will not just explore the usual data of psychoanalysis: "dreams, failures, obsessions and neuroses". She will also and especially consider "the thoughts of waking life, successfully adjusted acts, style, etc." (BN1: 575; BN2: 595). She will understand that a person "expresses himself as a whole in even his most insignificant and his most superficial behavior" (BN1: 568; BN2: 589).

The result of this investigation must be self-evident "not because it is the poorest and the most abstract but because it is the richest" and most concrete (BN1: 563; BN2: 584). We must explore the analysand's unique way of solving the problem of being. If this person is psychotic, for example, we will want to know not only that he found the conditions of his existence intolerable and so needed to escape into fantasy or imagination. We will also want to know why he prefers to be Jesus Christ and not Adolf Hitler or Genghis Khan. We will want to encounter in so far as this is possible the very person, not a collection of drives or a bundle of unconscious wishes or generalized qualities or states. We must discover the person's fundamental project not behind concrete lived experience, but in that very experience itself.

Sartre's answer to the problem of self-deception

Existential psychoanalysis, like Freudian psychoanalysis, must account for the fact that the analysand's life is riddled with self-deception. Freud explains self-deception in terms of unconscious dynamics and wishes. Sartre explains it in terms of the division between pre-reflective and reflective consciousness and the structures of bad faith. Pre-reflective consciousness is simple gut-level awareness, basic intentionality. It is bodily lived, conscious and intentional, but not necessarily even verbal since, as Sartre says, language is fundamentally for others. Sartre says that pre-reflective consciousness "is penetrated by a great light without being able to express what this light is illuminating". This is so not because we are dealing with an "unsolved riddle as the Freudians believe" (BN1: 571; BN2: 591). Indeed all is there, luminous, available. What is lacking is the means that would allow conceptualization. The truth is not hidden in the unconscious. Indeed it is not unconscious at all but unknown in the sense of being not yet reflected on. The analysand, as Sartre says, must come to know what she already understands.

The reason that consciousness and knowledge are not identical is that there is a gulf of "impassable nothingness" between the consciousness reflecting and the consciousness reflected on (BN1: 274; BN2: 298). This gulf does not represent a resurgence of the Freudian unconscious by another name. The impassable gulf occurs because when consciousness turns and attempts to make a "pseudo" object of itself, the self reflecting and the self reflected on are not the same. This object of reflective consciousness is always a pseudo object because I cannot simultaneously see myself and be myself. At the moment of reflection, I am always reflecting on a past self. I am trying to grasp myself from the viewpoint of the other.

Hence arises the possibility for all kinds of distortions. Some of these come from my attempt to recapture my object self by looking at myself through the eyes of the other, especially the original powerful others, who were able to see me as an object out there in the world. The experience of what Sartre refers to as "the look" of the other makes me uncomfortably aware of this, since I experience the other's Look first in shame and later also in pride (BN1: 252–302; BN2: 276–326). I also need the other to see me, so that the failure of the original powerful others to accurately see and validate me has a negative impact as well. Their looks, touches and words are important to my development as a person. All of us have experienced the distortions stemming from the looks (or failure to look) of the original powerful others. Our ways of criticizing or ignoring ourselves mimic theirs. Hence Sartre says that Flaubert, whose physical needs were taken care of but who was disregarded as a person, develops a passive personality. Lack of recognition as a person also plays a major role in Laing's examples of "ontological insecurity" (Laing [1959] 1979). These include cases where psychotic patients, having not been treated as persons early on in their lives, come to treat themselves and/or others as not being real or as being objects rather than subjects.

Self-deception arises from the desire to view or make myself into a particular kind of object – for myself and/or others. Actually, the very belief that I can be an object like other objects in the world, a substantialized self as a table is a table, is a distortion. It is an act of what Sartre calls bad faith, or lying to myself about the nature of my existence, because I am not an object but a free subject. Hence all those attempts to grasp myself as an object, leading eventually to the development of the ego in the Sartrean sense as a construct of reflective consciousness (not a seat of reality orientation, as in Freud), are in bad faith. They deny my position as a free subject. While it is not possible or even desirable to live without an ego (one would probably be either psychotic or a mere weather vane moving about with every wind), a rigidly developed ego is a primary source of self-deception (see Barnes 1991 on the positive aspects of the ego). Hence Sartre says in *The Transcendence of the Ego* that "perhaps the essential role of the ego is to mask from consciousness its very spontaneity" (Sartre 1957a: 100).

Even viewing myself as a miserable, bad, inferior, ineffective, selfish or otherwise objectionable object is a matter of bad faith. Yet such a position, like all solidifications of the ego, serves the purpose of giving me at least a sense of identity. It allows me to imagine that I am something and to avoid the nothingness that I actually am. Hence people often stubbornly cling to such identities. Furthermore many of the Freudian defences emanate from this desire to objectify the self. We have already seen how introjecting the original others aids me in developing a solid (if distorted) sense of self. Similarly, Sartre describes in *Saint Genet* and *Anti-Semite and Jew* how the despised or "evil" other confirms the "just" man or the bigot in his sense of solid superiority by projecting all those potentially disowned qualities onto Genet the thief or the Jew as an outsider (Sartre 1963, 1965b). We are not dealing here with unconscious processes, but with manoeuvres in bad faith.

Since there are two poles to human reality – freedom and facticity – there are actually two poles to bad faith. What I actually am is a freedom in situation, not a simple facticity or an ungrounded freedom. If I find myself unwilling, for whatever reason, to accept the tension implied in these two poles, freedom and facticity, I may try to escape in one direction or the other. I may overemphasize facticity, trying to make myself into a solid something, as in the form of bad faith discussed above. Or else I may try to escape into ungrounded freedom, pretending to be absolutely free in the sense of not being impacted by my present circumstances, my past, my socioeconomic conditions, my relationships, and so on. This second form of bad faith, in its more extreme forms, might lead to mania or psychosis – just as the other form might lead to severe depression or the grandiosity of narcissism. In milder cases, the second form might lead to "commitment phobia" or denial.

Both forms of bad faith help to explain the phenomena of self-deception without resorting to the unconscious – though of course existential psychoanalysis does not deny that there is a personal history that provokes one to adopt one strategy or the other. The strategies themselves, however, are not from a Sartrean perspective unconscious processes but ways of fleeing the truth of the human condition in one direction or the other.

"Purifying reflection" and change

Reflective consciousness is not, however, something to be avoided in favour of an impulsive spontaneity. Indeed, reflection cannot be avoided. Sartre describes a certain kind of reflectivity that actually reveals to us our freedom. So far we have discussed reflectivity only on the plane of what Sartre calls accessory or impure reflection. It is "impure" because it is contaminated with the desire to make myself an object. Yet there are two other forms of reflection that Sartre discusses briefly in *Being and Nothingness*. They are pure reflection and purifying reflection. It is these forms of reflection that can lead a person to recognize the image of himself "as if he were seeing himself in a mirror" (BN1: 573; BN2: 594) – and thereby make a new choice of a way of being in the world. This indeed is the aim of psychoanalysis, Sartrean or Freudian, according to Sartre.

Pure reflection, which Sartre describes as the "simple presence" of the consciousness reflecting to the consciousness reflected on (BN1: 155; BN2: 177), is both "the original form of reflection and its ideal form". It is the original form since without it no other forms could exist.

It is the ideal form because it does not try to create an object self. The impassable gulf between reflective and pre-reflective consciousness does not disappear, but it is not contaminated by the motive to construct an object self. Purifying reflection goes a step further. It allows us to grasp all of those reflective distortions, with their roots in childhood, that keep us entangled in the structures of bad faith that form the neurosis. Sartre says that the nothingness that consciousness is cannot be known to pre-reflective consciousness nor grasped as a psychic object by impure reflection, but that it "is accessible only to the purifying reflection" (BN1: 199; BN2: 222).

Sartre associates purifying reflection with play (BN1: 582; BN2: 602). He says that "play as contrasted with the spirit of seriousness appears to be the least the possessive attitude" (BN1: 580; BN2: 601). The spirit of seriousness, of course, is that materialist deterministic bad faith position in which I claim to be an object rather than a subject. Play, on the other hand, allows for a lightness rather than a heaviness of being. Sartre says that play is able to "make manifest and to present ... the absolute freedom which is the very being of the person" (BN1: 581; BN2: 601). Hence, as I have suggested elsewhere, it might be appropriate to describe the antidote to the spirit of seriousness as the spirit of play (Cannon 2009, 2011, forthcoming). Indeed it might be appropriate to describe existential psychoanalysis itself, as D. W. Winnicott ([1971] 1985: 38) describes psychoanalysis, as "two people playing together" – or, where one of them (hopefully the analysand) is unable to play, learning to play together. The analysand would thereby be able to escape from the constraints of the "serious world" and to create something that is not a mere repetition of the past, but something irreducibly new.

Purifying reflection, in conjunction with play, can therefore be said to create a space for radical change in therapy. It can lead to the appearance of one of those psychological *instants* that Sartre says "furnish the clearest and most moving image of our freedom" (BN1: 476; BN2: 498). They are moments of "double nothingness" (BN1: 435; BN2: 457), where past and present, self and world, change together as I move towards the future in a new way. Often they are accompanied by feelings of anxiety as well as lightness and playfulness. The anxiety that arises at such moments is not neurotic anxiety about the "return of the repressed". It is instead existential anxiety about the encounter with nothingness, with one's freedom. The existential psychoanalyst, in moving toward the "cure", will be careful to encourage the client not simply to move from one sense of a solidified self to another. Rather she will keep in mind Sartre's idea that the "principal result" of existential psychoanalysis must be to make us "repudiate the spirit of seriousness" (BN1: 626; BN2: 646). Its task is to allow us to move to a place where we take freedom itself, our own and that of others, as value.

Freud's method, which Sartre says is "better than its principles" (BN1: 573; BN2: 594), may actually encourage purifying reflection. The fundamental rule and evenly hovering attention may create the space for a person to engage in purifying reflection by setting aside the demands of everyday reality and the motive to appear in a certain way in favour of a simple curiosity about what is going on (see Thompson 1994a, 1994b for an existential perspective on Freud's technique). Sartre, in fact, notes that Freudian psychoanalysis "is often in sight of an existential discovery, but it always stops part way" (BN1: 573; BN2: 594). Certainly that sense of gut-level recognition that the analysand experiences when the analysis has reached a certain point and the analysand feels he is seeing himself clearly as if reflected in a mirror is an existential discovery. This experience is no mere intellectual reconstruction. Sartre says that the analysand does not merely agree to a hypothesis. Instead he experiences its truth: "he touches it, he sees what it is" (BN1: 574; BN2: 595). The analyst finds the "involuntary testimony of the subject" to be "precious" since he can now "pass on from the investigation proper to the cure" (BN1: 573; BN2: 594).

Where Freudian psychoanalysis falls short is not so much in its method as in providing principles that might explain what has happened. Sartre says that the experience of the analysand cannot be explained in terms of unconscious material becoming conscious. If the complex were really unconscious, if it existed in a realm apart from consciousness, the analysand could not recognize it. Instead the "enlightenment" of the subject "is truly understandable only if the subject has never ceased being conscious of his deep tendencies; better yet, only if these drives are not distinguished from his conscious self". In other words, the analysand's experience only makes sense if "the traditional psychoanalytic interpretation does not cause him to attain consciousness of what he is; it causes him to attain knowledge of what he is" (BN1: 574; BN2: 595). It only makes sense if the analysand is able to articulate on the reflective level what he had previously only experienced pre-reflectively.

Sartre and contemporary psychoanalysis

I have discussed the implications of Sartre's philosophy for post-Freudian psychoanalysis up to 1991, when *Sartre and Psychoanalysis* was published (Cannon 1991). There I suggest that Sartre's ideas about the look of the other and the importance of relationship explain better than Freudian drive theory the relational and mirroring needs of infancy and early childhood discovered by many of the post-Freudians. I think the revolution in psychoanalytic metatheory has only accelerated since then. Contemporary relational, intersubjective, and interpersonal psychoanalysts have continued the abandonment of Freudian drive theory that had begun with the analysts discussed in *Sartre and Psychoanalysis*. In doing so, they have developed an even stronger relational emphasis (see Mitchell 2000). Following Daniel Stern (1985), many dismiss Freud's idea of "objectless primary narcissism" – noting that research shows infants to be relational from the beginning of life. Many also criticize the hierarchical nature of the classical analytic relationship along lines similar to Sartre's criticism, insisting that analysis must be a "two-person" venture.

Some contemporary psychoanalysts consider the unconscious itself to be "relational" (see especially Bromberg 2006, 2011). If they mean by this that there is a nonverbal bodily lived connection between analyst and analysand that must be explored, then Sartre would agree with the idea if not with the terminology. Indeed many contemporary analysts are now attending to the nonverbal aspects of analysis, to "implicit" as well as "explicit" knowing (including interpersonal knowing), to the body and the intuitive "right brain" as well as the rational "left brain", as important sources of analytic information and as important to understanding how analysis "cures". Researchers are even comparing "pre-reflective" interactions between mothers and infants with similar interactions in analysis (see Beebee *et al.* 2005). There is also an emphasis on spontaneity and novelty in the analytic interaction. One thinks of Philip Bromberg's emphasis on the importance of "surprise" and "novelty" and of Daniel Stern's (2004) "now moments", which remind one of Sartre's psychological instants. On the other hand, contemporary analysts sometimes mix levels of discourse, conflating biological body-brain language with the language of experience, in a way that Sartre would have objected to. Sartre, for example, would object to the idea of "right brains communicating with right brains" (Schore 2011). As he and R. D. Laing ([1959] 1979) after him insist, we do not experience brain structures but people communicating – albeit with the brain as an underlying substratum to consciousness.

Some contemporary analysts actually go beyond Cartesian dualism to develop a rapprochement with phenomenology and existentialism. They are beginning to refer to their work as "post-Cartesian psychoanalysis" (Stolorow 2011). Among these are Robert Stolorow and George Atwood, who we find discussing such things as the "pre-reflective unconscious" (Stolorow & Atwood 1992). According to my understanding, what they have in mind is something very close to Sartre's idea of pre-reflective consciousness. Donnell Stern's (2003) idea of the unconscious as "unformulated experience" and Christopher Bollas's (1987) conceptualization of the "unthought known" also remind us of Sartre's idea of pre-reflective experience. Certainly Roy Schafer's (1976) "action language," influenced by the work of Sartre, had long attempted to restore agency to the "unconscious". Yet the continued use of the word "unconscious" for "nonverbal" seems to me to be problematic in all these writers, especially since most of the bodily lived experience being described has little to do with the dynamic unconscious of Freud. It is actually pre-reflective in Sartre's sense: It is bodily lived and experienced, personally and interpersonally, but not conceptually or reflectively known.

Sartrean existential psychoanalysis has not yet found its Freud. No current psychoanalyst has used Sartre's philosophy to develop a systematic approach. Indeed no one since Laing has done so. With the exception of Roy Schafer, Roger Frie (1997) and myself, few have taken Sartre's work on existential psychoanalysis seriously. Current psychoanalysts interested in phenomenology and existentialism, like Ludwig Binswanger and Medard Boss before them, have been more often drawn to Heidegger than to Sartre. This group includes Robert Stolorow and M. Guy Thompson. Although I have developed a psychodynamically oriented approach based on the work of Sartre, it is not pure psychoanalysis. Applied existential psychotherapy (AEP) is instead a synthesis of existential and psychoanalytic insights with interventions drawn from Gestalt therapy, body-oriented psychotherapy, and other experiential approaches.

Sartre's work nonetheless appears to be fertile with insights and suggestions that could be useful to psychoanalysis and psychoanalytically oriented psychotherapy today – along with other forms of depth therapy.

Further reading

Barnes, H. E. 1981. *Sartre and Flaubert*. Chicago, IL: University of Chicago Press.
Barnes, H. E. 1991. "The Role of the Ego in Reciprocity". In *Sartre Alive*, R. Aronson & A. van den Hoven (eds), 151–9. Detroit, MI: Wayne State University Press.
Barnett, L. & G. Madison (eds) 2011. *Existential Therapy: Legacy, Vibrancy and Dialogue*. London: Routledge.

Cannon, B. 1991. *Sartre and Psychoanalysis: An Existentialist Challenge to Clinical Metatheory*. Lawrence, KS: University Press of Kansas.
Cannon, B. 2009. "Nothingness as the Ground for Change". *Existential Analysis* (July): 192–210.

EIGHT

Nothingness and negation
Sarah Richmond

Although the title of *Being and Nothingness* registers the importance of the concept of nothingness (*le néant*) to Sartre's major philosophical book, it would be a mistake to think that nothingness only entered his philosophical thinking – or writing – in 1943. The concept appears frequently, with some variations, in Sartre's earlier "phenomenological" essays.

In *The Imaginary* (*L'Imaginaire*), Sartre's 1940 study of the imagination, the concept of nothingness, and the concepts associated with it – negation, denial, annihilation, nothing – play an essential role (Sartre 1940, 2004a). A principal aim of that work is to reject an influential philosophical conception of imagination as a capacity to entertain mental images, where these are conceived as immanent states of consciousness that are similar in type to sensations. Sartre argues cogently against that view (of which the best-known proponent is probably David Hume), putting forward a number of objections to the very idea that imagination involves the presence of "images" to the mind. Sartre argues instead that imaginative activity involves a relationship to the imagined object that requires a radical *break*, on the part of consciousness, with the world. In addition, he denies the existence of any "images" in the mind. Instead we are to understand that the imagining consciousness, like consciousness in general, is directed to an object. But the objects with which the exercise of the imagination puts us in contact are *unreal*. The imagining consciousness "must be able to form and posit objects affected by a certain character of nothingness" (Sartre 2004a: 183).

The idea of nothingness, moreover, is already intimately connected, in Sartre's thinking about the imagination, with the freedom of consciousness. Sartre's "Conclusion" to *The Imaginary* argues that for any consciousness to have the capacity to imagine, it is a necessary condition that it be free – and, further, that the imagination makes manifest a freedom which, in fact, any conceivable consciousness must possess.

As the main aim of this chapter is to set out and evaluate the claims that Sartre makes about nothingness in *Being and Nothingness*, I will not discuss his earlier work on the imagination in further detail. However, it is important to note the extent to which *The Imaginary* was, for Sartre, a "rehearsal" for the more ambitious project of *Being and Nothingness*. A similar use of phenomenological methodology to support a specific ontological characterization of consciousness – in terms of freedom – is also apparent in other early works. From the outset, then, Sartre's interest in phenomenology co-existed with and was an instrument for his wish to demonstrate the existence of human freedom, and his sense that the way to do this was by establishing an essential connection of consciousness with nothingness.

It is fair to say, however, that in *Being and Nothingness* the concept of nothingness becomes far more prominent. In a letter to Simone de Beauvoir dated 24 January 1940 (the year that *L'Imaginaire* was published), Sartre announces that he has just discovered that nothingness can be given an organizing role in the "metaphysics" he is developing: "I have written a bit about metaphysics … 'What a jumble!', you will say. But not at all; it is neatly organized around the idea of Nothingness, or the pure event in the heart of being" (Sartre 1983a: II, 56; my translation) In *Being and Nothingness* Sartre announces that his project is "phenomenological ontology", and argues that an adequate ontology must take account of nothingness, "alongside" being. The promotion of the concept to a more pivotal role is reflected in the fact that after having introduced it, in the first chapter of part one, Sartre devotes two of the following sub-sections to a comparison of his conception of nothingness with those of two influential predecessors, Hegel and Heidegger. In other words, nothingness is shown to be sufficiently important in Sartre's philosophy to warrant inclusion in a detailed historical narrative, in which Sartre is also careful to point up the advantages of his own understanding of the concept, in comparison with the earlier ones.

Sartre's argument for nothingness in *Being and Nothingness*

Sartre introduces the topic at an early stage in *Being and Nothingness*. Following the introduction, which surveys the domain of being in general, part one is entitled "The Problem of Nothingness". Sartre's route to this problem has been the need, which the Introduction has left unmet, to understand how the two "regions" of being so far described – the for-itself and the in-itself – are related to each other. Since each of these types of being is, Sartre says, an "abstraction" – incapable of existing in isolation from the other – we need to find a "concrete" phenomenon that will allow us to examine them as they are instantiated in the world. Closely tracking Heidegger's methodology in *Being and Time*, Sartre suggests that we choose, as our initial example, the very activity in which we, as knowledge-seekers, are currently engaged: the activity of asking a question or, as Sartre often puts it, "interrogation". From here his path diverges from Heidegger's: Sartre wishes to focus specifically on the fact that, for any question, the possibility of a negative reply exists. This is true for every question, Sartre argues, not only for those that admit of a yes/no answer:

> There are questions which on the surface do not permit a negative reply – like, for example, the one which we put earlier: "What does this attitude reveal to us?" But actually we see that it is always possible with questions of this type to reply, "Nothing" or "Nobody" or "Never". (EN: 39; BN1: 5; BN2: 29)

Sartre goes on to argue that negative judgements of the type "S is not P" cannot fully account for nothingness (or non-being – *non-être* – an alternative term that Sartre uses interchangeably). Negative judgements are founded on nothingness, rather than the other way round. With this claim Sartre concurs with Heidegger, who had made the same point in his famous account of "*das Nichts*" put forward in his 1929 inaugural lecture at Freiburg, "What is Metaphysics?". Sartre's ideas about nothingness are heavily influenced by this lecture, to which he explicitly refers in *Being and Nothingness*. (It was from this lecture that Carnap took the sentences that he declared to be meaningless "pseudo-statements" in his equally famous 1932 article "The Elimination of Metaphysics Through Logical Analysis of Language"; Carnap [1932] 1959).

The core of Sartre's argument that, in addition to the negativity involved in negative judgements, *nothingness* requires ontological recognition is his well-known example of Pierre's failure to turn up in the café where he is expected. Sartre's strategy here is in the first instance phenomenological, not in Husserl's strict sense, but in the looser, philosophical sense associated with appeals to "what it is like" to undergo some type of experience. Sartre sets out to show that when we consider what it is like to discover Pierre's absence from the café, we see that the experience involves an element of "encounter" with Pierre's non-being which precedes the level at which a judgement might be made, and cannot therefore be accounted for in terms of judgement. At the same time, Sartre is in disagreement with Bergson's "eliminativist" treatment of the concept of nothingness, which denies that there is anything to that concept that cannot be derived from the idea of the logical function of negation.

Taking up the point of view of the person who, having made an appointment to meet Pierre in the cafe, is expecting to find him there, Sartre describes the activity of scanning the café visually in order to locate him. In this experience, Sartre suggests, there is an intuition of *Pierre's absence*, an experience that might subsequently be reported by saying "I saw that he was not there" (Sartre takes the term "intuition" from Husserl; we can take it here as equivalent to "perception"). Sartre's point is that if, in the course of looking out for Pierre, one sees, say, a female customer in a brown coat, that experience is not *just* a perception of a woman in a brown coat. Rather, part of what one sees, in seeing the woman, is that she is *not Pierre* – the experience of each person, as they are visually scanned, is *modified* by the possibility of their being Pierre, such that Pierre's non-appearing person "haunts" it. If one compares this with the experience of the cafe that another person, *not* expecting anyone in particular, might have, we can see how different the two experiences will be. The other person, looking at the woman in the brown coat, apprehends her in her own right. We could say that he sees her simply as a woman-in-a-brown-coat, whereas our person looking for Pierre sees her as a woman-in-a-brown-coat-who-is-not-Pierre.

To fill out this claim about perception Sartre draws, as elsewhere in his work, on the resources of Gestalt psychology. According to Gestalt theory, sensory experiences typically involve a perceptual "field", which may be differently organized by different subjects, according to their expectations and their practical orientation. The perceptual field is typically articulated into a salient *figure* – the object of explicit attention – against a more or less indifferently experienced *background*.

Borrowing this figure/background distinction, Sartre suggests that in the case of the person who has the appointment with Pierre, the café as a whole forms the background for a specific anticipated figure – that of Pierre. But as he is not there, the figure is experienced as an absence. It is worth quoting at length Sartre's explanation of how, in these circumstances, the "object" of my intuition turns out to be "a flickering of nothingness":

> When I enter this café to search for Pierre, there is formed a synthetic organization of all the objects in the café, on the ground of which Pierre is given as about to appear ... the original nihilation of all the figures which appear and are swallowed up in the total neutrality of a *ground* is the necessary condition for the appearance of the principle figure, which is here the person of Pierre. This nihilation is given to my intuition; I am witness to the successive disappearance of all the objects which I look at – in particular of the faces, which detain me for an instant (Could this be Pierre?) and which as quickly decompose precisely because they "are not" the face of Pierre. Nonetheless if I should finally discover Pierre, my intuition would be filled by a solid element, I should be suddenly arrested by his face and the whole café would organize itself around him as a discrete presence.
> But now Pierre is not here. Pierre is absent from the whole café ... the café remains ground; it persists in offering itself as an undifferentiated totality to my only marginal attention. Only it makes itself ground for a determined figure; it ... presents the figure everywhere to me. This figure which slips constantly between my look and the solid, real objects of the café is precisely a perpetual disappearance; it is Pierre raising himself as nothingness. So that what is offered to intuition is a flickering of nothingness.
> (EN: 44; BN1: 9–10; BN2: 34)

This nothingness-involving perceptual experience, then, forms the basis for the judgement that might subsequently be formed, that "P is not here": the negative judgement depends upon the antecedent, prejudicative "intuition".

What should we make of this? Sartre has, I think, convincingly demonstrated that there is something phenomenologically distinctive about experiences that appear to involve nothingness, but is this sufficient to establish, against the eliminativist, that nothingness needs to be acknowledged as an element of ontology? Sartre's account invites the objection that the experience of Pierre's absence from the café is merely subjective in so far as it depends on the prior belief or expectation that Pierre will be there: the "intuition" of his absence is not after all of something that is there "for all to see" but is a function of the spectator's expectation (indeed, Bergson would explain away the "intuition" in just this way, as registering a mismatch between the actual appearance of the café, and the way it was expected to appear).

Surprising as it may seem, in so far as this admission appears to weaken his case, Sartre is in fact happy to acknowledge that the experience of

Pierre's absence undergone by his friend *is* a function of the friend's expectation but, refusing to see this point as a problem for his account, he takes it in a completely different and non-deflationary direction.

Sartre agrees that Pierre's absence is subject-relative in so far as it depends upon the observer's expectation. Pierre's absence differs from that of a host of other equally absent characters (Sartre mentions Wellington and Valery) whose absences from the café are "purely formal", and do not figure intuitively in the experience of anyone there:

> To be sure, Pierre's absence supposes an original relation between me and this café; there is an infinity of people who are without any relation with this café for want of a real expectation which establishes their absence. I myself expected to see Pierre and my expectation has caused the absence of Pierre to happen as a real event. (EN: 44–5; BN1: 10; BN2: 34)

This admission, however, is not supposed to diminish the "reality" of nothingness; we are not to conclude that, because Pierre's absence is only apparent to his friend, the "intuition" is an illusion. Rather, Sartre claims, it shows that nothingness is *associated with* human consciousness, it tells us something about its "location". Sartre is happy to admit that without consciousness there would be no nothingness.

In section V of the chapter, Sartre pursues the question of where nothingness comes from. It must be kept in mind that nothingness, *qua* non-being, has no being. It cannot then be explained in terms of the in-itself, because that "region" of being, as Sartre has told us, is "full positivity": it cannot therefore "contain ... Nothingness as one of its structures" (EN: 57; BN1: 22; BN2: 46). But where then can "it" come from? As non-being, nothingness can have no power to produce itself, it cannot be or do anything.

Perhaps in order to distance himself from Heidegger's controversial assertion "*Das Nichts selbst nichtet*" (often translated as "The Nothing noths"), Sartre issues a logical caution about the risk of misusing the concept of "nothingness". Evincing a more orthodox attitude towards logic than Heidegger's and anticipating the objection (which I discuss in the following section) which A.J. Ayer would make against him – Sartre warns that it would be incorrect to use "nothingness" as the subject of *any* verb:

> we can not grant to nothingness the property of "nihilating itself". For although the expression "to nihilate itself" is thought of as removing from nothingness the last semblance of being, we must

recognize that only *Being* can nihilate itself ... in order to nihilate itself it must *be*. But Nothingness *is not*.
(EN: 57; BN1: 22; BN2: 46)

So if nothing cannot be produced either by being or by nothingness, Sartre concludes that there must be some being that in some way "is" its own nothingness: "*the being by which Nothingness comes to the world must be its own Nothingness*" (BN1: 23; BN2: 47; Sartre's emphasis). There must be a being "shot through" with nothingness, a dynamic being which "nihilates Nothingness in its being *in connection with its own being*" (BN1: 23; BN2: 47; Sartre's emphasis). And the only being that fits the bill, Sartre argues, is consciousness.

Indeed, Sartre argues, the very possibility of asking a question – the conduct which Sartre initially sets out to investigate – requires the capacity to "stand out" from being, in order to put it into question. A withdrawal, or detachment ("*recul*"), from being is required, and nothingness makes this possible.

The itinerary which has led us through Pierre's absence in the café now turns out to have been redundant. It looked as if the "negative reply" that any question may elicit had led us to see nothingness as a "real" element within the world – given to intuition – but the further question about its source shows that in fact it is consciousness which introduces it there in the first place. Sartre could have managed without this entire P-involving detour, by simply arguing, as he does, that nothingness – or, as it now takes on the guise of this new name – freedom, is a necessary condition of the human capacity to ask a question.

Sartre's assimilation of the nothingness of consciousness to its freedom, and the context of rational enquiry, in *Being and Nothingness*, might seem to align him with the tradition of thought, inspired by Kant, in which freedom is said to be a requirement of rationality. Indeed, our freedom *qua* rational beings is often illustrated by our capacity to "question" – as when we step back from our immediate beliefs in order to question their well-foundedness, and to decide, on the basis of reflective judgement, whether to endorse or dismiss them. In fact, the freedom that Sartre ascribes to human consciousness has no particular conceptual connection with rationality: for Sartre, adherence to the norms of rationality is *itself* a choice. In this respect, nothingness is a useful term for indicating the "thinness" of Sartre's characterization of consciousness.

We can see that Sartre's claim is simply a variant of his earlier claim, in *The Imaginary*, that nothingness is a precondition of the imagination. Indeed, the interchangeability of the two arguments can be seen in both texts: in *Being and Nothingness*, several pages after the discussion of Pierre in the café, Sartre makes it clear that the capacity for which he thinks nothingness is required is in fact a *general* human capacity to "tear itself away from the world" ("*s'arracher au monde*"), and refers the reader back to his earlier work on the imagination: "The image must enclose in its very structure a nihilating thesis" (BN1: 26; BN2: 50). Symmetrically, in the conclusion to *The Imaginary*, Sartre states that the freedom he has shown to be necessary for imagining is also manifested in conscious activity more generally. For example, Sartre says, we see its operation in the exercise of Cartesian doubt.

How acceptable is Sartre's account of nothingness? Our survey so far should already have made clear how mind-bogglingly slippery this concept is. In the next section I will focus more closely on some of the problems raised by Sartre's use of it.

Problems for Sartre

An important question is whether Sartre's use of nothingness requires us to tolerate a logical contradiction. Certainly Sartre appears at times to break the so-called "law of non-contradiction". According to this law, allegiance to which is commonly regarded as a necessary condition of rational belief, P and not-P cannot both be true. If Sartre appears to violate it, is there a way of making sense of what he says that we can accept?

At some points, Sartre seems explicitly to commit himself to the necessity of logical contradiction in his thought. In the Introduction, he asserts, for example, that the "principle of identity" has only a "regional" validity: it holds true of the in-itself, but not of the for-itself. Thus Sartre agrees that we can say, in relation to being-in-itself, that "*being is what it is*" (BN1: xlii; BN2: 21; Sartre's emphasis).

But, as he goes on to say, outside that domain the principle cannot be maintained:

> This statement is in appearance strictly analytical. Actually it is far from being reduced to that principle of identity which is the unconditioned principle of all analytical judgments. First the formula designates a particular region of being, that of *being-in-itself*. We shall see that the being of for-itself is defined, on the contrary, as being what it is not and not being what it is.
>
> (EN: 32; BN1: xli; BN2: 21; Sartre's emphasis)

This passage also contains, in the last sentence, the overtly paradoxical phrase – "being what it is not and not being what it is" – which Sartre uses throughout BN to characterize the for-itself. I will return to this phrase later.

In addition to this explicit statement, there are several passages where Sartre appears to make the concept of nothingness internally contradictory by reifying it – allowing it to stand as the subject of a verb – in just the way that, we noted earlier, his logical caution warns against.

The following passage, for example, illustrates Sartre's oscillation, in the space of a few lines, between a reified "nothing" – capable of "insinuating itself" between elements of being – and an incompatible acknowledgement of its non-being:

> This freedom which reveals itself to us in anguish can be characterized by the existence of that *nothing* which insinuates itself between motives and act. If someone asks what this *nothing* is which provides a foundation for freedom, we shall reply that we cannot describe it since it *is not*.
> (EN: 69; BN1: 34; BN2: 58; Sartre's emphasis)

In one of the earliest English-language commentaries on BN (written even before it had been translated into English), A. J. Ayer noticed this move. Ayer objected to the "Looking Glass logic" of Sartre's discussion of nothingness. Ayer's complaint is that Sartre uses the term "nothing" as if it *named* something (Ayer 1945: 17), closely paralleling Carnap's criticism of Heidegger's use of *"das Nichts"*. Ayer goes on to illustrate the sort of "trick" that Sartre plays:

> To say that two objects are separated by nothing is to say that they are *not* separated; and that is all that it amounts to. What Sartre does, however, is to say that, being separated by Nothing, the objects are both united and divided. There is a thread between them; only, it is a very peculiar thread, both invisible and intangible. But this is a trick that should not deceive anyone.
> (*Ibid.*: 18–19)

As the passage from *Being and Nothingness* that I have just quoted shows, it is undeniable that there are some passages in the text in which Sartre uses this "trick". However, it is also a rambling work, demonstrably in need of editing, and within its many pages Sartre is often inconsistent. It would be unfair to dismiss Sartre's endeavour as a failure merely on the basis of a few unfortunate passages. So a question remains as to whether some cogent position, which is either independent of those passages, or allows them an unproblematic interpretation, can be extracted from what Sartre says.

One interpretative strategy, which has been used by several defenders of Sartre, is to steer clear of the ontological aspects of his argument altogether. Anthony Manser, defending Sartre's use of *"le Néant"* against Ayer, deferred to the positivists' repudiation of metaphysics, arguing that Sartre was not in fact advancing metaphysical claims. Instead, Manser offered a reading of (parts of) Sartre's claims which likened them to Wittgensteinian insights about the limits of some of our concepts; he suggests, for example, that if we register our unwillingness to say of a machine that it is "following orders", we will have understood something about Sartre's opposition to psychological determinism. More recently, other philosophers have suggested that the most productive use of Sartre's claims is to construe them as *merely* phenomenological. Gregory McCulloch, for example, writes that Sartre "is interested in what is involved, from the phenomenological point of view, in existing ... consciously, rather than in what a conscious entity is (e.g. brain, biological organism, immaterial substance, or whatever)" (McCulloch 1994: 3–4).

Commentators have also accommodated Sartre's apparently contradictory claim that consciousness "is what it is not and is not what it is" by suggesting that we should qualify it – temporally or in some other way. There are passages in *Being and Nothingness* that support this reading: Sartre's suggestion as to what the homosexual in bad faith *should* say, were he to speak truly, incorporates just such a temporally qualified characterization of his identity: "To the extent that a pattern of conduct is defined as the conduct of a paederast and *to the extent that I have adopted* this conduct, I am a paederast. But to the extent that human reality cannot be finally defined by patterns of conduct, I am not one" (EN: 99; BN1: 64–5; BN2: 87; my emphasis).

But these strategies are misguided. In the first place, they make poor sense of a great deal of the text in question. As I have attempted to show, Sartre takes himself to be offering a chain of arguments that lead to the conclusion that consciousness "introduces" nothingness into the world, that it is *literally* its vehicle (Sartre's well-known statement "Nothingness lies coiled in the heart of being – like a worm" does not look remotely phenomenological; BN1: 21; BN2: 45). If Sartre's intention were to convince the reader of her freedom solely by means of phenomenological considerations, we would expect the experience of anguish to carry great weight. But Sartre actually points out that his claim that anguish manifests our consciousness of our freedom is not supposed to convince us, on its own, that we are not subject to determinism. He takes himself to have provided a distinct *proof* of that fact (which, moreover, does not rely on facts about the way in which we experience anything): "anguish has not appeared to us as a *proof* of human freedom; the latter was given to us as the necessary condition for the question" (BN1: 33; BN2: 57).

Second, removing the ontological force from Sartre's claims, by turning them into claims about how things must appear to us, makes them much weaker. Sartre himself concedes that these claims cannot secure the conclusion he wants: that is why, as we have just seen, he does not make our experience of anguish the central point by which we are to be persuaded. He is happy to admit, against an imaginary interlocutor, that anguish – despite the fact that it *feels* like a consciousness of freedom – could co-exist with a psychological determinism of which we were ignorant (BN1: 33; BN2: 57). Similarly, if we introduce temporal qualifications, in the way suggested above, to defuse the description of the for-itself as "being what it is not and not being what it is", the claim states only that consciousness is subject to change, which is, of course, quite compatible with psychological determinism.

It is clear then that Sartre intends nothingness to *ground* our freedom ontologically. But once this intention is given full recognition, it also becomes clear that the requirements made of the concept of nothingness cannot be met.

Things go awry in Sartre's account at a number of points. One problem is that his argument often moves much too fast. This is a serious flaw in Sartre's attempt to found negation as a logical category on nothingness *tout court*, in which the alternative explanation offered by Bergson's eliminativist approach is never convincingly ruled out: even if the putative experience of nothingness "precedes" the specific judgement that "Pierre is not here", Sartre has not shown that it is not *informed* by the subject's antecedent expectation of Pierre and thereby dependent on *prior* conceptual activity. So he has not shown that the concept of nothingness cannot in general be derived from our capacity for negation. Instead, Sartre jumps from the claim that nothingness is necessarily associated with human consciousness to the claim that it is somehow "woven into" the fabric of consciousness.

In any case, as we saw earlier, the example of Pierre is an unnecessary detour. It returns us to Sartre's claim, rehearsed in *The Imaginary*, that nothingness is a necessary condition for raising a question in the first place. But the necessity of some kind of withdrawal (*recul*) from the world is not enough to establish the necessity of nothingness. Sartre has pointed out that some attitude other than complete perceptual immersion in being is required, but this is not enough to rule out alternatives to his own nothingness-involving account. Sartre of course will dismiss any representational account of our capacity to conceive of things as being other than they are – but the reason for this dismissal – that consciousness can have no "content" – is not independent of the conclusion he is trying to establish. Rather than leading us to his ontology from some point outside it, then, Sartre's train of thought seems to circle around within it (Sebastian Gardner (2009: 22), one of Sartre's ablest defenders, suggests that we might make a virtue of Sartre's "methodological circularity", once we have recognized its unavoidability. I do not have space to discuss this sophisticated line of defence here, but the strategy needs to be noted.).

Most philosophical theories are obliged to acknowledge the existence of compelling philosophical alternatives; I am not suggesting either that the failure of Sartre's theory to adequately rule such alternatives out could have been avoided, or that it is fatal. There is, in addition, a general problem with the concept of nothingness that we have already touched on. The problem is the philosophical work that Sartre wants this concept to do. Even if we seem able to formulate a concept of nothingness, we cannot intelligibly grant it an *explanatory* role in relation to being. Sartre cannot at the same time respect his own logical caution about nothingness (by remaining faithful to its non-being) and establish that nothingness is the reason for our freedom. Sartre represents nothingness as "blocking" psychological determinism, but if determinism would hold "without" nothingness, then it must also hold "with" it, because non-being cannot *intervene* in the workings of being. Commentators have pointed out that one bizarre consequence of the ontology Sartre presents in BN is that, in terms of being, it amounts to no more than materialism. Adding non-being to the picture does not add any genuine further way of establishing human freedom.

Problems without Sartre

Sartre is often at his most brilliant when criticizing and noticing the weaknesses in the theories he rejects. And it is noteworthy that everyone who has taken a serious interest in the areas of philosophical thought that Sartre's own concept of nothingness aims to revolutionize has found them to be formidable and vexatious. In particular, Sartre is right to notice that the basic nature of human consciousness – and its capacity for self-consciousness – are especially resistant to explanation, either in naturalistic terms or by means of our "ordinary" concepts.

From the outset of the phenomenological tradition, philosophers found it impossible to articulate the structures of consciousness satisfactorily. For example, Franz Brentano (commonly regarded as the first phenomenologist) is committed to two doctrines about consciousness that cannot be reconciled: first, that the object of consciousness is a content of consciousness, a "proper part" of it; and second, that in the case of self-consciousness, or "secondary intentionality", the object of consciousness is itself. This is mereologically impossible. Related difficulties can be found in Brentano's phenomenological successors, for example, in Husserl, in the "splitting of the ego", which makes phenomenological reflection possible. More recent discussions of consciousness often make these challenges the starting point of discussion. (And David Chalmers's well-known phrase "the hard problem of consciousness" turned the difficulty of accounting for consciousness's subjective aspects into a slogan.) In light of this history, we could regard it as a merit of Sartre's account that it embraces the contradictions that have been such a stumbling block to others, and tries to put them to productive use.

In addition, Sartre shows great insight in grasping the many areas in philosophy in which the phenomenon of non-existence (as non-Sartreans would put it) features, and is poorly understood. Alongside the imaginary objects that Sartre discusses in *The Imaginary*, philosophers have struggled to explain the ontology of fictional entities, impossible objects (like the round square), and the objects referred to in statements of their non-existence. Sartre's elaboration of the concept of nothingness aims both to account for these strange objects and to unify them within its compass.

I have argued that Sartre's attempt to make the transition, from the phenomenon of negative judgements to a "nothingness" that allegedly provides their foundation, is insufficiently motivated. In relation to his philosophical rivals, we might see Sartre as making the same mistake: however apparent it may be that these rival theories *are not* successful, it does not, unfortunately, follow that the turn to nothingness provides a solution.

Further reading

Gardner, S. 2009. *Sartre's* Being and Nothingness: *A Reader's Guide*, 38–88. London: Continuum.
Manser, A. 1961. "Sartre and 'le Néant'", *Philosophy* 36(137): 177–87.
McCulloch, G. 1994. *Using Sartre*, chapter 3. London: Routledge.
Richmond, S. 2007. "Sartre and Bergson: A Disagreement about Nothingness". *International Journal of Philosophical Studies* 15(1): 77–95.

NINE

The look

Søren Overgaard

Introduction

Other people have a special place in our lives. Many of our favourite activities – from sports to serious conversations – essentially involve others, and numerous things that we *can* do by ourselves – watch a good movie, taste wine, visit museums – are just more fun if we can share the experience with someone. At the same time, other people are also the ones from whom we try to hide if we have done something dumb, embarrassing or morally wrong. And others can bore, annoy, threaten and harm us in a multitude of different ways. As we all know too well, life with others is not always pure bliss; indeed, as a character in Sartre's play *No Exit* (Sartre 1945b, 1955) puts it, other people can be "hell". An emphasis on the more negative aspects of human social life is evident in most of what Sartre writes about our relations with others in *Being and Nothingness*, including his famous analysis of the fundamental encounter with the other in the shape of what Sartre terms "the look".

The present chapter offers a presentation and defence of Sartre's analysis of the look. Since Sartre develops his account against the backdrop of what he views as the shortcomings of the analyses of the social encounter offered by his phenomenological predecessors, we need to have a basic grasp of what those analyses contain. The early parts of the chapter therefore offers brief summaries of Husserl's and Heidegger's analyses of intersubjectivity (Hegel, another of Sartre's stalking horses in this context, will not be discussed), after which I outline Sartre's most important criticisms.

Husserl: intersubjectivity

"Intersubjectivity" is Husserl's term of choice for anything having to do with the relations between subjects. In rough outline, his account of the most basic intersubjective encounter runs as follows.

We experience our immediate environment as part of an *objective* world. To appreciate this phenomenological point, look at the book in front of you. It appears to you as something whose existence is independent of your consciousness of it. You don't experience it as something that might cease to exist if you closed your eyes or turned away. You see also see it as containing more than what you perceive at this instant. It contains other pages beside the ones you are currently reading, a cover that you don't see because it is facing the desk, and so on. None of this can be reduced to something you *know*; rather, this is how the book *looks* to you.

Not only do you experience books as things that can exist unperceived by you and have more aspects or sides than you can experience at once – you also experience them as things that in principle could be different from the way they appear to you. According to Husserl, this reflects the fact that the book does not appear to be your *"private synthetic formation"* (Husserl 1995: 91), but strikes you as something others can experience as well. The book, as it appears to you, is not just your private experiential object, but potentially the object of other subjects' experiences too: it is given as "actually there for everyone" (*ibid.*). This makes it possible that the book as others experience it deviates from the book as you experience it. In this way, our immediately experienced world – what Husserl terms the "life-world" (*ibid.*: 136) – refers back to an experiencing intersubjectivity.

Husserl suggests that our experience of the intersubjective significance of the world is itself based upon a more direct experience of other subjects as such. Absent such an experience there is no way of confirming my experience of the life-world as shared with others. Husserl believes the direct experience of another subject as such is possible in the encounter between two *embodied* subjects. Recall that a physical object always has more sides or aspects than are strictly perceived in a single perceptual experience. This, of course, has to do with the fact that I always see a thing from a particular perspective; and this perspective, in turn, is determined by my bodily position in space. Not only that: Husserl also argues that the sense I have of there being more of the object than I currently see is connected with my awareness of my (bodily) potential for moving and thus changing my perspective. I am, in other words, aware of the hidden rear sides of things as sides I *would* see if I moved in particular ways. And since this experience of the object as containing "more" than is currently perceived is essential to its appearing as a physical object (and not, say, an afterimage), Husserl concludes that only an embodied subject can experience physical things *as such* (Husserl 2001b: 39–53).

This point is important to Husserl's account of the encounter with other subjects. Given that I can only have perceptual experiences of physical objects as such if I am embodied, Husserl's problem is not how I can reach other minds "behind" their bodies, but how their bodies can appear to me as bodies of the right sort – that is, as other embodied *subjects*. Husserl's guiding idea here is that I must experience my own body and the body of another as forming a "pair", appearing as two of a kind (Husserl 1995: 112). If I touch a table top with my hand, this action is at the same time subjective and bodily; and if I watch my hand as it explores the table top, it visually appears to me as such. If I notice another person's hand moving across the table top, I immediately see it as a subjective organ exploring the table top, just like my own hand.

Husserl emphasizes that although this experience is an immediate (perceptual) experience of the other's embodied subjectivity and not the result of an inference (*ibid.*: 111), this experience is fundamentally different from the perception of physical objects such as books, trees and coffee cups. While the cup never shows all of its sides at once, it nevertheless has no sides or aspects that cannot be perceived. Even the porcelain under the glaze can be perceived, if I am willing to scratch or otherwise damage the cup. Other subjects, by contrast, have aspects that essentially are unperceivable, Husserl thinks. I can see another's joy in her smile, but exactly what it is like for her to feel this joy is something in principle beyond my perceptual grasp (*ibid.*: 109). Unlike mere physical things, then, others "transcend" my experience: they so to speak always contain more than I will ever be able to experience.

Heidegger: being-with

Much like Husserl, Heidegger takes his point of departure in the observation that we experience the world as containing implicit references to others. As he puts it, "the world is always the one that I share with Others" (Heidegger 1962: 155). Yet Heidegger generally puts greater emphasis on our practical involvement with our surroundings than does Husserl, and so the former highlights others' role as potential *users* of worldly objects (rather than observers). A wedding dress, for example, is not merely an object perceivable by others as well as by me, but is "cut to the figure" (*ibid.*: 153) of the person who (unlike me) will wear it. "Similarly", Heidegger says, "when material is put to use, we encounter its producer or 'supplier'" (*ibid.*). The field that we pass when we are out for a walk refers to the farmer who neglects it or manages it well; my copy of *The Corrections* refers to its author, the bookshop where it was purchased and the person from whom it was a present; and so on.

Heidegger's term for what Husserl would call the "subject" is "*Dasein*", or "being-there". Consequently, he refers to other subjects as "*Dasein*-with" (*ibid.*: 155). Thereby he obviously wants to highlight that others are radically different from books, fields and wedding gowns. Others are my co-users, so to speak: other *Daseins* that *wear* clothes, *read* books, and *plough* fields. While Husserl's analysis suggested an image of the other as someone who was standing opposite me, and whom I recognized as another subject via similarities between our bodies and behaviours, Heidegger's account suggests the image of someone standing by my side, turned (like me) towards a world of objects-for-use.

This becomes more evident in what Heidegger says about "solicitude". Unlike tools and objects that we use – that are "objects of concern", in Heidegger's terminology (*ibid.*: 157) – solicitude is Heidegger's umbrella term for our ways of relating to others. The term must not be taken to imply sympathy or concern for the plight of others: "Being for, against, or without one another, passing one another by, not 'mattering' to one another – these are possible ways of solicitude" (*ibid.*: 158). Types of solicitude that *do* involve a modicum of caring or mattering, however, generally fall somewhere between two extremes, Heidegger thinks. On the one hand, I can "*leap in*" for the other, that is, take over "for the Other that with which he is to concern himself. The Other is thus thrown out of his own position" (*ibid.*: 158). The other extreme is the case where, as Heidegger puts it, I "leap ahead" of the other. The idea here is that I do not take over the other's projects (her "concern"), but facilitate her own taking care of them. Here one is preoccupied with "the existence of the Other, not … a '*what*' with which he is concerned" (*ibid.*: 159). The first type of solicitude, then, focuses on the other's projects, on that with which she is concerned, and regards the other as replaceable: in taking care of her projects for her, I take her place. The second type of solicitude is directed at the other *herself*, as the one whose projects they are, and who therefore cannot be replaced.

Heidegger's analysis – as also suggested by his discussion of these two types of solicitude – is generally oriented towards projects, work and collaboration. Simplifying a bit, we can say that, on the Heideggerian analysis, we encounter others in a context in which we are "concerned" with something – either individually or collectively. This highlights a difference between Heidegger's and Husserl's accounts. Perhaps one can say that whereas Husserl conceives of the fundamental encounter with the other as an encounter with a "you", or at least another "I" (alter ego), Heidegger's account suggests that the "we" is more fundamental. Moreover, while Husserl emphasized the transcendence of the other, Heidegger maintains that the others are precisely the ones from whom I initially (and for the most part) do *not* distinguish myself (*ibid.*: 154). Heidegger's well-known analysis of the role of the so-called "they" (or "one": *das Man*) further underscores this point. As Heidegger writes:

> We take pleasure and enjoy ourselves as *they* take pleasure; we read, see, and judge about literature and art as *they* see and judge; likewise we shrink back from the "great mass" as *they* shrink back; we find "shocking" what *they* find shocking. The "they", which is nothing definite, and which all are, though not as the sum, prescribes the kind of Being of everydayness. (*Ibid.*: 164)

As suggested towards the end of the quote, the neutral and anonymous "they" not only controls our choice of smartphone, takeaway food, and the like, but even our most basic ways of understanding ourselves, each other, and the world around us. In fact, Heidegger believes our inability to distance ourselves from what "they" say and "one" is supposed to do is so massive that we generally are not even ourselves, but "they-self" or "one-self" (*ibid.*: 167).

Sartre's critique

As mentioned, Sartre's account of "being-for-others" takes its point of departure in what Sartre perceives as the weaknesses of the Husserlian and Heideggerian accounts. According to Sartre, Husserl is unable to escape solipsism – the hopeless view that only I (Latin: *solus ipse*) exist – since on the Husserlian account the other can only appear "as an *object* to my knowledge" (BN1: 231; BN2: 255). Sartre discusses an example that may help to understand the reasoning behind this accusation.

Sartre imagines that he is sitting in a park. Suddenly he notices another man pass by a bench located at the edge of a lawn. Sartre sees the man "as an object and at the same time as a man" (BN1: 254; BN2: 277). What this involves, according to Sartre, is noticing how the surroundings – the lawn, the benches, and so on – organize themselves around the stranger (BN1: 254; BN2: 277–8). This has the further implication that these surroundings are no longer organized or grouped around me but flee from me towards a new centre in the shape of the other person:

> [The green lawn] turns toward the Other a face which escapes me. I apprehend the relation of the green to the Other as an objective relation, but I can not apprehend the green *as* it appears to the Other. Thus suddenly an object has appeared which has stolen the world from me. (BN1: 255; BN2: 279)

This "object" is of course the other person. The rather conflict-oriented slant Sartre gives his description of the example should not blind us to the fact that the description is supposed to illustrate the essence of Husserl's account (BN1: 256; BN2: 280). Just like Husserl, Sartre emphasizes how my experience of the embodied other is at the same time an experience that the world is not exhausted by its being for me, but is also what it is for the other. Since the world is in this sense no longer mine, one can (perhaps) say that the other has "stolen" it from me.

Sartre thinks the Husserlian account is alright as far as it goes, but that it will never give Husserl what he wants, namely an analysis of the most fundamental encounter with another *subject*. For as Sartre writes, "*the Other* is still an object *for me*" (BN1: 255; BN2: 279). Of course, the other is a very special object given his power to reorganize my surroundings; yet he is nevertheless still my experienced *object*. The problem now is the following: if the most fundamental relation to another is a relation between me as the experiencing subject and the other as an experienced object, then it is not possible to verify – it becomes "purely conjectural" (BN1: 253; BN2: 276) – that the other *is* an experiencing subject just like me. On the one hand, the other *seems* fundamentally different from the lawn, the benches, and so forth. On the other hand, he is an observed object just as they are. And unless there is some other, more direct way in which he can manifest himself as an *experiencing subject*, his special status seems merely an unfounded assumption. Consequently, Sartre concludes that Husserl cannot escape solipsism.

Sartre does not find Heidegger's account satisfactory either. While Husserl conceived of the encounter with the other along the lines of Sartre's example of the stranger in the park, the image suggested by Heidegger's description is that of "a *crew*. The original relation of the Other and my consciousness is not the *you* and *me*; it is the *we*. ... It is the mute existence in common of one member of the crew with his fellows" (BN1: 246–7; BN2: 270). The problem with this image is not that it reduces the other to an object and thereby collapses into solipsism. Rather, the problem is that the individual *Dasein*'s relationship with the "crew" is a relationship with an abstract, anonymous sociality, as opposed to concrete other individuals – such as "Pierre or Anny". More precisely, to the extent that the others with whom I am standing "side by side" are given to me as concrete individuals, then they must be so given in virtue of *another* type of experience I have had of them, in which they were presented as the individuals they are (BN1: 427; BN2: 448–9). I do not get to know other individual people by marching beside them (cf. BN1: 424; BN2: 446). So if I do know the ones with whom I march it must be because I have or have had other relations or encounters with them besides "being-with" them, shoulder to shoulder. But since "being-with" is supposed to designate the very structure that makes possible every encounter with other particular persons, no such more original encounter can be envisaged, on the Heideggerian account. Therefore, that account is ultimately solipsistic, Sartre argues (BN1: 247–9; BN2: 270–72).

Here we have only scratched the surface of Sartre's critical discussion of Husserl and Heidegger. Much more could be said not only to flesh out Sartre's criticisms, but also on behalf of the targets of his criticisms. But our main interest here is in the conclusions Sartre draws from this discussion in terms of the nature of a viable account of the encounter with the other.

The look

As Sartre views the situation, it has become clear that neither *my* experience of the other (my looking at the other), nor *our* experience of, or "concern" with, some common object or task, can constitute the most fundamental relation between me and another subject. The obvious alternative, Sartre thinks, is a relation such that *I am the other's* experienced object. I encounter the other as *subject* precisely when I experience myself as the one who is being looked at, as opposed to the one who is looking. Thus, Sartre claims that the most original encounter with the other is an encounter with "the *one who looks at me*" (BN1: 257; BN2: 281) – an encounter with the other's "look".

The other's look does not have to be in the shape of two eyes directed at me. The look "will be given just as well on occasion when there is a rustling of branches, or the sound of a footstep followed by silence, or the slight opening of the shutter, or a light movement of a curtain" (BN1: 257; BN2: 281). In fact, it is this sort of case, rather than my experience of "the convergence of two ocular globes in my direction" (*ibid.*), which is the paradigmatic experience of the look. For as Sartre's own formulations make clear, eyes are *objects*. If the other who is looking at me is herself visible to me, then I can – by looking at her – make the look disappear behind the two "ocular globes". Such formulations may sound strange, but Sartre's thought is by no means counterintuitive. There is a sense in which one can make another's look go away by staring at his or her eyes as if they were mere physical objects. "The Other's look", by contrast, "hides his eyes; he seems to go *in front of them*" (BN1: 258; BN2: 282). Indeed, "the Other's look is the disappearance of the Other's *eyes* as objects which manifest the look" (BN1: 268; BN2: 292).

"The look", therefore, refers more to a subjective experience than to a phenomenon "out there" in the world. It is supposed to articulate our experience of another subject's presence, an experience we may have when no one is actually there and may fail to have when another person is actually looking at us. This is also clear in one of Sartre's most famous examples of the look: the experience of being caught peeping through a keyhole. At first I am totally caught up in the scene revealed to me through the keyhole – I am pure looking, as it were. Suddenly I think I hear footsteps behind me, and everything changes: I am now the shameful, contemptible voyeur exposed by the look of the person behind me. As Sartre discusses the example, however, it turns out there is no one there after all. But this does not mean that the look goes away. When, turning around, I discover that no one is there, what is cancelled is only "the contingent connection between the Other and an object-being in *my* world", not the other's presence as subject, as look (BN1: 277; BN2: 301). That the look remains is evidenced my burning cheeks and my lingering feeling of having been exposed.

In fact, Sartre quite generally associates the experience of the look with feelings of vulnerability, disempowerment and even enslavement (BN1: 259, 265, 267; BN2: 282, 289, 291). The look paralyses me and makes it impossible for me to act naturally (or even look back). The nervousness we may feel if we have to speak, sing or dance in front of a large audience illustrates Sartre's point. We need not believe that the audience is a hostile one to feel that the sheer weight of their looks makes it difficult to act naturally. Even to walk or speak naturally can be almost impossible when one feels the others' looks piercing one's skin, as it were.

According to Sartre, the only way in which I can escape my role as the other's paralysed object is by making the other *my* object, thereby again assuming the role of experiencing subject. But this means that the most fundamental relation with others becomes one of conflict, where we struggle to objectify each other: "While I attempt to free myself from the hold of the Other, the Other is trying to free himself from mine; while I seek to enslave the Other, the Other seeks to enslave me" (BN1: 364; BN2: 386). Not only is this perspective on social life pretty bleak in itself; what makes matters worse is that the conflict is quite irresolvable:

> if I look at his look in order to defend myself against the Other's freedom and to transcend it as freedom, then both the freedom and the look of the Other collapse. I see eyes; I see a being-in-the-midst-of-the-world. Henceforth the Other escapes me. ... everything happens as if I wished to get hold of a man who runs away and leaves only his coat in my hands. It is the coat, it is the outer shell which I possess. (BN1: 393; BN2: 415)

It is difficult to see how it could be otherwise. For the other's presence as a subject is her presence as the one who looks at me, objectifies me. Thus, if her exposure to my gaze merely places an object before my eyes, then any attempt on my part to conquer the other qua subjectivity must fail. I will never have more than the coat. And the problem with that is that the other has merely eluded my grasp, not disappeared entirely, and thus is still out there looking at me. As Sartre writes, "what is certain is that *I am* looked at: what is only probable is that the look is bound to this or that intra-mundane presence" (BN1: 277; BN2: 300). No matter how many such intra-mundane presences I am able to paralyse with my gaze, I am still looked at; I can never catch hold of the other as the one who looks at me. Sartre suggests that the other who looks at me consequently has an "unnumbered" or "prenumerical" presence (BN1: 281–2; BN2: 305). It is, then, not really this or that *particular* other that I encounter when I am being looked at, but rather something like Heidegger's neutral *Man*, which is everyone, yet no one in particular (cf. BN1: 282; BN2: 306).

In the chapter called "Concrete Relations with Others", Sartre painstakingly draws the consequences of his conflict-oriented understanding of our encounters with others, issuing, for example, in his notorious analyses of love and sadism. Much of what of Sartre says about concrete relations with others is clearly reminiscent of Hegel's dialectics of master and slave, but for Sartre mutual recognition is not in the cards. On the contrary, "we are indefinitely referred from the Other-as-object to the Other-as-subject and *vice versa*. The movement is never arrested, and this movement with its abrupt reversals of direction constitutes our relation with the Other" (BN1: 408; BN2: 430). Thus, "we shall never place ourselves concretely on a plane of equality; that is, on the plane where the recognition of the Other's freedom would involve the Other's recognition of our freedom" (*ibid.*).

Criticisms of Sartre

Perhaps the most common critical reaction to Sartre's account of the look – and his account of social life more generally – is to fault it for its extremely negative slant. On Sartre's analysis, even sexual desire and love are ultimately types of irresolvable conflict. But, as Gregory McCulloch nicely put it, "many of us seem often to rub along rather more harmoniously than Sartre would have it, in and out of bed" (McCulloch 1994: 139). If so, isn't Sartre's account patently inadequate as an account of our most fundamental encounter with others?

Not necessarily. Jonathan Webber makes a distinction between two aspects of the experience of the look, which is pertinent in this context. According to Webber, Sartre's account of the look weaves together an account of my "awareness of [my] being-for-others, of the gaze of the Other" with an account of the experience of the other person as "ascribing to one a fixed nature" (Webber 2011: 191–2). These, however, are different experiences, and it is only the latter experience, not the former, which underlies "the conflict that [Sartre] finds in our interpersonal relationships" (*ibid.*: 192). Yet the experience in question predominantly occurs "within the project of bad faith" (*ibid.*: 191; see also Chapter 10 of this volume), and is consequently not an experience Sartre thinks characteristic of our social existence as such. If this interpretation is sound, Sartre may perhaps be faulted for not keeping these points clearly apart. But his failing to do so, on Webber's reading, is merely a consequence of Sartre's general decision to weave together phenomenological ontology and cultural critique. At any rate, if Webber is right, we can distinguish a "neutral" account of the experience of the look – of the pure presence of another subject – from the conflict-oriented elaboration of the relations with others characteristic of the person in bad faith. And thereby the first criticism would be deflected.

Webber's distinction may also help to address other criticisms. Several critics have noted the strange fact that whereas Sartre is very insistent, in his critique of Heidegger, that the encounter with the other must be an encounter with a concrete, particular other, Sartre himself ultimately associates the look with a pre-numerical other, which is precisely not a particular other at all (Theunissen 1984: 241–3; Zahavi

2002: 271–2; Overgaard 2007: 107–13). It thus seems that Sartre is inconsistent on this point. In fact, he seems to renounce all attempts to make a concrete encounter with a particular other intelligible as an original encounter. Such encounters can ultimately only be encounters with the other-as-object, and thus not original modes of intersubjectivity at all. The original intersubjective encounter is an encounter with an omnipresent, invisible and strangely abstract other.

Perhaps, however, this criticism rests on a double misunderstanding. First, what Sartre clearly suggests is that the attempt to "fight back" by objectifying the other is of no use, as it only allows me to conquer an object. But we now know that this struggle of looks is something characteristic of bad faith – not something that must be part and parcel of each and every experience of the look. Second, Sartre does not positively say that I *cannot* experience the look in the shape of a concrete person looking at me. In fact, he explicitly contradicts that claim: "what *most often* manifests a look is the convergence of two ocular globes in my direction" (BN1: 257; BN2: 281; Sartre's emphasis). Sartre seems to argue, then, that there is a way of seeing the other *through* feeling exposed to her look, and that this is quite different from looking *at* the other (as in Sartre's park example). This makes it possible for him to maintain that the encounter with the look can be an encounter with a particular, individual other.

Moreover, if Sartre was to say that it is this experience of exposure to the look in a concrete face-to-face encounter that is the most original encounter with another subject as such, there is evidence to suggest that his claim might be true, in at least one sense of "most original". Developmental psychologist Vasudevi Reddy has argued that it is an infant's felt emotional responses (for example, of coyness) to being the object of another's attention that makes them aware of other people's attention as such (Reddy 2008: ch. 6). As Reddy writes, "in the first instance, infants are aware of others' attention when it is directed to themselves", and "this awareness is based upon the capacity to respond emotionally" to others' attention when so directed. Then, "as the infant's engagement with others' intention develops in complexity, the infant becomes aware others' attention when it is directed to other things in the world" (*ibid.*: 92). Read through a Sartrean lens, Reddy's work seems to confirm that it is indeed the experience of the other's look that first reveals the other to us as a subject – as someone able, among other things, to attend to his or her surroundings.

Further reading

McCulloch, G. 1994. *Using Sartre*, chapter 8. London: Routledge.
Theunissen, M. 1984. *The Other: Studies in the Social Ontology of Husserl, Heidegger, Sartre, and Buber*, C. Macann (trans.), chapter 6. Cambridge, MA: MIT Press.
Webber, J. (ed.) 2011. *Reading Sartre: On Phenomenology and Existentialism*, chapters 12, 14. London: Routledge.
Zahavi, D. 2002. "Intersubjectivity in Sartre's *Being and Nothingness*". *Alter* 10: 265–81.

TEN

Bad faith
David Detmer

"Bad faith", as a first approximation, refers to self-deception. While lying to oneself might be the clearest example of what is meant by bad faith, most of the examples that Sartre discusses involve techniques that are subtler than overt lying, and might better be characterized as attempts to evade the truth and to keep it hidden from oneself. Such conduct is widespread and common, according to Sartre, especially when the truth to be evaded concerns one's own freedom and consequent responsibility. Accordingly, Sartre, as a champion of both freedom and truth, devotes a great deal of attention to describing, explaining, and attacking bad faith. Indeed, bad faith emerges as a central concept in his thought, one that is repeatedly taken up both in his philosophical work and (implicitly) in his literary writings, and throughout all phases of his career.

The concept of bad faith serves a number of functions in Sartre's work. For example:

- It helps him to explain the widespread acceptance of certain beliefs that he regards as obviously false.
- It aids him in his attempt to prove that the being of consciousness must be radically different from that of non-conscious things.
- As a central concept in his "existential psychoanalysis", it serves as an indispensable tool in his attempt to understand human lives, both real (as in his biographical studies of Genet and Flaubert) and fictional (as in his development of characters in the story "The Childhood of a Leader" and the play *No Exit*, among other works).

- Implicitly in his early works, and explicitly in his later ones, it functions as an instrument of moral criticism, as it is identified as a vice to be overcome, and is contrasted with a corresponding virtue, that of "authenticity".

The challenge of bad faith

The very existence of bad faith poses a challenge to Sartre, since it appears, on the face of it, to be impossible. The reason is that bad faith seems to imply a contradiction. If I deceive myself, "I must know in my capacity as deceiver the truth which is hidden from me in my capacity as the one deceived" (BN1: 49; BN2: 72). In this way bad faith differs both from cases of simple intellectual mistake and from cases in which one person deceives another. For when I make a mistake there is no inconsistent conjoining of true and false belief; I simply believe a falsehood. And when I deceive another the truth and the falsehood are distributed among two consciousnesses; I know the truth, and I lead the other to believe a falsehood that I do not myself believe. But if I successfully deceive myself it would appear that I must, at one and the same time, both know the truth (so that my denial of it counts as a deception, rather than as a mere mistake) and not know it (so that I am genuinely deceived). But how can I both know something and not know it at the same time?

The answer, according to Sartre, has to do with the strange character of the being of consciousness. A conscious being, according to Sartre, differs radically from other kinds of beings in that it fails fully to coincide with itself, but rather always stands somewhat at a distance from itself. Its manner of being is shot through with negations, dualities, and ambiguities; and it is precisely the exploitation of these that facilitates bad faith. Sartre even goes so far as to say that consciousness, or, in some formulations, "human reality", "is a being which is what it is not and which is not what it is". He insists, further, that it is precisely this paradoxical fact that serves as "the condition of the possibility for bad faith" (BN1: 67; BN2: 90).

Anguish

But what can Sartre possibly mean by such baffling claims? Perhaps the easiest route into grasping his meaning is to consider his discussion of anguish. Sartre begins his analysis by distinguishing anguish from fear.

Whereas fear refers to concern about an external threat, "anguish" is Sartre's term for the reflective awareness of one's own freedom. But why should the consciousness of one's freedom be identified with worry or concern, analogous to fear, and differing from it only in that it takes a different object?

Sartre explains by offering an example. Suppose that I am walking in the mountains, and suddenly come upon a long, narrow path, with no guard rail, at the edge of an abyss. I will experience fear when I realize that a threat from without – a sudden gust of wind, the sliding of rocks or dirt under my feet – could easily cause me to plunge to my death. But now suppose that I respond to my fear by resolving to proceed slowly, and with maximum caution. I will pay careful attention to each and every step, and I will maintain maximum vigilance in noting at all times the wind, the rocks, the dirt, and any other dangerous element in my surroundings. In this way I can greatly minimize the risk posed by these external threats, and feel confident that I will be able to reach the end of the path safely.

But now a new worry emerges. How can I know *now* that I will maintain this caution throughout the period in which I will be in danger? Perhaps after walking a way without incident I will, in spite of myself, gain confidence, and gradually become more relaxed and less careful. Notice that this new worry is addressed, not to any external danger, but rather to my own future attitudes, choices and actions. I am concerned, in short, about my own freedom. This is anguish.

The phenomenon of anguish thus exposes one of the ways in which I fail to coincide with myself. Though I exist as a temporal being, because I am always engaged in projects that are rooted in my past and which aim to bring about a specific future for me (such as one in which I return safely from my walk in the mountains), still, I am temporally separated from my past and my future, both of which, at least to that extent, therefore elude me and remain separate from me. My relationship to my future is thus shown to be thoroughly ambiguous. On the one hand, the reason I am so worried about the mountain hiker who might fall to his death is that this hiker is, in some obvious sense, me, and not someone else. But in so far as that hiker is temporally separated from me, and therefore beyond my present control, he is not me. So "I am what I am not, and am not what I am". Or, to be more precise, "I am the self which I will be, in the mode of not being it" (BN1: 32; BN2: 56). Anguish in the face of the future, then, "is precisely my consciousness of being my own future, in the mode of not-being", since "the decisive conduct will emanate from a self which I am not yet" (*ibid.*).

Freedom and negation

My lack of self-identity, my standing apart from myself, can also be approached by means of an analysis of freedom. On Sartre's view, every free action involves a double negation. On the one hand, to act is to attempt to bring about a state of affairs that currently is not. On the other hand, every act is also an attempt to negate what currently is. For example, suppose that I feel cold and consequently get up and put on a sweater. By this action I attempt to bring about a desideratum (a state of affairs in which I feel warm and comfortable) that currently is not, and I attempt to overturn the present situation (one in which I feel cold and uncomfortable). Such double negativity characterizes the way of being of all consciousnesses. I am constantly oriented towards, aiming at, and striving for, what is not; and I do so on the basis of a standing apart from, and a fleeing from, what is.

Moreover, that towards which I strive both is and is not me. It is me in the sense that I conceive of myself as persisting over time, so that the future I am attempting to bring about is *my* future, rather than someone else's. But it is not me in the sense that I am temporally separated from it, and it is to some degree beyond my present capacity to control (for example, perhaps I will not be able to find my sweater; or, if I do, it might fail to make me warm). Similarly, I both am and am not everything that characterizes me at present, such as my age, my nationality, my occupation, my social role, my current emotional state, or even my "ego". I obviously am them in the sense that they do accurately pertain to me and describe me, such that it would be folly to deny that I am, for example, an American philosophy professor in his fifties. But I am not them in the sense that I put a distance between myself and all of these facticities as soon as I perceive them or think about them. At that point they become not so much me as objects *for* me. I evaluate them, adopt attitudes toward them, and undertake projects on the basis of them or in spite of them. They are neither me nor my actions, but rather constitute that on the basis of which I act as I attempt to negate what is and to bring about what is not.

It is in this way that my way of being differs most radically from that of non-conscious things. A rock or a chair neither aims towards what is not nor attempts to negate what is. It forms no attitude towards any aspect of itself and does not take itself for an object. Thus, it fails to stand apart from itself, but rather coincides with itself perfectly. It is what it is. A conscious being, by contrast, escapes, evades and negates itself at every turn. It is what it is not and is not what it is.

How to deceive successfully: general principles

But how, exactly, does the slippery, ambiguous, paradoxical nature of the being of consciousness facilitate bad faith? The answer to this question has everything to do with the fact that it is usually easier to deceive with unclear and misleading half-truths than it is with clear statements of blatant falsehoods. For one thing, clarity aids, and vagueness inhibits, the critical project of investigating a claim so as to determine whether or not it is true. In order to refute an assertion, one ordinarily needs a reasonably clear understanding of what it means. So an effective method of deception is to employ ambiguity and vagueness, coupled with an appeal to the intended audience's interests and prejudices, so as to *suggest* a message that would not be received so uncritically if it were stated clearly. Similarly, while it is often easy to expose deceptive statements in which the deceptive element resides in what is explicitly stated, it is vastly more difficult (it generally requires much more imagination, energy and critical thinking skills) to expose as deceptive statements that are, strictly speaking, true (or, at least, partly true), but which mislead by means of omission and emphasis. If one asks whether or not a given claim is true, often it is fairly obvious how one might go about finding the answer. For claims that are false are all false in the same way: they assert something that is not the case. But misleading statements can deceive in an almost unlimited number of ways. To anticipate, and thus to be able to investigate, all of the different ways in which a statement might mislead because it simply leaves out (rather than lies about) something of crucial importance, or because it puts undue emphasis on something else (even without lying about it), is often well beyond the critical resources of the intended audience for the deception.

So the ambiguity of consciousness, its character of being what it is not and not being what it is, enables bad faith by rendering deceptive beliefs about oneself merely misleading partial-truths rather than clear thoroughgoing falsehoods. I deceive myself about myself by playing up one aspect of the complex being of my consciousness while playing down another, rather than by telling myself stories about myself that are clearly and wholly false.

The specific mechanisms of bad faith

Exploiting the facticity/transcendence duality
One such pair of aspects that Sartre discusses at length is that of "facticity" and "transcendence". Roughly speaking, the former term refers

to everything about me that is "given", that "is". It refers to all of the facts that pertain to me, such as the fact that I was born at a certain time and in a certain place, that I now hold a specific job, that I am the father of a specific person, that I have done certain definite things in the past, and so forth. "Transcendence", on the other hand, refers to all of the ways in which I go beyond these givens by thinking about them, evaluating them, and, most importantly, by undertaking actions on the basis of them (or in spite of them or in opposition to them). In short, "transcendence" is a synonym for "freedom", which Sartre understands in terms of a negating of facticity in the context of a reaching towards a desideratum that currently is not.

This "double property of the human being" (BN1: 56; BN2: 79) facilitates bad faith because it allows me to deceive myself by (1) identifying myself with my facticity while ignoring my transcendence, (2) identifying myself with my transcendence while ignoring my facticity, or (3) sliding back and forth, in an unprincipled way, between identifying myself with my facticity and doing so with my transcendence. Such behaviours can be undertaken with a great deal of subtlety, so that they amount to nothing more than a selective focusing on one thing while averting one's gaze from something else. They need not involve the denial of truths that one is staring in the face, for such lies would indeed "fall back and collapse beneath my look" (BN1: 49; BN2: 73).

Bad faith is further facilitated by the fact that, according to Sartre, the meaning of facticities is never self-announcing, but rather always depends on transcendence. He argues, on the basis of a careful description of our perceptual experience, that seeing is almost always seeing-as. We encounter things in our perceptual field under the colour of concepts and categories. An apple might be noticed and seen as an apple, or as a specific kind of apple (such as golden delicious), or as a yellow thing, or as a roundish thing, or as a thing on the table, or as a fruit, or as an edible thing, or as a small thing, or as a thing from the grocery store, or as a thing to be included in a still life painting, and so on, or it might not be noticed at all, or noticed only vaguely and marginally, as part of the undifferentiated background of some more interesting object that is demanding my attention. Whether something is noticed at all, and if so, as what, and with what meaning, is usually determined by my interests and projects. (And Sartre holds that in all perception there is an elevation of part of the perceptual field to the foreground and a relegation of other parts to the background.) If I am interested in eating, I see the apple as an apple. If I am interested in painting, I see it as an element in a still life. And if I am intensely engaged in a project with respect to which the apple has no relevance, I am likely either to ignore it or to notice it only marginally.

So it is only as I am going beyond, or transcending, facticity that it emerges as meaningful. This is significant because, were it the case that I ignored some things so as to focus on others, and saw the things that I did focus on under the interpretive colour of some concepts rather than others, only or especially when I wanted to deceive myself, then I would be on my guard whenever I engaged in such behaviours, and my attempts at deception would be likely to fail. But because conceptual interpretation and selective focusing are essential parts of the phenomenon of perception as such, I can have no principled objection to their use in any given case. So my deceptive and misleading selective focusing on transcendence at the expense of facticity (or the reverse) in any given case need not lead to suspicion. And the same is true of my subsuming what I am focusing on under a deceptive and misleading interpretation. In short, the fact that omission, emphasis and interpretation are necessary and legitimate in principle makes their illegitimate and dishonest use much harder to detect.

Sartre is quick to point out, however, that the slippery and ambiguous character of our way of being does not preclude accurate and honest thought about it. For example, specifically with regard to facticity and transcendence, Sartre insists that "these two aspects of human reality are and ought to be capable of a valid coordination" (BN1: 56; BN2: 79). To show this, he presents the example of a gay man who wishes to deny his homosexuality, as well as that of his friend, "the champion of sincerity", who wishes him to affirm it. The gay man is in bad faith because he denies his facticity. He acknowledges all of the facts that would lead an impartial observer to regard his orientation as homosexual, but "he refuses to draw from them the conclusion which they impose" (BN1: 63; BN2: 87). He does so by engaging in a double strategy. On the one hand, he identifies himself almost exclusively with his transcendence, minimizing his facticity. And on the other hand, to the extent that he does confront his facticity, in the form of the history of his sexual conduct, he adopts an interpretation (he is sexually adventurous, but has merely had very bad luck in meeting women) whereby that conduct is not indicative of a deeply rooted tendency. The champion of sincerity, on the other hand, is in bad faith in that he denies his friend's transcendence, seeing him as a kind of thing, who is a homosexual in the same way that a paper clip is a paper clip. He regards his friend as having a fixed essence, so that his past conduct also constitutes his future destiny.

On Sartre's view, both of these men assert a half-truth, and neglect one or the other half of the facticity/transcendence duality. To avoid bad faith, they would need to attain, and to confront honestly, a clear understanding of the coordinated interplay of these two aspects of human existence. As Sartre puts it, the gay man would not be in bad faith were he to say:

> to the extent that a pattern of conduct is defined as the conduct of a homosexual and to the extent that I have adopted this conduct, I am a homosexual. But to the extent that human reality can not be finally defined by patterns of conduct, I am not one.
> (BN1: 64; BN2: 88; translation modified)

Exploiting other dualities

Bad faith can also be facilitated by several other dualities pertaining to the being of conscious agents. For example, recall from the discussion of anguish that we are temporal beings, ambiguously situated with respect to our past and future: I both am and am not my future and my past. While instances of bad faith involving the past/future duality are often identical to cases based on the facticity/transcendence duality (with the past playing the role of facticity and the future playing the role of transcendence), other cases have a different structure. For example, suppose that I habitually engage in behaviours that are likely to destroy my health gradually over time. While the bad faith that supports such self-destructive conduct might take the form of a denial of facticity (I ignore the abundant evidence concerning, say, the hazards of smoking), it might have nothing to do with a denial of either facticity or transcendence, but might, instead, simply be based on the ambiguity of my relationship to my future self. By identifying myself exclusively with my past and present I might wholly affirm the half-truth that the old man who will suffer from my behaviour is "not me", but rather someone else for whom I will do no more now than feel pity.

Or again, consider Sartre's distinction between thetic and non-thetic (or positional or non-positional) awareness of things. The point of this distinction is that to be conscious is to focus, so that some things get my full attention (thetic awareness), whereas I am only marginally (nonthetically) aware of other things in my perceptual field. This distinction (which, once again, refers not to an occasional or optional feature of conscious experience, but rather to an ineliminable part of its essential structure, thus ruling out the possibility of a quick, principled objection to its use in instances of bad faith) facilitates bad faith by the simple means of selective focusing. Whenever something that might displease me about myself begins to call itself to my attention, I can simply avert my gaze, focus on something else, and cause this item to melt into the relatively undifferentiated ground of my marginal attention. Similarly, if I am, perhaps against my will, confronted with clear instances in my past of some kind of misconduct, I can still refrain from investigating them, inquiring into them, bringing them to full and lucid clarity, and asking myself what sort of pattern they suggest. This is surely self-deception, but it falls short of the kind of full-blooded lie to oneself that would entail a contradiction. It relies, instead, on the technique of keeping vague things vague, and of exploiting the ambiguities and self-divisions of consciousness so as to enable me to emphasize what I want to emphasize and to omit what I want to omit.

The bad faith of selective focusing is further enabled by another essential structure of consciousness, that of the pre-reflective/reflective duality. Sartre argues that the primary mode of consciousness is pre-reflective. In this mode consciousness is fired out towards the objects in the world with which it is concerned. It does not reflectively focus on itself. That is a secondary mode of consciousness, made possible by consciousness's non-thetic, or marginal, awareness of its own activities when it is engaged pre-reflectively with other objects. When I am counting, the content of my thought is "1, 2, 3, 4, 5", and so forth. However, if someone were suddenly to interrupt me and demand to know what I am doing, I would easily be able to shift from the pre-reflective to the reflective mode and report, "I am counting". This pre-reflective/reflective duality facilitates bad faith through selective focusing in that it allows me to remain in the pre-reflective mode while I am doing despicable things (so that my attention remains riveted to the objects with which I am dealing, and takes no notice of me, or of issues concerning the meaning or interpretation of my actions, let alone what they, in concert with other actions of the same sort, might imply about my character), while at the same time allowing me to visit the reflective mode, and to return to it often, during the (perhaps much rarer) cases when I am doing laudable things. In this way I can become skilled at noticing, and basking in, my nobility and virtue, while scarcely noticing my vices.

Handling evidence

Probably the most important technique of bad faith is simply the ability to allow oneself to be persuaded by weak evidence. This is not usually accomplished by first noticing that the evidence for a given belief is weak, and then persuading oneself that the evidence is nonetheless adequate to support the belief. Rather, the more common progression would be something like this: First, I want to believe something. Then, rather than engaging in an honest inquiry into the evidence concerning it, I search, in a one-sided way, for evidence that will justify my belief. Finally, without explicitly focusing on it or formulating the point to myself in words, I respond to a dimly perceived vague worry that the evidence might not turn out to be good enough by resolving to use a low evidentiary standard. As Sartre puts it:

> Bad faith does not hold the norms and criteria of truth as they are accepted by the critical thought of good faith. What it decides first, in fact, is the nature of truth ... [Bad faith] stands forth in the firm resolution *not to demand too much*, to count itself satisfied when it is barely persuaded, to force itself in decisions to adhere to uncertain truths. (BN1: 68; BN2: 91)

An extremely common related technique of bad faith is to employ, in an inconsistent and unprincipled way, different standards of evidence for different beliefs, so that one adopts a low standard of evidence for beliefs one wants to affirm, while simultaneously insisting on a high standard for beliefs one wishes to reject. For example, if I wish to criticize a head of state, I might accept weak evidence that his policies are responsible for high gasoline prices. But if gas prices are high when someone I approve of is in office, I find the evidence that the policies of a head of state can significantly affect such prices to be inconclusive and unconvincing.

Notice, once again, that these are methods of self-deception that do not involve overt lying. With them there is no denying of plain facts that one is staring in the face. Rather, they deal with matters of judgment in weighing and evaluating evidence, issues that are difficult and controversial, making the transgression of valid norms concerning them often difficult to detect, and impossible to dismiss in a quick and principled way. The project of believing something on the basis of weak evidence does not impose the sort of psychological barriers that would be put in play by an attempt to lie to oneself about an obvious truth of which one is lucidly aware. After all, in the former case I do not *know* that the belief I wish to affirm is false. Moreover, there is *some* evidence to support the claim that it is true. Finally, it is unclear *how much* evidence is needed to make a belief defensible in the first place, so that it is not obvious that I am doing anything wrong by believing this – or so I, perhaps convincingly, tell myself.

Bad faith as an explanation of widely held false beliefs

Ordinarily, false beliefs require no special explanation. Some issues are difficult; information regarding them is often lacking; and people can make honest mistakes in attempting to reason about them. In addition, in this world of advertising, public relations, political propaganda, and the like, many false beliefs can be attributed, in part, to successful efforts on the part of some to deceive others. Why, then, does Sartre so frequently invoke bad faith as an explanation for false beliefs?

One reason is that Sartre holds a distinctive conception of consciousness, maintaining that it is always self-aware. In this same vein, he rejects any kind of psychoanalytic notion of an unconscious mind in which some contents might be hidden from consciousness. Were it not for his analysis of bad faith, these positions would render it difficult for him to explain why there are, as he also insists, commonly held false beliefs about consciousness itself.

Bad faith emerges as a plausible explanation, however, in light of the fact that the false beliefs in question are comforting, and involve denials of truths that would be demanding, disturbing, or threatening. For example, as we have seen, Sartre claims that when we are reflectively aware of our freedom, we experience it as anguish. One reason why we so seldom focus on our freedom and face up to its implications, and why so many of us deny it entirely in favour of a deterministic worldview, is, for Sartre, precisely that we wish to flee our anguish and to escape the irksome obligations it imposes, namely, the obligation to act, and to take responsibility for our actions.

Bad faith in Sartre's fictional works and biographical studies

Many of Sartre's stories and plays feature characters in bad faith. For example, in his play *No Exit* (Sartre 1945b, 1955), the character Garcin, dead and in hell, attempts to flee from the realization that he had lived his life as a coward. His main technique of bad faith is the denial of facticity. He desperately attempts to avoid confronting the pattern suggested by his past actions, and seeks instead to identify himself with his lofty aims and intentions, which he had not lived long enough to fulfil. Because the evidence of his cowardice is so strong, he does not go so far as to try to convince himself that he had been a hero. Instead, he merely claims that, because of his premature death, the matter "had been left in suspense, forever" (Sartre 1955: 39).

Bad faith also figures strongly in Sartre's biographical works, in which he makes use of his "existential psychoanalysis" in an attempt to understand a human life. For example, in his biography of Jean Genet, he suggests that the initial course of Genet's life was set in his early childhood, when he, in stark contrast to Garcin, identified himself solely in terms of his facticity and denied his transcendence. This identification sprang from an incident in which he was caught stealing, and heard an adult say of him: "you are a thief". Referring to this incident, Sartre comments:

> He who was not yet anyone suddenly becomes Jean Genet ... It is revealed to him that he *is* a thief and he pleads guilty, crushed by a fallacy which he is unable to refute; he stole, he is therefore a thief ... What he *wanted* was to steal; what he *did*, a theft; what he *was*, a thief ... *Genet is a thief*; that is his truth, his eternal essence. And if he *is* a thief, he must therefore always be one, everywhere, not only when he steals, but when he eats, when he sleeps, when he kisses his foster mother.   (Sartre 1964a: 26–8)

Bad faith as an instrument of moral criticism

While in *Being and Nothingness* Sartre claims to be employing the term "bad faith" merely descriptively, with no moral connotation, he drops this pretence in his later works. In these writings he criticizes bad faith and calls, instead, for "authenticity", which he defines in terms of "having a true and lucid consciousness of the situation [and] in assuming the responsibilities and risks that it involves" (Sartre 1965b: 90). He adds that "there is no doubt that authenticity demands courage and more than courage. Thus it is not surprising that one finds it so rarely" (*ibid*.).

His reasons for condemning the flight from truth are presented most clearly in some of his posthumously published works, such as *Notebooks for an Ethics* (Sartre 1983b, 1992) and *Truth and Existence* (Sartre 1989b, 1995). His main point is that if we do not know the truth about the world, we will not know what needs to be changed. Nor will we know what means are likely to be effective in changing it. Consequently, we will be unable to carry out successfully our moral obligation to change the world for the better.

Further reading

Catalano, J. S. 1996a. *Good Faith and Other Essays: Perspectives on a Sartrean Ethics*. Lanham, MD: Rowman & Littlefield.

Detmer, D. 2008. *Sartre Explained: From Bad Faith to Authenticity*. Peru, IL: Open Court.
Sontoni, R. E. 1995. *Bad Faith, Good Faith and Authenticity in Sartre's Early Philosophy*. Philadelphia, PA: Temple University Press.
Webber, J. (ed.) 2011. *Reading Sartre: On Phenomenology and Existentialism*. New York: Routledge.

ELEVEN

Authenticity
Jonathan Webber

Introduction

Sartre's concern with individual authenticity pervades his early philosophical and literary writings. Yet his conception of authenticity is somewhat elusive. The only significant point he makes directly about authenticity in *Being and Nothingness* is in a footnote. There, he tells us that authenticity is the opposite of bad faith, but goes on to say that the description of authenticity "has no place here" (BN1: 70n; BN2: 94n). In two immediately subsequent works, *Existentialism Is a Humanism* and *Anti-Semite and Jew*, Sartre argues that authenticity is the fundamental virtue in his ethical outlook and he characterizes various examples of authentic and inauthentic ways of living, but in neither work does he give a clear explication of the idea of authenticity itself. His notes from that period, posthumously published as *Notebooks for an Ethics* (Sartre 1983b, 1992), make it abundantly clear that he intended to construct a complete account of ethics on the basis of authenticity, but since that project never came to fruition we are left without a detailed statement of the idea itself that Sartre considered worthy of publication.

Despite this, a commitment to the importance of authenticity drives Sartre's existentialism. It does so primarily through an exploration of its absence. In plays and novels as well as in *Being and Nothingness*, Sartre explores the ways in which people fail to be authentic and the damage this causes to their own lives and to the lives of those they affect. Indeed, one might even view these explorations of bad faith as attempts to discern the contours of its negation, his ideal of authenticity. These discussions make it clear, moreover, that for Sartre authenticity should not be confused with sincerity or good faith. The ideal of sincerity requires us to recognize and accept the motivations that drive our behaviour. The ideal of good faith requires us to inspect our own motivations honestly with a view to accepting who we are. But in Sartre's view, the very idea that we must accept the motivations that we have, rather than seek to shape our motivations, is at the very core of bad faith.

The importance of this is brought out well in Charles Larmore's recent book, *The Practices of the Self*. If authenticity is being true to the person that you really are, then this need not be understood in terms of some set of fixed motivations. Larmore sets this idea up in two dimensions. He rejects the idea of authenticity as identifying with a fixed or essential self, embracing instead the idea that inauthenticity is the denial of the formal structure of human existence. In this respect, Larmore agrees with Sartre. The second dimension concerns the relation between oneself and society. For the idea of being true to one's essential motivations has often been seen to require resisting pressure to conform to the tastes, goals and values of society. Larmore retains this traditional aspect of the idea of authenticity, though he refines it in a certain way. Through this aspect of his idea of authenticity, Larmore develops a critique of Sartre's ideas that authenticity is the opposite of bad faith and is the fundamental virtue.

In this chapter, I argue that Larmore is mistaken about the nature of authenticity and that Sartre's position is preferable. I begin by presenting Larmore's position in more detail. Next, I raise a problem for Larmore that reflects a consideration that shapes Sartre's discussion of bad faith. I then trace this problem to Larmore's understanding of our epistemic access to ourselves through reflection. Larmore bases his account on Sartre's theory of pure and impure reflection, but I will present a different reading of Sartre here. Finally, I will show how the account of reflection that I ascribe to Sartre grounds a conception of authenticity in which identifying with the formal structure of oneself as a being that undertakes commitments is allied not with absence of external influence, but rather with recognition of the motivations to which one has already committed oneself. The basic structure of Sartre's account of authenticity is thereby uncovered, and his ideas that authenticity is the opposite of bad faith and is the fundamental virtue are both shown to survive Larmore's critique.

Larmore's account of authenticity

If authenticity includes being true to the kind of being that you are, then to give this idea substance we need an account of the kind of being that you are. Larmore (2011) argues that we are essentially normative beings, meaning that our identities are determined by the commitments we undertake to think, speak and act in certain ways. He argues that such commitment is essential to both belief and desire. Beliefs "function as standing directives that give the agent the (rational) obligation to think and act in accord with their presumed truth", while desires likewise consist in "orienting the conduct, intellectual as well as practical, of the individual" (*ibid.*: 81). Larmore presents this as a more precise rendering of Sartre's thesis that subjectivity consists in a relationship to oneself that is not a matter of introspective knowledge. "The intimacy in which the subject necessarily lives with himself and that Sartre intended to express", writes Larmore, "is practical in nature, consisting in the subject's thinking or acting only by way of committing himself" (*ibid.*).

Although all thought and action makes such commitment, Larmore argues, we sometimes think and act in ways that imply that this is not so. Thought and action are authentic only when they do not imply the denial that our beliefs, desires and actions consist in undertaking commitments. When we are entirely absorbed in what we are thinking about or what we are doing, there is no possibility of such a denial, and hence no possibility of inauthenticity: we coincide perfectly with ourselves. Larmore calls this "being natural" (for example, *ibid.*: 27–30, 144–5). The possibility of inauthenticity arises only when we are reflectively aware of ourselves.

Larmore divides reflection into two categories, "cognitive reflection" and "practical reflection" (*ibid.*: 24). These differ in their basic structure: cognitive reflection is a kind of thought, practical reflection a kind of action. When directed towards oneself, cognitive reflection is the consideration of how one would look to other people (*ibid.*: 83–8). When directed towards the world, cognitive reflection is consideration of what reasons other people would have for believing, desiring or acting in a particular way (*ibid.*: 68–76). Cognitive reflection, then, is thinking about oneself or about the world from the perspective of others. These others can be particular people one knows, imaginary people, or the impersonal abstraction of society in general. Because this cognitive reflection is concerned with the perspective of others, it is always inauthentic: one commits oneself to a particular thought or desire, but one does so on the basis that someone else would do so (*ibid.*: 144).

Practical reflection, on the other hand, has authentic and inauthentic varieties. Practical reflection is the explicit endorsement of beliefs, feelings or actions (*ibid.*: 24). "I love wearing my leather jacket!" is one of Larmore's examples of such conscious avowal (*ibid.*: 147). This act of avowal is not "a judgment about what we should do", but "an explicit intention to do this or that" (*ibid.*: 71). It is inauthentic when we simultaneously distance ourselves from the fact that we are making this commitment. Larmore gives two examples. One is avowing an intention as though it were merely the effect of an outside force. "Duty compels me to do it!", one might announce, as though one has not chosen to do it (*ibid.*: 148). The other is Emma Bovary's decision to pursue a love affair, on grounds that it would follow from the nature that she likes to see herself as sharing with her literary heroines (*ibid.*: 147–8). In this kind of practical reflection, as in cognitive reflection, "we assimilate ourselves to another" and so "are denying, in effect, the very nature of what we are doing" (*ibid.*: 150).

Authentic practical reflection is the avowal or endorsement of a commitment without this denial. It is authentic because it affirms one's status as a normative being, as living by the commitments one undertakes. This and unreflective absorption in thought, feeling or action are the only two kinds of authenticity. Of the two kinds of inauthenticity, cognitive reflection and inauthentic practical reflection, only inauthentic practical reflection is a form of bad faith. Only in this case do we experience our thoughts, feelings and actions in a way that is "contrary to their true tenor" and "disfigure them by clinging to the standpoint of an onlooker" (*ibid.*: 159). In cognitive reflection, we experience ourselves as considering ourselves or the world from the standpoint of an onlooker, and that is indeed what we are doing. For this reason, Larmore rejects Sartre's equation of inauthenticity with bad faith (*ibid.*: 149, 159). What is more, argues Larmore, cognitive reflection is essential to living well, so inauthenticity is not always a bad thing. Thus, authenticity cannot be the supreme or fundamental virtue on which ethics is founded (*ibid.*: 145, 153–4, 159).

Depth of commitment

Larmore's conceptual framework clarifies part of the structure of Sartre's idea of authenticity. Larmore is right to describe Sartre's account of being human in terms of undertaking commitments, and to identify authenticity as the recognition of this. But there is a dimension of Sartre's account of human existence that is missing from Larmore's reading of Sartre. This is the ongoing effect of commitments once they are made. Sartre thinks that attempts to undertake new commitments can run into practical difficulties rooted in other commitments one has already undertaken and that now run deep in one's overall psychology.

Sartre illustrates this in a vignette in his novel *The Age of Reason* (Sartre 1945a, 1986b), published two years after *Being and Nothingness*. Daniel is aware that others see him as a sentimental person, partly on account of the cats he cares for, and he wants to prove to himself that they have got him wrong. So he resolves to drown his cats in the river. But when he reaches the water's edge, he finds that he cannot bring himself to do so (Sartre 1986b: 81–91). Sartre describes intentions like this, which one cannot really go through with, as "cheques without funds to meet them" (*ibid.*: 86). He makes a similar point in his discussion of freedom in *Being and Nothingness*. Freedom does not simply consist in the ability to do anything at any time, he argues, because one's motives and the reasons one finds in the world reflect one's existing projects. Freedom therefore consists in the ability to change those underlying projects. For any action of mine, it is indeed true that I "could have done otherwise", but the important question is, "at what price?" (BN1: 464; BN2: 476). There is a sense in which Daniel could have drowned his cats. But he found, when the time came, that the price of doing so was one that he would not pay.

Daniel formed his intention in bad faith. He had not taken into account the resistance to carrying out this intention rooted in his love of his cats. It was, we might say, an inauthentic intention. He had not committed *himself*, the self constrained by his existing commitments, to the goal of drowning the cats (Sartre 198bc: 90). In this regard, Daniel resembles a character in Sartre's central discussion of bad faith in *Being and Nothingness*, the man who has had many affairs with men in the past but resists the advice of his friend, "the champion of sincerity", to identify with his homosexuality. He resists the idea that his actions show he has a fixed nature that includes sexual attraction to men and not women. Sartre, of course, thinks that he is right to resist this idea. But the character goes wrong, Sartre thinks, in taking this as a reason to deny his homosexuality altogether. Just as the champion of sincerity is in bad faith because he pretends that we are not normative beings whose identity is bestowed by our commitments, his friend is in bad faith because his stated intention to settle down with the right woman does not take account of the homosexual desires that he does indeed have and to which he has committed himself (BN1: 63–4; BN2: 86–7).

Unless an undertaking is informed by one's existing commitments, therefore, whether these are to be respected and preserved through the undertaking or are to be overthrown in its name, the undertaking is too shallow to count as an authentic commitment. Yet such a shallow undertaking does fit Larmore's account of authentic practical reflection. Its lack of depth is not a denial of one's status as a normative being. On the contrary, it involves overplaying this status, as though one can easily commit to anything at all.

Larmore comes close to addressing this problem in three passages of his book. In one, he argues that the aim of becoming a certain sort of person should be understood as undertaking a commitment that then constrains our thought and action in general (Larmore 2011: 158). The kind of constraint he describes is rational: one rationally ought to respect the commitment in thought and action. The difficulty of following through on such commitments is due to the fact that they do not, of themselves, exert psychological pressure towards respecting them. The kind of commitment we are concerned with, on the other hand, is one that has been acted on repeatedly and through such habituation has come to exert psychological pressure of its own.

Larmore also comes close to addressing habituated commitment when he discusses clarifying commitments one has unreflectively undertaken in order to endorse them in practical reflection. "Mary, for instance, is convinced that Mark has become the love of her life", he writes, "but observing that she feels more tender toward him when he is not there than when they are together, she starts to question the nature of her attachment" (*ibid.*: 86). "Before deciding to espouse some religious belief", he points out, "we may want to establish whether we find it attractive because of its consoling power and not by virtue of its apparent truth"; so "in order to know whether we are really a believer" he recommends we "undertake to perform all the rituals and recite all the prayers in order to observe whether we are carrying them out with the sort of conviction that is the proof of faith" (*ibid.*: 162). The observations these characters make about themselves, according to Larmore, are instances of cognitive reflection, since only cognitive reflection aims at knowledge. Practical reflection is the explicit endorsement of a commitment, but these characters are only aiming to discover what their commitments truly are. Cognitive reflection is always a form of inauthenticity, for Larmore, even though in cases like these it is a prelude to authentic practical reflection.

Public behaviour and private experience

These passages indicate the shape that an account of practical difficulty rooted in existing commitments would have to take within Larmore's framework. One can learn of the pressure these commitments exert, on Larmore's view, only through cognitive reflection on oneself. Daniel should have taken into account what those around him already knew, that he loves his cats. The man who will not admit his homosexuality is denying something that is obvious to his friend, whether or not his friend is mistaken to see it as part of a fixed essence. Larmore holds cognitive reflection to be our only form of epistemic access to our own motivations: "everything we know about ourselves is founded on the fundamentally public procedures of observation and inference" (Larmore 2011: 135). He grounds this claim in the failure of successive philosophers to make sense of the metaphor of "introspection" as a mode of direct access to the contents of our own minds (*ibid.*: 123–6). Sartre sometimes sounds as though he endorses a similar claim. "Consciousness does not know its own character – unless in determining itself reflectively from the standpoint of another's point of view", he writes (BN1: 349; BN2: 372).

But if this is the only way in which one can become aware of one's own motivations, then it is difficult to see where Daniel or the man who will not admit his homosexuality are going wrong. For both of these characters have looked at their own past from an external perspective. Each has understood that their behaviour can be interpreted as manifesting a certain trait, but each insists that it is compatible with the absence of that trait. What these characters fail to take into account is not behaviour. Daniel fails to take into account the value his cats have for him. The man who denies his homosexuality fails to take into account his sexual attraction to men. Such values and feelings are not directly observable from an external perspective. Indeed, it seems to be Sartre's point in these vignettes that the bad faith of these characters rests on taking up an external perspective in order to conceal this crucial information.

Yet this does not commit Sartre to the view that values and feelings are inner mental states that one can become aware of through "introspection". In his early *Sketch for a Theory of the Emotions*, Sartre argued that an emotion is "a specific manner of apprehending the world" (Sartre 2002: 35). To be frightened is to experience the world as a fearful place, to be angry is to find the object of one's anger hateful (*ibid.*: 34–61). In *Being and Nothingness*, Sartre generalizes this idea to all feelings. Disgust is experienced as the repulsiveness of disgusting objects (BN1: 605, 616; BN2: 625–6, 635–6). But he goes further, and applies the idea to evaluative attitudes as well as to affectivity. For something to be valuable to you, on this account, is for it to be experienced as valuable in everyday engagement with the world (BN1: 38–9; BN2: 62–3). This suggests that our knowledge of values and feelings requires neither introspection nor inference from behaviour. Rather, awareness of the way the world seems to us can furnish knowledge of our values and feelings. Daniel should have taken into account the value that he experiences his cats as having for him. The man who denies his homosexual desires should consider the ways in which men and women feature in his experience.

What is required is a particular kind of reflection on one's own experience. In unreflective experience, the world has a particular evaluative and affective structure, but this structure is not where one's attention is focused. One is attending to the world itself. The evaluative and affective structure is the way that world appears. To make this structure, this mode of presentation, the object of attention is to move to another kind of experience. This is reflection on the unreflective experience of the world. Such reflection does not simply present the world again, for attention is no longer directed towards the objects that make up that world. Neither does such reflection involve an external perspective on oneself. It is not a form of Larmore's "cognitive reflection". Neither, finally, is it aimed at endorsing a commitment. It is not Larmore's "practical reflection". It is aimed at gathering information, but information about how things seem rather than about how they are. That is to say, it is concerned with phenomena, or appearances. For this reason, it is rightly called "phenomenological reflection".

Pure and impure reflection

Because values and feelings are manifested in the way the world appears, phenomenological reflection can reveal those values and feelings. Consider again Larmore's examples of cognitive reflection in the service of authentic practical reflection. Mary learns something about her relationship with Mark by reflecting on the difference between the way he features in her experience when he is absent and when he is present. When one reflects on one's own religious practice to ascertain whether one is a genuine believer, one is not reflecting on the motions one goes through but on how one experiences those rituals. These are not really cases of cognitive reflection as Larmore defines it. Phenomenological reflection is inherently first-personal. Since it is reflection on the way the world appears in experience, only the subject of that experience can reflect on it in this way. Only you have direct access to the way the world seems to you.

Although phenomenological reflection is required for understanding one's existing commitments, Sartre does not hold that all phenomenological reflection is conducive to authenticity. He divides such reflection into two categories, "pure reflection" and "impure reflection". Pure reflection preserves the sense of oneself as a normative being whose identity is conferred by commitments one undertakes and that one can revoke. Impure reflection, on the other hand, denies this. Sartre does not make this account of the difference between pure and impure reflection very clear in *Being and Nothingness*. The terminology in which he describes it is generally ambiguous. Larmore's distinction between cognitive reflection and practical reflection is inspired by a reading of it. "Pure reflection, according to *Being and Nothingness*, 'delivers the reflected-on [i.e. ourselves] to us, not as a given [i.e. an object of knowledge] but as the being which we have to be'", writes Larmore (2011: 151), quoting Sartre (the notes in brackets are Larmore's). This is the basis for Larmore's idea of "practical reflection", in which one features as the person undertaking the commitment, in contrast to "cognitive reflection" in which one is an object of knowledge.

Rather than taking the phrase "the reflected-on" to refer to oneself, however, we should take it to refer to the experience that is the object of phenomenological reflection. For example, if I think about an absent friend and then reflect on that experience, the "reflected-on" is my thinking about that absent friend. Moreover, rather than take the term "given" in an epistemic sense, to denote an object of knowledge, we should understand it here in a metaphysical or ontological sense, to denote something beyond our control.

Read in this way, the passage quoted by Larmore claims that pure and impure reflection differ not in what they present, which in both cases is the way the world appears, but in how they present it. Pure reflection presents it, correctly, as a manifestation of my commitments. Impure reflection presents it as just a given. From impure reflection, one could infer that the way the world seems is the way the world is, or that the way the world seems is a result of unchangeable facts about oneself. Impure reflection thus supports inauthenticity, since it allows one to live as though the evaluative and affective texture of the world is not the result of one's commitments. Pure reflection supports authenticity, since it delivers knowledge of that texture as resulting from one's commitments.

Authenticity and bad faith

Understood in this way, authenticity does not essentially require resisting social pressure. Neither does it essentially require viewing oneself and the world from one's own perspective, rather than taking up the perspective of other people. The difference between authenticity and inauthenticity, that is to say, is not based on the role that other people play in one's life at all. Authenticity is rather the recognition of the particular person that you are. This has two dimensions. One is recognition of what it is to be a person, which is to be a normative being whose identity is conferred by their commitments. The other is recognition of the particular commitments that one has, as these are manifested in the way the world seems in experience. Once we understand Sartre's conception of authenticity in this way, we can see that the two criticisms that Larmore raises against it are misplaced.

One of Larmore's criticisms is that Sartre is wrong to identify inauthenticity with bad faith. Cognitive reflection, he argues, is a form of inauthenticity that does not in itself involve bad faith. One is taking up an external perspective, so one is not wholly identified with oneself, but one can be perfectly well aware that one is doing so. However, on Sartre's account inauthenticity does not consist in taking up an external perspective, so cognitive reflection is not in itself an instance of inauthenticity. The identification of inauthenticity with bad faith is therefore consistent with the claim that cognitive reflection is not a form of bad faith. Larmore's other criticism fails for essentially the same reason. This is the criticism that authenticity cannot be the fundamental virtue, since one cannot live well, indeed one cannot engage in authentic practical reflection, without engaging in cognitive reflection. Since cognitive reflection is not an instance of inauthenticity, on Sartre's view, the role of cognitive reflection in living well does not entail that inauthenticity can be a good thing.

Authenticity and inauthenticity, according to Sartre, concern how one understands oneself to be. One kind of inauthenticity involves affirming one's traits as though they were fixed. Sartre calls this "sincerity", illustrating it with his character "the champion of sincerity", who encourages his friend to embrace his homosexual desires. The other kind involves denying one's actual traits and pretending to have contrary traits that explain one's behaviour. This is what the champion of sincerity's friend does when he denies his homosexuality. Sartre calls this kind "bad faith", but he also holds that this and sincerity are both forms of bad faith in a larger sense (BN1: 66–7; BN2: 89–90).

Bad faith in this larger sense is asserting a claim about oneself despite being aware, to some extent, that this claim is not true. According to Sartre, the champion of sincerity is aware that desires are the result of commitments just as his friend is aware of his homosexuality (BN1: 64–5; BN2: 87–8). Larmore's examples of inauthentic practical reflection are indeed both cases of inauthenticity on this account, but not for the reason Larmore gives. Undertaking a commitment on the pretext that duty requires one to do so is a denial that the values one finds in the world are only a function of one's existing commitments. Endorsing an affair as following the path of one's heroines is pretending that this outcome is determined by traits one shares with those heroines.

The ethics of authenticity

Larmore presents one further reason to reject Sartre's claim that authenticity is the fundamental virtue that underpins the rest of ethics. This is a general scepticism about such monistic approaches to ethical value. With respect to authenticity, the objection is "that in certain circumstances the pursuit of authenticity can lead to undesirable consequences" (Larmore 2011: 6). More dramatically, is it not possible to be perfectly authentic and thoroughly evil? If authenticity is understood in the way that Larmore describes it, then this certainly is possible. For if authenticity is just coinciding with oneself in a way that does not deny one's status as a normative being, then this sets no constraints at all on the effects one's actions can have on other people. Understood in this way, that is to say, authenticity is an entirely self-regarding virtue. Larmore does not see this as a reason to reject the idea that authenticity is valuable. His recommendation is rather that we abandon any attempt to cast it as the supreme value, and admit instead that its role is tempered by other values.

Sartre's attempt to cast authenticity as the supreme value need not face this problem. This is because Sartre does not think of authenticity as coinciding with oneself. It is possible, therefore, that authenticity can set constraints on one's attitudes towards others as well as towards oneself. If authenticity can be shown to require the recognition that people in general are normative beings with ongoing commitments, that is to say then this might be argued to set important constraints on the ways in which one treats people in general. It seems clear from *Existentialism and Humanism* (Sartre 1946b, 1973), *Anti-Semite and Jew* (Sartre 1946a, 1948b) and *Notebooks for an Ethics* (Sartre 1983b, 1992) that this is the direction in which Sartre wanted his ethical theory to develop. But if it is to be developed in this way, there are two immediate problems that need to be solved.

One problem stems from Sartre's account of values as rooted in the commitments one has already undertaken. This is integral to his idea of authenticity, since authenticity requires recognizing the values to which one's existing commitments give rise. How is this compatible with the claim that authenticity is objectively valuable, something to which all people ought to aspire irrespective of their existing commitments? The answer to that meta-ethical question needs to lead either directly or indirectly to a form of authenticity that concerns other people as well as oneself. If one argues, for example, that inauthenticity necessarily frustrates one's own projects, then this could directly support only a self-regarding form of authenticity. An argument from here to the need to recognize other people as the particular normative beings that they are would still need to be provided. Herein lies the second problem, one parallel to Larmore's concern about authentic evildoers. For it is not at all clear why merely recognizing that somebody is a normative being with a particular set of commitments should require one to treat that person with any respect or concern for their wellbeing. It might constrain the ways in which one can successfully oppress people, for example, but it is not at all obvious that it should preclude oppressing them.

These are the problems with the ethics of authenticity that Sartre was grappling with in the years following the publication of *Being and Nothingness*. That he never published his promised work on ethics could be taken to indicate that he could not resolve them. Alternatively, it could be taken to indicate an endorsement of the ethical writings of Simone de Beauvoir, which build on this conception of authenticity. Either way, it remains an open question whether an account of authenticity of roughly the shape drawn by Sartre could provide the basis of ethics. If such an account of authenticity could not answer this perennial foundational question, moreover, it does not follow that it could not make other substantial contributions to ethical theory.

Further reading

de Beauvoir, S. 1948. *The Ethics of Ambiguity*, B. Frechtman (trans.). Chicago, IL: Citadel.
de Beauvoir, S. 2005. *Philosophical Writings*, M. A. Simons (ed.). Chicago, IL: University of Illinois Press.
Guignon, C. 2004. *On Being Authentic*. London: Routledge.
Webber, J. 2009. *The Existentialism of Jean-Paul Sartre*. New York: Routledge.
Webber, J. Forthcoming. "Sartre on Knowing Our Own Motivations". In *Pre-flective Consciousness: Early Sartre in the Content of Contemporary Philosophy of Mind*, S. Miguens, C. Bravo Morando & G. Preyer (eds).

TWELVE
Knowledge
Anthony Hatzimoysis

Introduction

Knowledge is a notion that occurs throughout Sartre's philosophical writings. From his early forays in phenomenology (Sartre 1970: 200a; 2004c: part A) to his late engagement with dialectical reason (Sartre 1960b: 30n, 31n, 502; 1985b), *connaissance* is a term that appears in almost every twist and turn of Sartrean argumentation.

Yet discussions of Sartre's conception of knowledge are anything but common. How may we best interpret that peculiar phenomenon of paucity of references to knowledge in the secondary literature, and overabundance of that term in Sartre's own texts? Part of the explanation, in my view, lies in the fact that knowledge for Sartre is what we may call a contrastive notion: knowledge is what consciousness – including one's primary relation to oneself, to one's own body, to other beings in a situation, and to the world – is not.

But what exactly is that notion with which so many other notions apparently get mixed up, and with which they ought not to be confused? In this chapter I shall sketch an answer to that question by considering a section from *Being and Nothingness* where Sartre sets knowledge itself as the focus of his discussion (BN1: 172–80; BN2: 195–203).

Our discussion will be limited in its focus: it will not address Sartre's views on knowledge throughout his voluminous output, nor will it try to account for every occurrence of "knowledge" in *Being and Nothingness*; instead, it will pay close attention to particular paragraphs of one section of that book. However, the discussion will be quite broad in its intended implications as it will provide the required background for exploring a general question, which here will be simply stated, but not addressed: whether Sartre's positive claims about knowledge allow it to fulfil the contrastive role with which it is bestowed in his philosophy.

I begin with a brief statement of Sartre's account of knowledge, for the benefit of readers unfamiliar with his philosophy. Sartre's account includes some standard philosophical terms, sometimes employed in a non-standard way; hence, I clarify the meaning of those terms, by showing how it differs from the meaning they carry in the work of other philosophers, and by drawing on parts of Sartre's work that are relevant to a correct understanding of those terms. In the course of my presentation I pose some critical queries and sketch some answers, so as to better clarify the Sartrean approach to knowledge.

Intuition and belief

Knowledge worthy of its name is intuitive; any non-intuitive relation to an object is withdrawn as soon as intuition is attained; and intuition concerns the presence of consciousness to its object. Those are, in outline, the three pillars on which Sartre's theory of knowledge stands. Let us take a closer look at them.

Sartre begins his discussion by discriminating genuine from substitute forms of knowledge: there is only one type of knowledge, properly speaking, and that is "intuitive knowledge" (BN1: 172; BN2: 195). Before we explore the exact meaning of that phrase, it is worth noting that Sartre introduces knowledge not in terms of what it is about (thus, he does not claim, for instance, that nothing can count as knowledge unless it captures Platonic forms, Aristotelian *eide*, or Husserlian *essences*); nor in terms of how it relates to other doxastic phenomena (such as justified belief, or warranted opinion); nor in terms of the alternative grammatical constructions of the relevant verb ("to know that", "to know how", or "to know an object"). Yet specific views about each of those matters are entailed by his analysis, as we shall soon see.

Intuitive knowledge, simply put, is knowledge procured by intuition. But what is intuition? In ordinary parlance, intuition stands for the (seemingly) ungrounded but (apparently) indubitable apprehension of some fact. In contemporary epistemology, intuition has been systematically examined under different headings. Take, first, a cluster of theories that approach intuition through the notion of belief, asserting that intuitions are beliefs (Lewis 1983), or that they are dispositions to believe (Van Inwagen 1997), or that they are attitudes in which a proposition seems to be true, as opposed to a belief's wholehearted commitment to a proposition being true (Bealer 1998). Those are all important suggestions but, unfortunately, not very helpful in making sense of the Sartrean approach to intuition. Sartre does not relate intuition to belief or to a similar kind of propositional attitude. In the section on knowledge, belief is peculiarly absent, and when it does enter the discussion in other parts of *Being and Nothingness*, it is not in order to illuminate intuition, but with a view to highlight, for instance, the ontological interplay between *croyance*, on the one hand, and *mauvaise* or *bonne foi*, on the other (BN1: 69–70; BN2: 93–4).

Apart from the absence of relevant textual evidence, there is an important reason for being reluctant to think of intuition as identical to, or otherwise dependent on, belief. If intuition were similar to belief, the question would promptly arise as to how, for Sartre, intuition is justified. But that question simply does not arise: within the Sartrean system, intuition is not in need of justification because intuition itself is the ultimate source of justification.

"Intuition" has also been the name given to a method, according to which philosophy advances through an experience of focused sympathy, which enables us to move into the inner being of a phenomenon, such as duration, or the self (Bergson 1992: 159, 172, 185–8). The influence of the "method of intuition" is evident in Sartre's aversion to both rationalism and empiricism in their dogmatic versions, his emphasis on lived experience (*le vecu*), and his understanding of temporality as an "original synthesis" rather than a mere aggregate of unrelated instances. However, what is valuable and distinctive in the Bergsonian method of intuition is its emphasis on the intellectually demanding and time-consuming character of meticulously attending to the various aspects of an ever-unfolding process – and such emphasis is lacking in Sartre's use of intuition, in the current context. As soon as intuition is achieved, an object is given effortlessly, and for what it is. This does not commit Sartre to the view that all sides of an object are given at once, and in the same manner (see chapters 2 and 5 of Hatzimoysis 2011 for a sketch of the Sartrean analysis of visual experience, and chapter 6 of the same work for the concomitant issues pertaining to Sartre's phenomenological account of a thing's essence).

If we are to identify correctly the theoretical precedents of the Sartrean employment of "intuition", we might as well look at the two philosophers mentioned in the section on knowledge: one is Husserl, and the other is Descartes.

Intuition and discourse

The section on knowledge opens with a distinction between "intuition" and "deduction"; and that distinction appears to be a direct descendant of Descartes's view that when we "review all the actions of the intellect by means of which we are able to arrive at knowledge", we "recognize only two: intuition and deduction". Intuition is "the conception which an unclouded and attentive mind gives us", whereas deduction denotes "all necessary inference from other facts that are known with certainty" (Descartes 1988: rule III). The Cartesian view, however, could illuminate the Sartrean theory, subject to two important qualifications.

First, the order of intuition and deduction is reversed: for Descartes, intuition provides the principles from which deductive reasoning ought to proceed; for Sartre, "deduction and discursive argument ... are only instruments which lead to intuition"; and when intuition is achieved, discourse and deduction "are effaced before it" (BN1: 172; BN2: 195).

Second, a Cartesian intuition is primarily a means by which we acquire secure knowledge of conceptual relations; just by examining various concepts, and thus *a priori*, we can intellectually grasp that one includes the other – for instance, that the concept of God includes the notion of eternal existence; Cartesian intuition, in other words, informs us primarily about true propositions. In Sartre's discussion, though, intuition is not the revealing of *a priori*, conceptual truths: intuition is "of a thing" and pertains to the relation of consciousness to "the being" (BN1: 173; BN2: 196).

It is evident that Sartre subscribes to the traditional distinction between "discourse and deduction", on the one hand, and "intuition" on the other. What is perhaps less clear is why exactly he gives priority to the latter. It might be suggested that Sartre simply takes for granted the ordinary distinction between two French verbs for knowing: *connaitre*, which is of persons or things, and *savoir*, which is about true propositions. Intuition, as we saw above, concerns not propositions but things. And since Sartre here examines not *savoir*, but *connaissance*, he is right to privilege intuition over alternative types of knowledge that concern propositions, such as deduction or discourse.

That suggestion is correct, but it simply elaborates on what Sartre is doing, not on the reasons why he is doing it; we are still owed an explanation for Sartre's choice of *connaitre* rather than *savoir* as the focus of his philosophical analysis. Such an explanation can be constructed with elements from Sartre's account of knowledge. To correctly identify, though, those elements, as well as the pattern in which they are weaved, we need to shift the focus of our discussion from epistemology to ontology.

Intuition and presence

We have been told so far to what intuition is opposed (discourse and deduction) and what it is of (a thing or the being). Sartre completes his introduction of intuition by bringing in another notion: presence. He writes that "intuition is the presence of consciousness to the thing" (BN1: 172; BN2: 196).

We may understand this definition of intuition by invoking, and slightly elaborating upon, an example, offered by Sartre, about the different ways in which some one person – call him "Pierre" – is experientially given to me: as a mental image, through photograph, and in a drawing. In imagining Pierre:

> certain details are lacking, others are suspect, the whole is very blurred. There is a certain feeling of sympathy and pleasantness that I want to restore to the face but which will not come. I grab a photograph from a drawer, and that gives me "all the details of his face … but the photograph lacks life; it presents perfectly the external traits of Pierre's face; it does not give his expression. I then find a caricature where his features are deliberately distorted … yet, what is missing in the photograph, vitality, expression, is clearly there in the drawing: I "rediscover" Pierre.
> (Sartre 2004a: 40–41)

In this example an object (Pierre) is given to (Sartre's) consciousness through different media: first as a mental image, then through a photograph, and then by a vivid caricature. Despite the differences between the cases, aptly captured by Sartre's narrative, there is a common experiential theme: Pierre is given to consciousness as absent.

Consider now what would happen if, while Sartre was ruminating about a recent conversation he had with his friend, Pierre knocked on the door and walked into the study: he would no longer be conveyed by some medium, through which Sartre would try to capture his friend: Pierre would be unmediatedly given to Sartre. Pierre also would no longer be well or badly indicated by various (psychological, photographic, or drawn) pieces of evidence: Pierre himself is not evidence about Pierre, or something that indicates Pierre, or from which we may deduce Pierre; being in the room, Pierre is no longer re-presented;

rather, he is presented to Sartre. This unmediated experience of presence gives the core meaning of intuition.

Sartre, to be sure, is not the first philosopher to think of intuition in those terms. Husserl, as Sartre is happy to acknowledge, was there well before him. Husserl's talk of "originally presentive consciousness" and "originally presentive intuitions" purports to convey the kind of conscious event from which genuine knowledge originates (Husserl 1983: §19). Sartre locates the difference between Husserl and himself in what might sound like a pedantic point, that is, that whereas Husserl thinks that in intuition it is the object that is present to consciousness, for Sartre, "being-present-to" is only possible for a being that is conscious of itself being in a certain situation: "being-present is an ekstatic mode of being of the for-itself", and, therefore, intuition is not the presence of the thing to consciousness but "the presence of consciousness to the thing" (BN1: 172; BN2: 195–6).

Sartre then devotes a section of seven densely written pages in spelling out this sentence (BN1: 172–80; BN2: 196–202). The reader will more easily follow that section if she appreciates its basic argumentative point: Sartre defends his conception of intuition as consciousness's presence to an object, by laying out what has to be the case about consciousness, so that knowledge of an object be possible.

Consciousness and knowledge

Sartre's oft-repeated claim, throughout his writings, that conscience is not *connaissance*, should not make us lose sight of the fact that, properly speaking, knowledge is one of the many modes of consciousness. It would be absurd to claim that while someone is acquiring knowledge of an object, her consciousness is switched off, or even that it is directed away from the object of knowledge to which she is currently attending. In Sartrean terms, we may say that knowledge is first and foremost an instance of "being-in-the-world", which is a "synthetic totality of which consciousness, like the phenomenon, constitutes only moments" (BN1: 3; BN2: 27). Hence, to understand knowledge, we need, first, to make sense of how consciousness is related to whatever it is conscious of; and, second, to see what sets knowing apart from other modes of one's conscious relation to the world.

The former task is what preoccupies Sartre, in the section under consideration. He argues, briefly, as follows: for consciousness to be, it has to be consciousness of some thing; but to be conscious of any thing, it has, at a minimum, to be conscious of itself as not being the thing of which it is conscious. However, consciousness cannot be conscious of itself before being directed to its object, simply because consciousness is not a thing – it is itself no thing, but the revealing intuition of things. Consciousness's intending of a thing reflects back on itself, rendering consciousness the reflection of that thing on which it is reflected; the reflection is something of which consciousness is always necessarily (non-positionally) aware, while it is (positionally) aware of its object. Indeed, consciousness is (nothing but) that (non-positional) presence to itself being (positionally) present to its object. The conscious being is self-presenting, a being for-itself, directed towards a being in-itself, of which it is conscious.

This line of reasoning effects the transition from discussion of consciousness to an analysis of being. Driven by his view of intentionality as a conscious being's transcendence towards the world, Sartre maintains that the for-itself is outside itself, in the in-itself, since it defines itself by what it is not: "In knowledge, taken as a bond of ontological being, the being which I am not represents the absolute plenitude of the in-itself" (BN1: 177; BN2: 200). That further entails that in knowledge, "the only type of being which can be encountered and which is perpetually there is the known. The knower is not ... [in the sense that] he is nothing other than that which brings it about that there is a being-there on the part of the known – a presence" (*ibid.*).

Sartre puts emphasis on the immediacy of the relation between consciousness and the world. However, immediacy may not be mistaken for fusion. The knower cannot disappear in the known, and the known can never be absorbed by the knower. The absorption of the known by the knower is disallowed by Sartre's forceful critique of idealism: the object of knowledge is not an ethereal item locked in a mental box, but part of the reality towards which consciousness is directed. And the total disappearance of the subject in the object is not possible because consciousness never ceases to be (non-positionally) aware of itself being (positionally) conscious of its objects.

Nevertheless, the emphasis on immediacy appears, to me, to jar with Sartre's frequent allusions to the unbridgeable duality that characterizes knowledge. If there is one claim about knowledge that readers of *Being and Nothingness* will find repeated in almost every section of that book, it is Sartre's warning that conscience ought not to be modelled on *connaisance*, since the latter involves a "subject–object dualism" that is destructive of the seamless unity that characterizes consciousness's immediate relation to itself (BN1: xxviii; BN2: 8–9; cf. BN1/BN2: part I, ch. 1, §V and part II, ch. 1, §§I, V, and most of Sartre 2004c: part A). An attempt to render "dualism" compatible with "immediacy" in the case of knowledge, should take into account Sartre's ontology of negation; but that is a topic for another occasion.

Concluding remark

Sartre offers an analysis of knowledge in terms of presence, and unpacks that notion by showing the ontological bond that connects consciousness with the world. A careful study of his theory will reward the reader both for the rigour of its argumentation, and the richness of its phenomenological detail. Nevertheless, certain conceptual issues remain unaddressed by Sartre – and it is not clear to me how they might be resolved in the context of his analysis. I shall close on a critical note, by briefly articulating one of those issues.

Let us grant Sartre the view that knowledge of an object is indeed a matter of presence. Does this view allow for consciousness being present to an object, without acquiring knowledge of it? The question arises because it is not unreasonable to claim that you may be present to an object, even carefully attend to it, yet fail to know it.

If Sartre acknowledges that one's being present to an object does not entail that one knows it, he should have been more explicit about it. He could have specified, for instance, the circumstances under which the ontological bond between the for-itself and the in-itself does not guarantee knowledge; or, in simpler terms, the cases in which consciousness's attending to a thing, does not deliver knowledge of it. However, no indication as to how we may tell the successful from the failed cases is given in the section devoted to knowledge. We may distinguish, here, between two groups of epistemically unsuccessful cases. One concerns the main topic of Sartre's discussion, that is, perceptual, especially visual knowledge. The relevant cases of illusion and hallucination are not explored in the section on knowledge; and when they are discussed by Sartre, it is in a very different context and with a different purpose, that is, for illuminating the workings of imagination (Sartre 2004a: part 3). The other group of cases of epistemic failure concerns a type of consciousness's relation to an object, which is, again, not addressed by Sartre. Those are cases in which consciousness is present to its object, yet one fails to have knowledge of that object, because one lacks understanding, as it is evidenced by one's inability to give an account of that which one claims to know. But "giving an account" to back one's cognitive claims is a discursive phenomenon, and as such lies outside the province of Sartre's, otherwise masterful, analysis of intuitive knowledge.

Further reading

de Coorebyter, V. 2000. *Sartre face à la phénoménologie*. Brussels: OUSIA.
Gardner, S. 2009. *Sartre's* Being and Nothingness: *A Reader's Guide*. London: Continuum.
Hatzimoysis, A. 2011. *The Philosophy of Sartre*. Durham: Acumen.
Mouillie, J.-M. (ed.) 2001. *Sartre et la phénoménologie*. Paris: ENS.

THIRTEEN

The fundamental project
Paul Crittenden

Freedom: the free project and action

"Project" is a basic term in Sartre's ontology, for in its separation from in-itself being, the for-itself is at once thrown into the world and engaged in a free project. The free project, in his description, is "the impulse [*élan*] by which the for-itself thrusts itself toward its end" (BN1: 557; BN2: 578). Consciousness is one with freedom and thereby with engagement in free projects for "the freedom of the for-itself is always *engaged*; there is no question here of a freedom which could be undetermined and which would pre-exist its choice ... freedom is simply the fact that this choice is unconditioned" (BN1: 479; BN2: 501).

This claim relates to particular projects aimed at this or that specific end, but embraces more profoundly the idea that all our projects "are united in the global project which we are" (BN1: 481; BN2: 503). The free project in this sense points to the notion of the *fundamental project*, understood as my being, what I make myself to be in choosing the person I am in what I do. Following his account of consciousness and freedom earlier in *Being and Nothingness*, Sartre devotes the concluding part 4 of the work to a study of action and the relations of *doing* (and *having*) to *being*. This leads to the claim that "each human reality is at the same time a direct project to metamorphose its own for-itself into an in-itself-for-itself and a project of the appropriation of the world as a totality of being-in-itself" (BN1: 615; BN2: 636). How does he arrive at this conclusion?

Sartre says that "to act is to modify the *shape* of the world; it is to arrange means in view of an end" (BN1: 433: BN2: 455). Tired and hungry, I seek food and rest. On becoming aware of growing social inequality, I join a movement for a more just society. An action is on principle intentional, directed to an end that is linked in turn with the recognition of a lack that is to be made good. Moreover, the desired end refers back to reasons and motives. These too must be understood as part of the intentional structure of the act as an occurrence outside the causal relationships of in-itself being. In these terms, no factual state, in the world at large or in one's past, can by itself give rise to action for "an act is a projection of the for-itself toward what is not" (BN1: 435; BN2: 458).

In bringing negation to the world, the for-itself is "a being who can realize a nihilating rupture with the world and with himself" (BN1: 439; BN2: 461). This possibility is freedom, and in nihilating itself, the for-itself nihilates its own past, constituted by its past acts bearing on the present as facticity. Freedom "makes itself an act"; it is "an existence which perpetually makes itself" (BN1: 438; BN2: 460). What I do yields an essence, indicative of past acts: "my essence is what I have been" (BN1: 450; BN2: 472). But freedom itself has no essence and cannot be defined. Drawing on Heidegger, Sartre says, "in [freedom], existence precedes and commands essence" (BN1: 438; BN2: 460).

What cannot be defined can nonetheless be described on the basis of experience: "I am indeed an existent who *learns* his freedom through his acts." More specifically, "I am an existent whose individual and unique existence temporalizes itself as freedom" (carrying one's past and always projecting oneself towards what is not yet; BN1: 439; BN2: 461). As such, each for-itself is necessarily aware of its freedom in the (self)-consciousness of existing that accompanies all consciousness. Elsewhere he appeals to the experience of anguish in the face of freedom. In either case, the claim is the same: that, in acting, the for-itself cannot avoid the experience of itself as the permanent possibility of putting its past out of play and perpetually faced with having to make itself to be. Freedom is precisely "the nothingness which is *made-to-be* at the heart of man and which forces human-reality *to make itself* instead of *to be* ... it is entirely abandoned to the intolerable necessity of making itself be – down to the slightest detail" (BN1: 440–41; BN2: 463).

For Sartre, freedom is manifested in passion no less than will. He therefore rejects the view that will and passion are opposed – that the will to do something leads to free action, and passion to causally determined behaviour. He argues rather that a passion or emotion, such as fear, is itself a type of free conduct, a response adapted to the situation as a means to pursuing ends posited by freedom. Will, as the choice of proceeding in a reflective and deliberative way, differs from passion only as a different means to the end. Will and passion both presuppose an original freedom, not as prior to the voluntary or passionate act, but rather as "a foundation which is strictly contemporary with the will or the passion and which these *manifest*, each in its own way" (BN1: 444; BN2: 466).

Reasons and motives similarly belong to the intentional structure of action. A reason for action, as Sartre specifies it, arises when a person assesses an objective state of affairs in the light of an end and sees that it offers a means to the desired goal. So in seeking the conquest of Gaul, Clovis noted the power of the Catholic episcopate and saw a reason to convert to Catholicism (BN1: 446; BN2: 468). A motive, arising within the subject (and incorporating relevant reasons), is "the ensemble of the desires, emotions, and passions which urge me to accomplish a certain act" (*ibid.*). The argument overall is that reason, motive and end are all "organized in an indissoluble unity by the very upsurge of a freedom which is beyond reasons, motives, and ends" (BN1: 450; BN2: 472).

Freedom and original choice

The upsurge of freedom "beyond reasons, motives, and ends" appears mysterious. Sartre must say of it what he says of consciousness – that it comes from itself, that *nothing* is its cause, that the for-itself is "a being which exists by-itself", a (non-substantial) absolute that creates and supports its essence (BN1: xxxi–xxxii, 80). Freedom makes itself perpetually and spontaneously. Assuming this as a postulate, why is the upsurge a thrust towards this end rather than that? Or if one is always free to put the past out of play, may one choose to do anything? Acknowledging that freedom appears as an unanalysable totality in which reasons, motives and ends form a unity within its compass, Sartre asks:

> Does this mean that one must view freedom as a series of capricious jerks comparable to the Epicurean clinamen? Am I free to wish anything whatsoever at any moment whatsoever? And must I at each instant when I wish to explain this or that project encounter the irrationality of a free and contingent choice?
> (BN1: 452; BN2: 474)

Insisting that he does not intend anything arbitrary or capricious, Sartre refers to the common understanding that to be free means, not just to exercise choice, but also that one's choice "could have been other than what it is" (BN1: 453; BN2: 475). He opens the way to reflection on original choice and the fundamental project with an example.

A hiker on a walk with friends becomes tired; at first he resists, but the fatigue increases and suddenly he gives up, throws his pack down and slumps beside it. Could he have resisted and walked on with the others? Sartre's starting point is that each for-itself is "the organic totality of the projects it is". The question then is whether resistance would involve no more than a minor behavioural change or whether "it could be effected only by means of a radical transformation of [one's] being-in-the-world – a transformation, moreover, which is *possible*". Allowing that the hiker could have done otherwise, the question is "*at what price?*" (BN1: 454; 464; BN2: 476, 486).

One hiker suffers fatigue and gives up, another who is equally tired carries on. Sartre argues that a fully adequate explanation would need to situate the act in each case in a framework of each person's past acts, how each "exists his body", how each relates to the world. His guiding principle is that "every act is integrated in global structures and finally in the totality I am" (BN1: 459; BN2: 471). To this end, he supposes that a method could be developed that would lead by regressive analysis from the act back to the "original relation which the for-itself chooses with its facticity and with the world". This, in anticipatory terms, "is nothing other than the for-itself's being in the world inasmuch as this being-in-the-world is a choice – that is, we have reached the original type of nihilation by which the for-itself has to be its own nothingness" (BN1: 457; BN2: 479). In related terms, regressive analysis promises to disengage the meaning of the particular act and proceed to "richer and more profound meanings until we encounter the meaning which does not imply any other meaning and which refers only to itself" (BN1: 457; BN2: 479). At this bedrock point no further interpretation is possible.

Every act is comprehensible inasmuch as it offers accessible rational content – the hiker drops his pack *in order to rest* – but fully comprehensible only through the regressive analysis that uncovers the "totality I am" together with a synthetic progression back to the act in "the total form" (BN1: 460; BN2: 482). This is my-being-in-the-world conceived as a choice – not a particular choice, but the basic or original choice in which I choose myself as a whole in every particular choice, the fundamental project which is my total being-in-the-world in every particular project, the fundamental act of freedom which gives meaning to my every act. Sartre describes this choice as a "constantly renewed act [which] is not distinct from my being"; we are conscious of it because "it is simply one with the consciousness which we have of ourselves"

(BN1: 461–2; BN2: 483). Original choice, one with consciousness and freedom, unfolds time and being so that I am conscious of the place of any particular act "within the compass of what I am", not with analytical or detailed awareness, but in the consciousness expressed "by the twofold 'feeling' of anguish and responsibility" related to myself as a whole (BN1: 463–4; BN2: 486).

The idea of original choice/fundamental project calls for assessment. But one can see that it provides Sartre with a *formal* basis for rejecting the view that he portrays a capricious freedom. In addition, he can now say that the price of resistance for the tired hiker would be to effect a radical change in his fundamental project. Is this possible? The difficulty is that original choice creates my reasons and motives and arranges my being-in-the-world in terms of possibilities and values. How then could I possibly find an effective motive from outside this frame? How is radical transformation possible? Sartre proceeds by comparing his approach with Leibniz's account of freedom.

Leibniz says that Adam took the apple. He freely chose to do this and his choice was contingent. Could he have refused? Yes, Leibniz responds, but only if he were another Adam in another possible world. In the world chosen by God, Adam's taking the apple is a contingent act, yet part of a necessary complex of events. In this world, therefore, Adam did what he wanted to do, but could not have done otherwise. Sartre objects that, while Adam chose to take the apple, he did not choose to be Adam, for that was settled in God's choice of this world. By contrast, he locates the problem of freedom in Adam's choice of himself as a whole in the world. He can agree with Leibniz that "another gesture of Adam, implying another Adam, implies another world", but only in the sense that "another face of the world will correspond with another being-in-the-world of Adam" (BN1: 469; BN2: 490–91). For Sartre, the Adam who refuses the apple is the same Adam in the same world, but an Adam who has changed his being-in-the-world.

This comparative analysis, he comments, has been purely theoretical, for reality is more complex and does not follow the order of logic. Understanding an act in terms of freely posited original ends is an exercise of interpretation, and the connection between a secondary possible (resisting fatigue or giving in) and the fundamental possible is not a logical deduction; it is, rather, "the connection between a totality and a partial structure" (BN1: 469; BN2: 491). In interpreting this relationship, he continues, there is no universal system for making connections between secondary and fundamental possibles; one must always rely on personal criteria provided by the subject (BN1: 471; BN2: 493). One must also recognize that various acts are "indifferent" in that they have no bearing on original choice. Moreover, mere voluntary effort to overcome fundamental choice will prove ineffectual. Radical change in one's fundamental project must occur, not in the will, but at the deeper level of freedom. How then does it occur? How can it be explained?

Sartre appeals to anguish as evidence that I am conscious of the choice that I am. Anguish also shows that we are aware that this choice cannot bind our future freedom, for, as the basis for all particular choices, it is contingent and unjustifiable. Specifically, he insists that radical change is possible because, in "temporalizing itself", the for-itself makes choices that begin a new project in ending a prior one. This is a continuous process, not from instant to instant, for there is no instant. However, in the continuous recovery of its original choice, the freedom of the for-itself "is haunted by the spectre of the instant". This is because the for-itself always has the possibility of positing its immediate past as object and making a new choice of ends in the unity of a single act, causing "the instant to spring forth as the nihilating rupture of the temporalization" (BN1: 467; BN2: 489).

The idea of radical conversion finds support in life and literature. But in fixing its occurrence in a moment and basing it on a permanent possibility, Sartre fails to explain why it occurs in any particular transition. Again, how does the for-itself create a new ensemble of reasons, motives and ends from within the original choice? He can say of it only what he says of original choice: it is incomprehensible; freedom acts *by itself* to create a fundamentally new complex of meaning. The question, then, concerns the creation of meaning in (initial) original choice. Must we simply accept that this is incomprehensible?

Sartre makes clear that freedom arises always and only in a situation constituted by the for-itself and the facticity of its surrounding world. Now, in his discussion of freedom and facticity, he includes the circumstances of my being in the midst of others and meeting a world full of meanings which are "*mine* and which I have not given to myself" (BN1: 510; BN2: 532). His whole focus in this context is on insisting that this factor does not limit freedom since the for-itself "must choose itself by taking account of these circumstances and not *ad libitum*" (BN1: 520; BN2: 541). But the consideration of my meeting a world full of meanings (as in language) could point to a different understanding of original choice. For, in taking account of shared meanings in choosing itself in its choices, the for-itself must already have these meanings in its grasp. They could then appear, not as facticity, but as an enabling element of freedom and choice. To lack command of meanings would be to lack freedom. Furthermore, their role would confirm that one's choice is not an absolute foundation.

The claim that freedom creates meaning "by itself" in original choice is therefore questionable (and with it the notion of foundational meaning). Nonetheless, the idea that I make myself the person I am and that I am responsible for myself as a whole seems entirely plausible. This would support an understanding of the human subject as a unity engaged in a project of unification in what it does, always bearing its past and its way of "existing its body" into the present, and always remaining free (within limits) to change the way it relates to its past and the world as a whole. But noting that this is not Sartre's own notion of original choice and freedom, I will return to consider his views further – specifically the proposal that in interpreting behaviour one seeks connections between a totality and a partial structure.

Making connections of this kind seems relatively unproblematic when we have access to parts and whole, as with a painting or a piece of music, or in grasping an object in seeing aspects of it. The idea of interpreting particular acts in terms of the subject as a larger whole seems right. But with original choice, the totality always remains in question, always subject to change, always out of reach. How might typical original choice be indicated? Sartre says "whatever our being may be, it is a choice; and it depends on us to choose ourselves as 'great', or 'noble' or 'base' or 'humiliated'" (BN1: 472; BN2: 494). Clearly, these choices, or others such as "ambition, the passion to be loved, [or] the inferiority complex", do not satisfy the requirement for a fundamental project "which can no longer be interpreted in terms of any other and which is total" (BN1: 479; BN2: 501). Committed to the ideal of bedrock explanation, Sartre returns to the theme of regressive analysis, this time in the form of a special phenomenological method called existential psychoanalysis.

Existential psychoanalysis and the fundamental project/desire

Existential psychoanalysis is "a method destined to bring to light, in a strictly objective form, the subjective choice by which each living person makes himself a person; that is, makes known to himself what he is" (BN1: 574; BN2: 595). Since "what the method seeks is a *choice of being* at the same time as a *being*, it must reduce particular behaviour patterns to fundamental relations – not of sexuality or of the will to power, but *of being* – which are expressed in this behaviour" (*ibid.*). This proposal grows out of his account of action and original choice, this time with a focus on the ends of action and desire. The basic principle once again is that the human being is a totality, a unity responsible for itself and its world, not a collection. And the aim is to show how each tendency, each inclination of a person has a meaning that goes beyond itself and which expresses in some way the subject's choice of being as a whole.

Freudian psychoanalysis provides an immediate context for Sartre's proposal, and he seeks common ground with it, especially in the emphasis on the symbolic character of behaviour and the search for underlying meaning. But he rejects the recourse to mechanistic explanation in Freudian theory and the idea of the unconscious. For similar reasons, he is critical of empirical psychology, especially in its failure to recognize the significance of the intentional structure of action. He objects, for instance, to the treatment of desire as if it were a thing *in* consciousness, rather than consciousness itself in its free project towards an end. This does not mean that existential psychoanalysis will be any less focused on the subject's empirical existence. Its concern is precisely with the subject's empirical tendencies and choices conceived as particular expressions of the postulated original choice. The task is to compare the various tendencies in the attempt "to discover and disengage the fundamental project which is common to them all" on the understanding that each "is the entire person" (BN1: 564; BN2: 585).

Given an infinite number of possible projects for an infinity of possible human beings, Sartre says that one would need to begin with individual investigations with a view to identifying common characteristics for classification into larger categories. That is a task for the future. In the meantime, he is confident that ontology can throw light on the ultimate stopping-point of an evident irreducibility. For, what could be more basic than the very *being* of the subject? It is clear then that the fundamental project of a for-itself *"can aim only at its being"* (BN1: 564; BN2: 585). Moreover, this desire for being is obviously indistinguishable from the being of the for-itself, which has already been defined as a *lack of being*. In short, the self-evident irreducible is the *project of being* or *the desire to be*. This, it must be understood, is not a desire existing in advance of particular concrete desires. Rather, "the desire to be exists and manifests itself only in and through jealousy, greed, love of art, cowardice, courage, and a thousand contingent empirical expressions" in the life of the particular person (BN1: 565; BN2: 586).

The final step is to recognize that the object of the desire to be can only be being-in-itself. What the for-itself lacks, what it desires and values is "the ideal of a consciousness that would be the foundation of its own being-in-itself by the pure consciousness which it would have of itself" (BN1: 566; BN2: 587). This, for Sartre, is the (contradictory) idea of God (as being for-itself-in-itself). Thus, "the best way to conceive of the fundamental project of human reality is to say that man is the being whose project is to be God ... Or, if you prefer, man fundamentally is the desire to be God" (BN1: 566; BN2: 587).

What does this mean for freedom? For it appears that the desire for being channels all choice into a single possibility and constitutes in effect a human "essence". Sartre responds by noting that "while the *meaning* of the desire is ultimately the project of being God, the desire is never *constituted* by this meaning" (BN1: 566–7; BN2: 587–8). This relates to the consideration that the desire of being, which is always a desire for a mode of being, "expresses itself in turn as the meaning of the myriads of concrete desires which constitute the web of our conscious life" (BN1: 567; BN2: 588). In this connection, he introduces a distinction between the concrete fundamental desire of the individual subject and an "abstract meaningful structure which is the desire of being in general" (*ibid*.). The free and fundamental desire is the unique person, with absolute concreteness and existence as a totality; this is everywhere in all the empirical desires of the particular for-itself and is never apprehended except through them. At the same time, for every for-itself in every situation, the general meaning of its concrete fundamental desire and particular choices lies in the desire for being. This latter, he observes, "must be considered as human reality in the person", that is, something one shares with all others, and a truth about human beings generally (*ibid*.). But while the ontological desire of being is the truth of the concrete fundamental desire, it "does not exist by virtue of reality" and cannot represent "the fundamental *human* structure of the individual; [hence] it cannot be an obstacle to his freedom" (*ibid*.).

Sartre's depiction of existential psychoanalysis appears as a bold sketch. The first stage, which he sets aside as beyond ontology, is the detailed psychological, social, historical and moral study of individuals designed to uncover in each case their particular fundamental project. (He expresses the hope of writing biographies of Flaubert and Dostoevsky on these lines.) The results would then be classified and compared as a basis for establishing "general considerations about human reality as an empirical choice of its own ends" (BN1: 575; BN2: 595). The important point in the meantime, he suggests, is not that existential psychoanalysis does not yet exist, but that it is possible. But its possibility, in the strong form he proposes, is precisely what is in question.

To provide more groundwork for the psychoanalytic proposal and a future work on ethics, Sartre turns finally to the question of what ontology can teach us about desire (BN1: 575ff; BN2: 595ff). In a wide-ranging discussion of human activities and practices – in art, science, play and endeavour generally – he argues that the *meaning* of all our striving lies, as previously announced, in the desire of being, that is, in the general project of appropriating the world as a totality of being-in-itself, the project of being God. If asked why the individual person chooses to possess the world in this way rather than that, he will reply that "here we see the peculiar character of freedom" (BN1: 599; BN2: 620).

Yet in thinking about ethical implications beyond ontology, he revives the idea that existential psychoanalysis could throw light on the desire for being and even provide an escape from this "futile passion". For existential psychoanalysis involves moral description concerned with the ethical meaning of what we do; it could have bearing, therefore, on the fundamental desire for being and the associated conviction that value, as object of desire, lies in things. On this basis he concludes that "existential psychoanalysis is going to reveal to man the real goal of his pursuit, which is being as a synthetic fusion of the in-itself with the for-itself; existential psychoanalysis is going to acquaint man with his passion" – and in this way, a person might find in its principles "a means of deliverance and salvation" (BN1: 626–7; BN2: 646).

With an eye to his forthcoming study of ethics, Sartre asks whether it is "possible for freedom to take itself for a value as the source of all value, or must it necessarily be defined by a transcendent value [the in-itself-for-itself] which haunts it" (BN1: 627; BN2: 647). This question involves an impossible leap. How, in the terms of his ontology, could anyone effect a change of this kind? For the desire for being is a truth concerning human reality, arising in the fundamental relation of the for-itself to the in-itself. Acquaintance with this passion might lead some people to change their particular fundamental project (a radical transformation such as Sartre appealed to in his discussion of Leibniz on freedom). But the new concrete fundamental project would retain the same general meaning uncovered in the ontology. It could only be another instance of the peculiar character of freedom, another way in which the individual person chooses to appropriate the world as a totality of being-in-itself.

The only escape lies at an entirely different level: one would need to challenge the ontology itself. Sartre himself followed this path in time, not by rejecting his past thought entirely, but by treating consciousness in terms of a more nuanced notion of "lived experience" (*le vécu*), and by adopting a diminished conception of freedom and an enlarged account of how we live in time. He also developed a much-enhanced, but still over-ambitious regressive/progressive method of inquiry, which he put to work in the study of individuals – notably Flaubert – and in considering moral, social and historical relationships more generally.

Further reading

Caws, P. 1979. "Freedom and Existential Morality". In his *Sartre*, 112–30. London: Routledge & Kegan Paul.
Deutscher, M. 2003. "On Lacking Reason for Desire". In his *Genre and Void: Looking Back at Sartre and Beauvoir*, 89–109. Aldershot: Ashgate.
Flajoliet, A. 2010. "Sartre's Phenomenological Anthropology between Psychoanalysis and '*Daseinanalysis*'". *Sartre Studies International* 16(1): 40–59.
Jopling. D. A. 1997. "Sartre's Moral Psychology". In *The Cambridge Companion to Sartre*, C. Howells (ed.), 103–39. Cambridge: Cambridge University Press.
Taylor, C. 1976. "Responsibility for Self". In *The Identities of Persons*, A. O. Rorty (ed.), 281–99. Berkeley, CA: University of California Press.

FOURTEEN

Self-making and alienation: from bad faith to revolution
Thomas W. Busch

In the autumn of 1933 Sartre took leave of absence from his teaching position at the Lycée François Premier in Le Havre and travelled to the French Institute (Maison Académique Française) in Berlin to begin a fellowship to study phenomenology. He cut short what was to be a year's stay, returning to France in June 1934. This was a politically tumultuous time in Germany, as Hitler had taken over nine months before Sartre's arrival. It was not, however, the political situation that hastened Sartre's departure. Sartre's full-time commitment was to philosophy and literature, reading Husserl on his own, appropriating ideas and writing furiously. His biographer, Annie Cohen-Solal, remarks on Sartre's lack of concern with politics during this time:

> The students of Le Havre had watched him scribble away, for hours, at the café, in the public library, between classes; his colleagues in Berlin now watch with great astonishment as he busies himself in his research at bars and in his first-floor bedroom, oblivious to the book burnings of 1933 and van Papen's speeches in front of Humboldt University. (Cohen-Solal 1987: 95)

In an interview, Sartre, looking back on this time, acknowledges his former apolitical attitude:

> Before the war I thought of myself simply as an individual. I was not aware of any ties between my individual existence and the society I was living in. At the time I graduated from the École

Normale, I had based an entire theory on that feeling. I was "a man alone", an individual who opposes society through the independence of his thinking but who owes nothing to society and whom society cannot affect, because he is free.

(Sartre 1977a: 45)

The centrepiece of *Being and Nothingness* is this free individual, and while it was written during wartime very seldom is the war mentioned. A case in point is Sartre's reference to living as a Jew in occupied France, which occurs in part 4 during his discussion of possible limits on freedom. The Jewish person encounters many apparently restrictive "prohibitions", which would seem to curtail his/her freedom. Yet Sartre uses the highly charged example only to defend the position of radical freedom he has proposed earlier in the book: "In fact according to the free possibilities which I choose, I can disobey the prohibition, pay no attention to it, or, on the contrary, confer upon it a coercive value which it can hold only because of the weight which I attach to it" (BN1: 524; BN2: 545). This defence exemplifies the ontological claim he made several pages earlier that: "The given in no way enters into the constitution of freedom since freedom is interiorized as the internal negation of the given" (BN1: 487; BN2: 508). No matter what given situation one is in, for Sartre, one can always assume various attitudes towards it. His concern is to refute determinism and to do this he promotes a strong view of the autonomous individual subject. Subjectivity, ontologized as being-for-itself, is constituted by a perpetually secreted negativity, which precludes identity with itself or its environment, confirming his "theory" of the individual "whom society cannot affect, because he is free". Absent a stable identity, this volatile subjectivity must choose its way in the world, on its own, creating and sustaining, but never "being", an identity.

By the war's end though, Sartre's thinking had begun to change course. When looking for a reason to account for "why my outlook changed so fundamentally after the Second World War", he claimed that:

a simple formula would be to say that life taught me *la force des choses* – the power of circumstances. In a way, *L'Être et le néant* itself should have been the beginning of a discovery of this power of circumstances, since I had already been made a soldier, when I had not wanted to be one. Thus I had already encountered something that was [not] my freedom and which steered me from without out.

(Sartre 1974b: 33)

The discovery of the power of circumstances marks the beginning of Sartre's politicization. Right after the war, in his editorial introduction to the first issue of his journal, *Les Temps modernes*, Sartre boldly proclaims that "our intention is to help effect certain changes in the society that surrounds us. By which we do not mean changes in people's souls" (Sartre 1988: 255). Ironically, the message of *Being and Nothingness* was none other than a call to change one's attitude, to effect a "conversion" of one's life to accept and live out one's radical freedom. That is evidently no longer enough. While one is "totally free", yet "it is the free man who must be *delivered*, by enlarging his possibilities of choice" (*ibid*.: 265). While here not taking back his ontological claims about total freedom in *Being and Nothingness*, Sartre appears to be conceding that these claims are incomplete. In fact, as his attention turns to the issue of "possibilities of choice", his hyperbolic claims about free subjectivity in *Being and Nothingness* are marginalized and minimized:

> Thus, in *L'Être et le néant*, what you could call "subjectivity" is not what it is for me now, the small margin in an operation whereby an interiorization re-exteriorizes itself in an act. But "subjectivity" and "objectivity" seem to me entirely useless notions today, anyway. (Sartre 1974b: 35)

To understand what freedom is for Sartre, it is necessary to see his understanding of it develop throughout his works. Too often his views are identified with *Being and Nothingness*. He realized this and protested "that they all stop too soon. I think that a study of my philosophical thought should follow its evolution. But no, they don't do it. It's odd" (Sartre 1981b: 8). One way of bringing out the evolution of his thinking, particularly his turn to politics, is to consider what he has said about self-making and alienation.

Self-making: existence precedes essence

The ground for Sartre's ontology of self-making in *Being and Nothingness* is found in *The Transcendence of the Ego*, his "existentialist theory of consciousness". Consciousness is a priority for Sartre because for him what is distinctively human is a unique awareness of self and world. He appropriates Husserl's intentional understanding of consciousness, that consciousness is always consciousness of an object, that consciousness is relational in nature, while transforming it into his existentialist view that existence precedes essence. For Sartre, consciousness operates on two different levels, pre-reflective and reflective. A reflective, or secondary level of consciousness, intends or posits an object that is another act of consciousness, as in Descartes's *cogito*, whereby he becomes aware of his own thinking. Prior to this secondary consciousness, when he was actually doing his thinking (and not thinking about his thinking) Descartes operated on the pre-reflective level of consciousness. On this level, while engaged for example in doubting, Descartes's consciousness was intending or positing a dubious object. Thus, while operating on either level, reflective or pre-reflective, consciousness is revealed to be intentional, directed toward an object. Now Sartre's adds a crucial aspect to his understanding of intentional consciousness. While consciousness, whether pre-reflective or reflective, is intentionally directed to an object (and not to itself), Sartre insists that consciousness is not unconscious of itself, but is aware of itself. However, this awareness of itself is not positional or focal. Rather it is non-positional, tacit and in the background. The structure of consciousness is to be intentional or positional of an object and simultaneously non-positionally self-aware. The reflexivity of non-positional self-awareness marks the creation of a "self" that necessarily comprehends its difference from its objects.

Sartre distinguishes the "ego" from the "self". While the latter is integral to the structure of consciousness, the former is constituted through acts of reflection. In reflecting on the pre-reflective life of consciousness, reflection transforms it through objectifying it with some serious consequences. He presents the example of a wife who was shaken by the thought of being unfaithful to her husband. Her first line of defence was to deflect this possibility as a real possibility, by identifying herself with her "ego", or objectified representation of herself. She considered herself to be a "faithful" person, one thus incapable of infidelity. In her eyes, she was not the type of person to engage in that sort of behaviour. But this defence collapsed with the vertiginous experience that nothing actually prevented her from acting unfaithfully, that it was, after all, a real possibility. Sartre comments: "But this vertigo is comprehensible only if consciousness suddenly appeared to itself as infinitely overflowing in its possibilities the *I* which ordinarily serves as its unity" (Sartre 1957b: 100). Sartre uses this example to argue that having a deep identity (nature or essence) is incompatible with radical freedom. If the woman had an essence which constituted her being and identity, then her actions would arise out of that ground and be circumscribed by it. The experience of vertigo or anguish revealed her radically free existential self to be beyond fixed identity. Sartre's existential lesson from this example is that one must create oneself, ungrounded by essence, by freely choosing, committing, and sustaining oneself faithfully or unfaithfully as a way of life.

In *Being and Nothingness*, Sartre takes up the structure of consciousness explored in *The Transcendence of the Ego* in terms of an ontology that stresses subjectivity, particularly defending its radical freedom. Epistemologically, all human experience, for Sartre, is dichotomized into subject/object and ontologically into self/other. The difference embedded in and making possible the dichotomy is *néant*, the break or fission in the continuity of being (in non-positional self-awareness) that allows for radical freedom. "The being of consciousness qua consciousness is to exist *at a distance from itself* as presence to itself, and this empty distance which being carries in its being is Nothingness" (BN1: 78; BN2: 102). The disruption of being from coincidence with itself temporalizes the being of consciousness, projecting it into the non-being of the future, haunting it with the imaginary. Exiled from identity with itself, human reality cannot rest in the stasis of being, but exhausts itself in temporalizing action, creating and supporting a way of life, projecting meaning and value. "In anguish I apprehend myself at once as totally free and as not being able to derive the meaning of the world except as coming from myself" (BN1: 40; BN2: 63).

The self as the place of the break with the causal continuity of being is radically free, that is, not determined by any factual state of affairs: "No factual state whatever it may be (the political and economic structure of society, the psychological 'state,' etc.) is capable by itself of motivating any act whatsoever" (BN1: 435; BN2: 457). Since radical freedom is the very being of the self, there is no middle ground, one is either determined or radically free: "Either man is wholly determined (which is inadmissible, especially because a determined consciousness – *i.e.*, a consciousness externally motivated – becomes itself pure exteriority and ceases to be consciousness) or else man is wholly free" (BN1: 442; BN2: 464). Human actions are not grounded in the foundation of an essence of being, but in the choices of a self by definition exiled from such a foundation.

From bad faith to revolution

Sartre referred to *Being and Nothingness* as his "eidetic of bad faith", and it is crucial to keep this in mind or it is easy to misunderstand that "essay on phenomenological ontology". After revealing the radical freedom of being-for-itself through phenomenological examples of questioning, imagining and experiences of anguish, Sartre tells the reader that two paths are possible for such a being, the path of "non-being", which is the acceptance of radical freedom, and the path of "being", which is that of flight or bad faith. The path of "non-being", or authenticity, "supposes a special transcendence needing separate study" (BN1: 44; BN2: 68) and will not be dealt with in *Being and Nothingness*. The path of "being" (bad faith) will be taken up, its forms exposed, its motivation revealed and its cure suggested. In no way is *Being and Nothingness* a full picture of the possibilities of human existence.

Two chapters explicitly deal with bad faith: "Bad Faith" and "Concrete Relations with Others". Bad faith is presented as a self-deception. Deception or lying presupposes a duality of liar and lied to wherein the liar hides the truth from the lied to. In the case of self-deception, one is hiding from oneself what one thinks to be true.

> I can in fact "not wish to see" a certain aspect of my being only if I am acquainted with the aspect which I do not wish to see. This means that in my being I must indicate this aspect in order to be able to turn myself away from it … In a word, I flee in order not to know, but I cannot avoid knowing that I am fleeing.
> (BN1: 43; BN2: 67)

This self-deceptive behaviour is applied to the defining aspects of human reality, freedom and facticity. The very condition of radical freedom is its break in the continuum of being and from essential identity. Yet, as a contingent factical being in the world, human reality must choose and commit itself in a process of self-making. Sartre expresses this in somewhat awkward language: "We have to deal with human reality as a being which is what it is not and which is not what it is" (BN1: 58; BN2: 82). While human reality is not what it is in the sense of essence, it "is what it is not" in the sense of self-making, a creation and support of a mode of life for which it is responsible. A person in bad faith is in denial of one of its terms. The waiter who believes himself to be a waiter as an essence must not notice how he is producing a way of life through choice, while the thief who denies all identity must not notice that his or her lifestyle is a committed project, creating a moral identity.

The ontological mode of being-for-others affords more opportunities for self-deception. The look of the Other objectifies the for-itself revealing a dimension of its reality unknown to the individual for-itself, as a factical object in the world. In its objectivity for the Other, the for-itself apprehends the meaning of its being and world slip from its control, producing new tensions between subjectivity and objectivity. Sartre discusses at length various forms of self-deception that can arise out of the situation introduced by Others. "I can", for example, "attempt to deny that being which is conferred on me from outside", by making an object of the Other since, "the Other's objectness destroys my objectness for him". On the other hand, "I can seek to recover that freedom and to possess it" (BN1: 363; BN2: 386), thereby reducing the Other to instrumentality. Once again, in these forms of bad faith (indifference, false love, sadism, masochism) there is a refusal of the human condition, a resistance to accepting both freedom and facticity. The remaining questions regard the motivation of this resistance and its possible cure.

Sartre offers a motivation for bad faith by considering the "break" in being, which he located in the non-positional self-awareness of being-for-itself, as a *lack* of self-identity, which provokes a desire for self-identity. Exiled from the identity of being, dispersed temporally and self-divided, being-for-itself seeks to catch up with itself, to recover its dispersion and split identity in order to give itself meaning in the form of self-identity. Being factical, the for-itself is not its own foundation; it has no fundamental justification, no intrinsic meaningfulness. In its self-making, the for-itself creates and sustains a meaningful life, but cannot actually *be* that mode of life in self-identity, the mode of being-in-itself. If being-for-itself could actually *be* the life that it makes and sustains as a project, it would be self-justifying, its own foundation. But, of course, if the for-itself were to *be*, it would no longer exist as a for-itself, a self-maker. It would lose itself as a self because a self is a "break" in the identity of being. Thus, the goal desired "can not be given by nature, since it combines in itself the incompatible characteristics of the in-itself and the for-itself" (BN1: 90; BN2: 114). Sartre has informed us as early as his work on emotion that people are prone, when in an untenable situation, one that has no real solution, to attempt magical solutions. Thus bad faith is a way to live the impossibility ever fulfilling an always-deferred self-foundation through a belief that one has achieved it. But as we have seen this demands that we deceive ourselves by denying those aspects of our situation (either our freedom or our facticity) that get in the way of sustaining that belief.

From time to time in *Being and Nothingness* Sartre reminds us that it is possible to overcome bad faith, to effect a "conversion" to authentic life. While authenticity is reserved for "separate study", the path to it is suggested in his treatment of existential psychoanalysis. At the very end of *Being and Nothingness* he tells us that "existential psychoanalysis is going to reveal to man the real goal of his pursuit, which is being as a synthetic fusion of the in-itself with the for itself" (BN1: 626; BN2: 646), in order to make use of this revelation as "a means of deliverance and salvation". No longer would one's life be frustrated in attempts to achieve the unachievable, but one would accept one's very break in being as the worthy life of freedom itself.

Being and Nothingness is a mix of phenomenological description, ontological categorization and metaphysical narrative. Its register is highly individual and intensely psychological, while the political seems irrelevant to the existential drama. That would soon change. "Every man is political. But I did not discover that for myself until the war and I did not truly understand it until 1945" (Sartre 1977a: 44). The war taught Sartre "the force of circumstances", an awakened sense of his implication in history and social structures. "*L'Être et le néant* traced an interior experience without any co-ordination with the exterior experience of a petty bourgeois intellectual, which had become catastrophic at a certain moment" (Sartre 1974b: 35). Sartre is moved now to explore a "concrete" freedom which takes into account the formative influence on the subject of its situation and in doing so encounter forms of *alienation* absent from the discussion of "abstract" freedom in *Being and Nothingness*. On a number of occasions (e.g. *ibid.*) he tells us that the book where he has best explained what he means by freedom is, in fact, *Saint Genet*. Here, in his attempt to understand Jean Genet's life, Sartre is led to speak of "the making of Genet" (Sartre 1963).

Contrasting with the adult world of *Being and Nothingness*, Sartre emphasizes the pivotal role of Genet's childhood in the development of his subjectivity. The vulnerable child, marked by social meanings attached to his illegitimacy, is "provided with a monstrous and guilty ego" (*ibid.*: 27). His attempts to be like other children are twisted by others into a nightmarish stigma. The child accepts the social verdicts levelled at him and, knowing no other recourse, sets out to enact them, "progressively internalizing the sentence imposed by adults" (*ibid.*: 49). *Being and Nothingness* is ill suited to make Genet's situation intelligible, for only two options in life were there offered, bad faith and authenticity. However, the child Genet was not running away from a radical freedom he did not know. He sees himself through the eyes of others, which in turn are conditioned by social structures alienating to him. As he internalizes the definitions and judgments of others, Genet makes them his self-definitions and judgments, resulting in his "alienation". But alienation cannot happen to things, Sartre argues, only to free people. In internalizing the definitions of others Genet can only enact them through projects of self-making, even though it is a self-making trapped in the definitions of others. As he "lives" the sentences imposed by others, Genet begins to express his life in writing, which, according to Sartre's reconstruction, ultimately leads Genet to experience his freedom and self-making as he gradually realizes his power to shape himself to others. What we learn from Genet is that "in the end one is always responsible for what is made of one. Even if one can do nothing else besides assuming this responsibility for I believe that a man always makes something out of what is made of him" (Sartre 1974b: 34–5).

In his later work Sartre vigorously delves into the processes by which people are "made" by their environment. It is not a question of rejecting existential self-making, but of taking into account social processes of "making". A concrete appreciation of freedom in this sense provokes a "dialectical" understanding of the subject and its world. He drops the ontological terminology of for-itself and in-itself in favour of praxis and practico-inert, emphatically more actional and material notions than ontological and psychological. Praxis, the actional subject, works on the world, engraves its projects upon it, and it in turn, modified by these imprints, constrains praxis. While ontological freedom stressed the "break" with given conditions in the ability to surpass them, concrete freedom stresses the situational terms which condition surpassing and circumscribe it.

> Every man is defined negatively by the sum total of possibles which are impossible for him; that is, by a future more or less blocked off. For the underprivileged classes, each cultural, technical, or material enrichment of society represents a diminution, an impoverishment; the future is almost entirely barred. Thus, both positively and negatively, the social possibles are lived as schematic determinations of the individual future. And the most individual possible is only the enrichment of a social possible.
> (Sartre 1958b: 95)

The tie between individual and social possible is the basis for Sartre's understanding of "class", which can be seen not only to constrain lives but to mediate them in relation to one another. Class consists of "the *social Being* of man at the fundamental level, that is to say, in so far as there are *several people* within a practical field totalized by the mode of production" (Sartre 1976a: 230). When he refers to class, Sartre invariably uses Marx's terminology and is concerned with liberating the proletariat whose lives are defined by their role in economic production. To survive in the present scheme of things the proletariat must employ means that recoil against their freedom: "individuals find an existence already sketched out for them at birth; they 'have their position in life' and their personal development assigned to them by their class" (*ibid.*: 232). The destiny portrayed here is not one grounded in an essence, but rather in the stasis of an entrenched situation that results in a repetitious existence as long as the constraining conditions prevail. One remains ontologically free under those conditions, one makes choices, but the choices are limited by the structural conditions of one's situation. The commitment to individual freedom in the overcoming of bad faith in Sartre's early writings develops into the commitment, in his later writings to overcoming structural forms of alienation in the realization "for *everyone* [of] a margin of *real* freedom beyond the production of life" (Sartre 1958b: 34), the political creation of a "city of ends". While overcoming bad faith required a conversion of attitude, changing structural forms of alienation requires "*material* work and revolutionary *praxis*" (*ibid*.: 13).

Until his death Sartre continued to do what he could to combat colonialism, racism and economic oppression. It is not an exaggeration to consider him a major voice of conscience in his age. He died still hopeful that a liberated society would materialize, a hope based upon his unwavering conviction that human beings are not stuck in the continuum of being but can always project a future different from the past.

Further reading

Busch, T. W. 1990. *The Power of Consciousness and the Force of Circumstances in Sartre's Philosophy*. Bloomington, IN: Indiana University Press.
Flynn, T. 1997. *Sartre, Foucault and Historical Reason, vol.1: Toward an Existentialist Theory of History*. Chicago, IL: University of Chicago Press.
Jeanson, F. 1980. *Sartre and the Problem of Morality*, R. Stone (trans.). Bloomington, IN: Indiana University Press. Originally published as *Le probleme moral et la pensee de Sartre* (Paris: Editions du Seuil, 1965).
McBride, W. L. 1991. *Sartre's Political Theory*. Bloomington, IN: Indiana University Press.

FIFTEEN

Politics and the engaged intellectual
William L. McBride

Having been relatively apolitical during the early stages of his career – he spent a fellowship year in Berlin soon after Hitler's appointment as German Chancellor without showing much apparent interest in what was beginning to take place in the political realm – Sartre became, in the years following the Second World War, the quintessential public intellectual. The chronology of his path is well documented, and it is intertwined with the evolution of his philosophy. In this chapter, that path will be quickly retraced, with brief pauses at some of its most salient markers.

Sartre's path to political engagement

Sartre had a fairly strong sense of identification with his generation; he was not alone in regarding it, in retrospect, as the "between the wars generation". His studies dominated his life in the years immediately following the First World War, and he then performed eighteen months of military service, compulsory for French males, as a meteorologist. His first career appointment was at the *lycée* in Le Havre, where he taught philosophy for several years before and after his time in Germany. Meanwhile, he was undertaking various writing ventures, with mixed success, including the ongoing rewriting of the novel, eventually entitled *Nausea*, which, when finally published in 1938, brought him considerable acclaim. Little by little, political realities began increasingly to impinge on his consciousness and his life. The most important of these developments for him was the civil war in Spain, which began in 1936; one of Sartre's best friends, the painter Fernando Gerassi, abruptly left Paris to fight against Franco on the Republican side, which ultimately suffered defeat. In short order thereafter, despite the Anglo-French effort at Munich to prevent all-out war by appeasing Hitler, there ensued the latter's invasion of Poland and the inevitable declarations of war and military call-ups – a sequence of events that Sartre proceeded to translate into personal terms in his fictional trilogy, The Roads to Freedom (Sartre 1945a, 1945c, 1949a). He himself was called up and spent the period of the so-called "phoney war", at the end of which the French Vichy government acceded to the Nazis after relatively little actual combat had occurred, reading and writing at a furious pace. He was taken prisoner along with his fellow combatants and spent nine months in a *Stalag* before escaping and returning to Paris. It was during this period that Sartre's earlier individualistic outlook on the world began to give way to a certain sense of human camaraderie – the prisoner-of-war camp experience was especially influential in this respect – and that he began seriously to reflect, as his friend and confidante Simone de Beauvoir affirmed in her memoirs, on the idea of commitment, *engagement*.

Sartre's post-war commitments

The time between Sartre's escape from the camp and the liberation of Paris from the Nazis in 1944 was comparatively brief – less than three and a half years. He participated in a short-lived resistance group that took the name "Socialism and Freedom" and resumed his teaching career, for the last time, at the Lycée Condorcet in Paris, but above all he wrote and published prodigiously. Two of his best plays – *The Flies*, with its veiled anti-Occupation message, and *No Exit* (Sartre 2005a) – were first produced then. Most important of all, his first philosophical *magnum opus*, *Being and Nothingness*, appeared in print in mid-1943. Although Sartre had already published two books on the imagination and other essays in philosophy prior to the war (most notably his outline of a theory of the emotions), *Being and Nothingness* was of an entirely different order both of magnitude and of importance.

In light of Sartre's later development it is worth considering to what extent, if any, *Being and Nothingness* may be considered to have political significance. The simple answer is, very little. It is above all a work of systematic ontology, aspects of which are explored in other essays in the present volume, and it contains virtually no text of a sort that might have appeared politically provocative to Nazi censors. One heavily veiled possible exception to this is Sartre's critical reference, on the penultimate page of the conclusion, to the "spirit of seriousness" that he indicates will be one focus of a future work of his on ethics. To those imbued with this spirit, he says, the actions of a solitary drunkard and the "vain agitation of the leader of nations [*conducteur de peuples*]" (BN1: 627; BN2: 647) are on a par with one another, or perhaps the former is in a better position. "*Conducteur*" can be translated as "*Führer*", the title usually given to Hitler. There is also one rather dramatic earlier sub-section entitled "Freedom and Responsibility" in which Sartre argues that, in a wartime situation, I am responsible for whatever stance I take towards the war, whether combat or escape or suicide, and so on (BN1: 553; BN2: 574); for anyone familiar with the period in which Sartre wrote and published *Being and Nothingness*, this part of the text exudes a sense of contemporaneity, but there is nothing obviously subversive about it. The types of interpersonal relationships with which much of this work is concerned are for the most part what Sartre will later call "dyadic", one-on-one (BN1: 592; BN2: 613), and the socio-political realm remains very much in the background.

Sartre as an "engaged writer"

This is not to say, however, that Sartre was still mostly ignorant of that realm by the time *Being and Nothingness* appeared. It is clear that, by that time, he was already planning to be a principal collaborator in a post-war initiative, in the form of an interdisciplinary and politically engaged revue that in fact took shape soon after the Liberation and was given the name *Les Temps modernes*. (The name was taken from the title of Charlie Chaplin's satirical film *Modern Times*.) Its original list of editorial board members included a number of prominent intellectuals, some of whom, such as Raymond Aron, soon left, while others, most notably Simone de Beauvoir and for some years Maurice Merleau-Ponty, formed its working core. Sartre's "Presentation" of the journal in its inaugural issue announced its intended general line, best characterized as "non-Communist Left" and committed to what it identified as a spirit of synthesis, attempting to understand human beings in their totality, as opposed to a spirit of analysis. While *Les Temps modernes* contained, over the years, many articles of general interest beyond the political realm (literature, psychiatry, history, etc.), the fundamentally political nature of its orientation never came into question.

Among the most notable essays of the early years of *Les Temps modernes*, three written by Sartre himself were exceptional both as defining statements of his own evolving political position and as highly influential in post-war intellectual life: "Réflexions sur la question juive", "Matérialisme et révolution" and "Qu'est-ce que la littérature?". The first (along with a large section that was not part of the original) and the third were eventually published in separate volumes (Sartre 1946a, 1948a), and the English translation of "Réflexions sur la question juive" was given the somewhat misleading title of *Anti-Semite and Jew* (Sartre 1948b).

Probably the most unforgettable part of the essay on "the Jewish question" is Sartre's opening portrait of the anti-Semite; it is forceful and devastating, and, of course, particularly poignant given the era in which it was written (*ibid.*: 36). Among Sartre's other achievements in this essay is his recognition of the inadequacies of an abstract, universalistic form of liberalism that pretends that, since we are all human after all, any solution to anti-Semitism does not have to involve coming to grips with the reality of it (*ibid.*: 143). As for "Materialism and Revolution" (Sartre 1962a, 1946c), it clearly delineates Sartre's philosophical distance from the Communist Party dogma that called itself "orthodox Marxism" and took a strongly deterministic view of history. Sartre here acknowledges the contribution of an uncompromisingly materialistic ontology to the morale, so to speak, of the ordinary worker, who is thereby reinforced in the conviction that he or she is on the same level as the owner of capital, no better or worse; but Sartre insists that the desirable goal of emancipation of the working class would ultimately be better served by a philosophical doctrine that retained the element of human freedom (*ibid.*: 220).

It is in "What Is Literature?", more than in any other writing, that Sartre most directly espouses a stance of commitment, *engagement*. After briefly surveying Western literary history of recent decades, with special emphasis on the "literature of consumption" (Sartre 1950a: 205), posing no threat to the dominance of the bourgeois class, that he ascribes to the late nineteenth century, he advocates an activist "literature of production" to be pursued by contemporary (prose) writers. Only such a literature, he maintains, can be taken seriously by today's public. Its ultimate and admittedly somewhat utopian goal should be to bring about a classless society. Literature and morality are, of course, not the same thing, Sartre acknowledges, and yet the purpose of engaged literature as he now conceived it is in the last analysis a moral one (*ibid.*: 258).

Sartre as political public intellectual

"What Is Literature?" was first published in instalments in *Les Temps modernes* throughout 1947. Hence, only four years after the publication of *Being and Nothingness* and three years after the Liberation of Paris, Sartre found himself in the position of public intellectual *par excellence*, a position that he was to occupy, in France and virtually worldwide, for some years to come. He was almost constantly called upon to respond to world events, the principal foci of which were, above all, the Cold War and, secondarily, the often bloody demise of Western colonial empires, especially that of France itself. Only for a brief period and without success did he play an overtly political role: he joined a short-lived party called the RDR (Rassemblement Démocratique Révolutionnaire), ostensibly designed to uphold an independent non-Communist left-wing position between East and West; but it soon became known that one of its leaders was in the pay of certain American interests, and this created a sense of disillusionment in Sartre and a number of other French intellectuals.

Equally (or perhaps even more) disillusioning for them was the documented revelation, within the same period (late 1949 to early 1950), of the existence of a network of slave labour camps in the Soviet Union, which were denounced in an editorial, written by Merleau-Ponty and approved by Sartre, in *Les Temps modernes*. A fictionalized version of some of the tensions surrounding the decision to print this editorial is a central part of Simone de Beauvoir's novel *The Mandarins*, published four years later (de Beauvoir 1954).

Within a few months war broke out on the Korean peninsula, exacerbating Cold War tensions even further. The Korean War was a major factor, though by no means the only one, in the eventual rupture between Sartre and Merleau-Ponty, which culminated in the latter's resignation from the editorial board of the journal in 1953, and which was slowly being overcome at the time of Merleau-Ponty's untimely death ten years later. "Merleau" had been, if anything, somewhat more sympathetic than Sartre to the general position of the Communist Party in the years prior to 1950; his 1949 book *Humanism and Terror* (Merleau-Ponty [1947] 1969) was such a serious, even-handed attempt to understand the mentality that had lain behind the notorious Moscow Purge Trials of the 1930s as to lead some critics to accuse him, wrongly, of endorsing those trials. But he came to regard the North Korean incursion into South Korea as part of a Soviet strategy of global dominance, whereas Sartre was more inclined to see certain American provocations as having played a significant role in precipitating the same event. In any case, by mutual agreement neither Sartre nor Merleau-Ponty published much of a directly political nature in *Les Temps modernes* during the ensuing period of roughly two years.

Breaking with Camus

During that same period (August 1952), however, one of the best-known and most controversial episodes in Sartre's life as engaged intellectual occurred with the publication of his famous "Reply to Albert Camus". The occasion for this was Camus's "Letter to the Director of *Les Temps modernes*" – the impersonality and extreme formality of this way of addressing him were of course deliberate – in response to a review of Camus's book *The Rebel* (Camus 1951; English translation 1954) that had been published in a prior issue. The review had been written by a younger member of the staff, Francis Jeanson, who had undertaken a task that all agreed was necessary (since it was a landmark work by a very prominent writer) but that they all, in a sense, dreaded. In his book, Camus, in effect, through numerous historical and literary analyses, concluded that, while individual revolt (the French title is *L'Homme révolté*, man in revolt) is often creative and productive, political revolutions are doomed to be counter-productive and to fail. Jeanson's lengthy critique of this position elicited a Camusian polemic that accused Sartre (Camus treated Jeanson as a Sartrean "mouthpiece" whom he never mentioned by name) of supporting the excesses of the Soviet Union under Stalin and of entertaining an unwarranted conviction concerning the inevitable future movement of history. Sartre, in turn, accused Camus of a moralism bordering on preaching and insisted that it is we human beings who make history, from which we cannot simply stand back as Camus appeared to wish to do. The polemic left Camus embittered. He and Sartre were never reconciled. Meanwhile, the French government's ultimately failed, sanguinary and very costly effort to quell the anti-colonial uprising in Algeria, where Camus had been born and his mother still lived (leading to his famous remark to the effect that if he had to choose between justice and his mother he would choose the latter), contributed even further to a sense of personal conflict during the years that followed. Among the French supporters of the Algerian revolutionaries, who risked serious consequences because of their stance, Francis Jeanson was prominent and active, while it was clear that Sartre, although not so deeply involved personally, was in agreement with him.

The rearguard military action in which the French government was most involved during the early 1950s, before the Algerian War had reached its height, was the war in Indochina, in which that government was attempting to keep control over Vietnam, Laos and Cambodia. A French sailor by the name of Henri Martin, who was, like many of his fellow citizens, a member of the Communist Party, was imprisoned for speaking out in favour of independence for Vietnam, and this soon became a *cause célèbre*. Sartre devoted a considerable amount of time and effort (including a visit to the French President) to obtaining Martin's release, which was granted shortly before the publication of a volume that Sartre had written for that purpose.

Sartre and communism: the need for a new Marxian methodology

Around the same period Sartre wrote a three-part essay, "The Communists and Peace", in which he argued in favour of this conjunction, and became involved in a peace movement in which Soviet and other Eastern Bloc intellectuals were prominent participants. He also made his first trip to the Soviet Union in 1954, returning with a very positive "take", which he later realized had been excessive, on what he had seen there. This was, in short, the time at which he came closest to being – to employ an expression of the time – a "fellow traveller"; it did not last very long.

The year 1956 was marked by the so-called "thaw," a partial softening of the hard-line communism of the USSR and its satellites that came about as a result of the acknowledgement of some of Stalin's crimes by his successor as Soviet Communist Party Secretary General, Nikita Khrushchev. But Khrushchev was apparently unprepared for the explosion of previously suppressed intellectual and political dissidence that ensued in some of the countries of the Eastern Bloc. He came quite close to ordering a military invasion of Poland, then actually did so in the case of Hungary. Sartre's strong reaction to this event was reflected in an essay entitled "Stalin's Ghost". Within a few months of its appearance in *Les Temps modernes*, a Polish journal, *Twórczość*, published a translation of Sartre's long essay on Marxism and existentialism, the French original of which was published in instalments later in the year under the title of "Questions de méthode". Although it had been "commissioned", so to speak, by a Polish editor who wished to avail himself of the more open intellectual climate by devoting an entire issue to analyses of Marxism in France, and so could be considered a *pièce d'occasion* similar to other Sartrean essays on politics of which I have highlighted just a few, *Search for a Method* (as the title of the English translation would have it; Sartre 1958b) is different in kind by virtue of returning to fundamental issues of political philosophy with which Sartre had begun to occupy himself especially in "Materialism and Revolution" (Sartre 1946c, 1962a). Indeed, although the English translation was published as a separate book on its own, Sartre eventually decided to treat the French original as a long introduction to volume one of his even longer *Critique of Dialectical Reason* (Sartre 1960c), the philosophical *magnum opus* of his later years. *Search for a Method* is thus an excellent example of the back-and-forth movement between essays in the public intellectual genre and philosophical treatises that Sartre was so successful in effecting.

The central question of method in *Search for a Method* is whether we have the intellectual tools today to enable us to understand the actions of any single individual – for example, the nineteenth-century writer Flaubert, who had fascinated Sartre throughout his career and became the focus of his last work, the three-volume *The Family Idiot* (Sartre 1971–2). Sartre's central premise is that neither Freudian psychoanalysis nor American behavioural science is adequate to this task and that Marxism, while it is the dominant worldview of the day and one to which he subscribes in principle, had, in its official, so-called "orthodox" version, sclerosed. Dogmatic communists, according to Sartre, seem to assume that individuals take on real identities only when they begin their first salaried jobs. It is in attending seriously to the problem of the human individual, then, that existentialism has a role to play – parasitic on Marxism, but nevertheless essential (Sartre 1958b: 30). The text of *Search for a Method* does not really resemble very closely the far more abstract and systematic account of human social wholes that is the first volume of the *Critique*, which is considered elsewhere in the present volume, but it serves as needed background to it – placing it "in situation", to use a favourite Sartrean term that he used as a label for his series, *Situations*, of published volumes of collected essays taken from *Les Temps modernes*.

Sartre as internationalist

Among Sartre's other major international involvements, special mention should be given to his concerns for Africa, Cuba and Israel. Among his sharpest works of political polemic is his preface to Franz Fanon's *The Wretched of the Earth* (Fanon 1963). Fanon was a French-educated Martiniquan psychiatrist who eventually moved to Algeria and became a strong proponent of the revolution there; but what Sartre has to say in this preface concerning the nature of colonialism and its very bitter fruits has implications for sub-Saharan Africa and other parts of the former French empire as well. Sartre travelled to Cuba in 1960, soon after Fidel Castro's revolution, and spent a considerable amount of time in his company. He wrote a series of newspaper articles, generally quite enthusiastic, about this experience, but he later became somewhat disillusioned with the authoritarian turn that was taken by that regime. As for Israel, Sartre remained a defender of it, though certainly not always of its government's policies, in the face of the anti-Israel stance of a portion of the French left.

The Algerian conflict having been settled by the dramatic re-entry of Charles de Gaulle into French politics and his decision to concede independence to Algeria against the wishes of the very "ultras" who had helped return him to power, the attention of Sartre and indeed of the world at large shifted back to Vietnam, where the United States began to undertake its ultimately disastrous military "escalation". France was not drawn back directly into this war, but Sartre wrote very forcefully in favour of the Vietnamese Communists' cause and, as an act of protest, disinvited himself from a lecture that he had agreed to give at Cornell University in the United States in 1965. Two years later, as the Vietnam War continued, Sartre accepted to serve as chair of a private Vietnam War Crimes Tribunal that was the creation of the elderly British philosopher Bertrand Russell. It was their wish to convene the tribunal in France, but President de Gaulle, whom Sartre always despised, refused permission for this in a letter addressed to him as "Mon cher maître" (Sartre famously commented that no one called him "master" except café waiters). During this same period Sartre refused to accept the Nobel Prize that had been awarded to him.

Sartre in the 1960s: revolt, repression and the "new intellectual"

The two, virtually simultaneous political climaxes of the 1960s were undoubtedly, first, the succession of worldwide student protests that began at the new, rather drab suburban university of Nanterre and soon spread to Paris proper, where other activities came nearly to a standstill and the government seemed at one point to be on the verge of falling; and second, the so-called "Prague Spring" in which Czechoslovakia seemed to be moving towards more open and democratic political institutions, only to be suppressed by invading Soviet forces. Both occurred in 1968. By this time Sartre's star was beginning to wane, as new philosophical movements variously labelled "structuralism" and "postmodernism" gradually occupied the intellectual scene, replacing existentialism at centre stage. Sartre appeared at a student meeting in the Sorbonne, but was told to keep his remarks brief. Many students, especially some of those at Sartre's *alma mater*, the École Normale Supérieure, who were in the vanguard of the protests, were greatly attracted to a Marxist instructor by the name of Louis Althusser, who endorsed an anti-humanistic line. But his ascendancy was short-lived, as the French Communist Party and he himself refrained from wholeheartedly supporting the movement, and a sort of normalcy gradually returned to Paris and to France as a whole. Meanwhile, the Soviet actions in Prague resulted in a final loss of confidence, on Sartre's part, that that regime would ever return from its long "detour" on the road to socialism; rather, he concluded, it had reached a hopeless impasse. He expressed this conviction in a brief preface, entitled "The Socialism that Came in from the Cold", to a collection of testimonials to the events written by Czech intellectuals and published in 1970 (reprinted in Sartre 1972c, 1979).

Sartre's final decade: ongoing engagement, new directions

The final decade of Sartre's life was marked by publication of *The Family Idiot* (1971–2); increasing health problems, especially failing eyesight; and involvement with a group of mostly younger people who, in a sort of aftermath to the failed student efforts of 1968, dedicated themselves to ongoing "revolutionary" activity under the name of "the Maos". (In fact, this label was intended primarily as a provocation, rather than as an expression of deep commitment to the thought of the Chinese leader Mao Tse-Tung.) Sartre even briefly assumed the editorship of their newspaper, *La Cause du Peuple*, as a way of shielding some of them from arrest. One member of the group, Benny Lévy, eventually became Sartre's private secretary and engaged in a series of recorded dialogues with him (since Sartre was by this time unable to write), of which a small portion was published in a mainstream newspaper under the title "Hope, Now" (later published in book form; Sartre 1991b, 1996). Although Simone de Beauvoir and some other members of the Sartrean "family", as they called themselves, opposed having this material published, because they considered Lévy to have been manipulative (and in fact the text appeared in some respects to be in contradiction with Sartre's earlier philosophical positions), Sartre himself insisted on going ahead with it. Only a few days later he died. The year was 1980; Sartre was nearly seventy-five years old.

Another French Lévy, Bernard-Henri, has called the twentieth century "Sartre's century" (the title of a book of his), and there is considerable merit to this. No other intellectual from that time was as widely known, as widely cited, or – to recall the title of another secondary work, this one by John Gerassi, Fernando's son – as widely hated. Some of his commitments were misplaced or at least proved to be disappointing to him, but his activism on behalf of those whom he saw as oppressed and in favour of enhancing human freedom as he understood it was remarkable and on the whole, in my view, positive. At the same time, it was generally in conformity with his philosophical principles, both early and late. In short, his legacy with respect to political engagement is formidable.

Further reading

Catalano, J. 2010. *Reading Sartre*. Cambridge: Cambridge University Press.
Cohen-Solal, A. 1987. *Sartre: A Life*, A. Cancogni (trans.), N. MacAfee (ed.). New York: Pantheon.
Flynn, T. 1994. *Sartre and Marxist Existentialism: The Test Case of Collective Responsibility*. Chicago, IL: University of Chicago Press.
Gerassi, J. 1989. *Jean-Paul Sartre: Hated Conscience of the Century*. Chicago, IL: University of Chicago Press.
Judaken, J. 2006. *Jean-Paul Sartre and the Jewish Question: Anti-Semitism and the Politics of the French Intellectual*. Lincoln, NE: University of Nebraska Press.

SIXTEEN

Sartre's theory of groups
Peter Caws

The existential subject

Sartre's ontology begins from the situation of the subject, not as an abstract category but as embodied and individual. Each of us is such a subject, and each of us knows only the subject that he or she is. As a subject I exist, that is to say I stand out (the root meaning of "exist") into a world that I encounter in its immediacy and its otherness. Objects in the world are what they are, but this implies also that they just are, that they have being. At first this being is apprehended only in its relation to me. Let me follow Sartre's example and take a simple case, an everyday object such as a letter-opener. The letter-opener presents itself to me as existing, that is as standing out into a world of other objects (including my physical body), but its being is in the first instance a "being-for-me".

Objects in the world disappear and reappear, and the simplest way of accounting for this is to assume that they have a form of being which is independent of their "being-for-me". Sartre calls this "being-in-itself". When the letter-opener is in my hand it has being-in-itself and being-for-me; when it is no longer present to me it has being-in-itself, but need not have being-for-me; but if it is lost or destroyed and I think of it, it still has being-for-me though it may no longer have being-in-itself.

But what kind of being do I as a subject have? I exist, but what am I? The fact that I can raise this question means at least that – like the letter-opener when merely thought of – I have being-for-me: being-for-myself. This is a new kind of being, and we may call it being-for-itself. Note, however, that in attributing this kind of being to myself I remain a subject – I have not turned myself into an object. My body is to be sure an object among objects, and like any other object can be taken to have being-in-itself, but the fact that I can call it my body suggests a difference in kind between the subject I am and the body I inhabit. I cannot grasp the subject, because I am it. Being-for-itself is perpetually in flight from itself, perpetually ahead of itself.

The restricted topic of this chapter precludes further development of this idea, which would lead us in the direction of the phenomenologists and the transcendental subject. I begin in this way because I want to trace an ascent from the situation of the bare individual to the ultimate collectivity of humanity and its history – or at least to trace this ascent as far as Sartre's theoretical insight can take it.

The Other and the look

I cannot turn the subject that I am into an object – if I lose my subjectivity the game is ended before it is begun. But what about other people? Courtesy and symmetry require that I attribute subjectivity to them, but I have no immediate access to that subjectivity, I can only infer it from similarities between their appearance and behaviour and my own. There is, however, one situation in which our roles – mine as subject, the Other's as object – are reversed. This may happen when I become aware that an Other is looking at me, objectifying me in ways which are unintelligible except under the hypothesis (which must however always remain a hypothesis) that he or she is a subject who sees me as an object. This awareness of being looked at may trigger an emotion, in Sartre's paradigm case the emotion of shame – he imagines for example that I am spying on someone through a keyhole and feel the Other's eyes upon me, so that suddenly I am no longer the subject and agent in control of the event, but a vulnerable object, at its mercy. This does not give me the Other's subjectivity directly – the same emotional response may be triggered by the mere suspicion of the presence of an Other, for example by a rustling of leaves which I interpret as bodily movement – but it makes clear to me that an account of my own situation as that of an isolated existential subject standing out into an emotionally neutral world must be seriously incomplete.

Emotions, for Sartre, are ways of being in the world; they colour the situation of the existential subject. The fact that he introduces the awareness of the Other by way of the emotion of shame is characteristic, but of course shame is only one of a whole spectrum of emotions, including fear and envy and desire and love, which may trigger the mutual acknowledgment and recognition, positive or negative, of one subject by another.

The Third

The look opens up my situation to the presence of Others. Once this step is taken from the singular to the plural it might seem that we are on the way from an individual to a social ontology, but things are not quite that simple. I have an inkling or a foreboding of the existence of the Other, but nothing binds us together into any sort of unity. Our relation is one of pure interiority, and one-sided interiority at that, since I have no access to the other pole of the relation. At this point Sartre invokes the concept of the Third (Sartre 1976a: 106, 114) – a spectator, perhaps, who sees me, and also the one who is looking at me, who sees my furtive apprehension at being observed, who embraces me and the Other in a dyad of psychological or philosophical interest. Our interior relation now has an exterior embodiment. The activity of the Third in constructing this dyad does not, however, depend on the interior relation: he or she may observe two individuals who are unaware of one another's presence or even existence, and group them under some concept for purposes of study or analysis or imagination or the like.

So this step towards the social has two components: on the one hand, my recognition that I am linked to Others internally by relations of presence or immediacy, as well as by the dialectics of practice (given that we can have reciprocal effects on one another – interpersonal praxis is for Sartre the domain of the dialectic), on the other, the need for the external objectifying regard that forms us into an entity, in the dyadic case a couple. The independence of these two elements and the contrast between them explain why, for example, a couple can cease to exist internally (by a refusal of recognition on the part of one of its members) but persist externally (by habits of recognition on the part of Others). These two modes of being of the social coexist in the individual even in more complex situations, up to and including his or her historical understanding – as a member of the human race alongside other members, as participating in a moment of a dialectical development that began far back in time and will continue far into the future. Two things, however, are to be noted here – Sartre's insistence on the radical equality of human beings (I could be or have been "just anyone") and his eventual rejection of the notion of history as an intelligible adventure of humanity. There must always be a Third standing outside in order to lend unity to any social being. Ontologically speaking, there is no higher level than the triad of subject, Other and Third; as we shall see things can get numerically more complex, but they can always be broken down to this elementary level, the crucial component of which remains the individual existential subject.

The series

The social world comprises very many individuals, some of whom know one other or interact with one another in groups of greater or lesser extent. One eventual question, to which an answer was suggested above, concerns the existence of a total and inclusive group worthy of the name of humanity, the subject of world history. This would be the outcome of the great dialectic, summing up the contributions of all the individuals who ever lived in their reciprocal relations to one another. Sartre lived at a time when history seemed to be in the making on a world scale – when communism and capitalism, in the wake of the Second World War, were in competition for the future of mankind. But he was a philosopher first, a politician or historian a distant second (though with striking talents in both domains); and philosophy, with its constitutive modesty and fierce self-criticism, could not bear the weight of that ambition. Nevertheless he started out boldly, in volume 1 of his *Critique of Dialectical Reason* (Sartre 1960b, 1976a), to tackle the ascent towards history, and on the way developed the original and very powerful theory of groups that is the subject of this chapter.

One obvious way of beginning the study of groups is to look to the external characteristics that mark everyday subdivisions between people: ethnicity, nationality, skin colour, gender, language, profession (etc.). Sartre chooses a quite different starting point. He occupies the position of the observing Third, and begins with the situation of a number of individuals each separately related to some object of common concern. The case he chooses is that of people waiting at a bus stop (Sartre 1976a: 256ff.). All of them have an interest in taking the bus, but this is not a collective interest; they do not all have the same destination or purpose in mind, there is no internal connection between them. Such a contingent assembly of unrelated subjects united only by a common object Sartre calls a series. Serial relations abound in daily life – customers in the market, spectators in the theatre, listeners to the radio or watchers of television, voters in an election, drivers on a highway, all constitute series whose members share a connection to an external object but have no internal connections between themselves.

A series may be ordered in such a way as to establish external connections between its members – for example the people waiting at the bus stop may form a queue in which relative position is determined by time of arrival – but in such cases no subject encounters an Other in an existential sense, the others just belong to what Sartre in other contexts calls the "practico-inert", the material or cultural context of life that, while it is a product of human praxis, is just as much a part of the subject's facticity as if it had arisen naturally. And a series may seem to behave like a group, as when for example spectators at a sporting event or in a theatre all applaud spontaneously at the same time because of some feat or performance, but again this does not establish a direct connection between the individuals concerned.

The group in fusion

True group formation begins when the members of a series become aware of one another not merely as accidental neighbours having no internal relations to one another, but as sharing a common interest that engages a common emotion. I now encounter my fellow bus riders, for example, as subjects who experience and suffer the same frustrations and inconveniences as I do when the bus is late or crowded or badly driven. We comment on these things while waiting in the queue; we resolve, perhaps, to write a joint letter to the directors of the bus company. Sartre calls such an informal association, establishing ties of sympathy and purpose, a "group in fusion". In Alan Sheridan-Smith's English translation of the *Critique* this is rendered as "fused group" (Sartre 1976a: 357), but such a designation is premature – at this point Sartre is exploring the process by which the group comes into being. His own examples are now drawn not from the business of daily life but from a moment in French history when the people, theretofore in a serial relation to the landowners and tax gatherers and court nobility of the Bourbon monarchy, realized that they could make common cause against their oppressors. The group that stormed the Bastille was an active group in fusion in Sartre's sense (*ibid.*: 381).

As that example shows, a group in fusion can be an effective force; it acts as if it were a single subject rather than a multiplicity of subjects. However, the introduction of a plural or collective subject poses an ontological conundrum – where do we take this subjectivity to be lodged? In the individual case the subject's body can be taken (in the first instance unproblematically – establishing this point would take us beyond the limits of this chapter) as his or her route to agency in the physical world, but it is one thing to fuse subjects into one group, quite another to fuse their bodies into one body. It seems that we have not quite succeeded in making an ontological ascent any further than the level of the triad of subject, Other and Third, or some purely arithmetical multiple thereof. On the one hand the group clearly has the effect it does because it acts in unison, and yet on the other this united action requires the separate participation of each member. Every one contributes to the cause; but anyone can betray it. Sartre's answer to this puzzle is to have all confer power on each – if I join with ninety-nine others to attack the Bastille, I do so with the strength of a hundred (*ibid.*: 393).

The sworn group

If I act with the strength of a hundred I can only succeed if the other ninety-nine actually play their part. At the stage of the group in fusion this principle is implicit – in the excitement of the moment we are carried along together without stopping to formalize our relations to one another. But over the longer term something more stable is needed. Groups of all kinds begin to form under all kinds of circumstances; some are short-lived and dissipate, but some may undergo a metamorphosis into something more permanent. Not uncommonly strangers who happen to be thrown together by some extraordinary circumstance – for example survivors of an accident or a blackout or a storm – organize themselves spontaneously into a functioning unit, taking care of the injured, sharing supplies and so on while waiting for relief. It may happen that when help arrives they find that this common experience has created something of value between them, and perhaps they promise to meet on the same day the following year, even every year from then on, to commemorate the event. Perhaps they actually do so, perhaps not – the point is that the commitment they are making turns the momentary group in fusion into something else. Sartre's example of this stage of the process is the Tennis Court Oath (Sartre 1976a: 419, 467), a mutual commitment made by some five hundred commoners or members of the Third Estate, who found themselves locked out of a meeting of the Estates-General in 1789, to the effect that they would meet together and continue to meet together until a new constitution had been written. This pledge transformed the group in fusion, which came together outside the locked doors and went looking for a place to meet, into what Sartre would call a "sworn group". This description would also fit, for example, the group of American patriots who had met in Philadelphia thirteen years earlier and pledged their lives, fortunes and sacred honour to the foundation of an independent nation.

The act of swearing or pledging to one another introduces a solemnity that may have far-reaching consequences. With some melodramatic flair Sartre introduces at this point the concept of "fraternity-terror": I promise my brothers that I will be faithful to our cause, and I authorize them to kill me if I fail in this commitment (*ibid.*: 427ff.). Not all sworn groups operate under such dire expectations – but at this point all that holds the group together is the word of each member. Note that the member, even having taken the oath, remains a free individual and does not become merely a function of the group, so the vertigo of freedom familiar from *Being and Nothingness* is still operative: the group depends on me, but the possibility remains that I may let it down.

The statutory group (the organization)

Up to this point the group does not have internal structure. But it seems desirable to formalize the mutual commitment of the members, so as to guarantee some kind of permanence. This is the stage, then, at which statutes may be drawn up and offices created (Sartre 1976a: 446ff). The group acquires a name, even a letterhead; members are designated as such and not merely self-selected; someone keeps a list, perhaps with dates of admission; an annual or other periodic meeting is scheduled, notices are sent out, attendance is recorded. The group acquires a stated purpose, which is spelled out in a constitution and by-laws. Members are recognized by other members with whom they have had no previous acquaintance, and by outsiders as belonging to the group, something that may arouse expectations or confer prestige. The variety here is endless: newsletters, badges, dinners, excursions, fund drives and the like; officers are elected to lead policy-making, receive and invest and disburse funds, keep records and archives. Groups may be small or large, short-lived or long-lasting, local or regional or national or international. What they have in common is the potential for totalization, the uniting of multiple individuals into a totality, which from the outside takes on solidity and objectivity. On the inside the member has acquired a new form of being, a "being-in-the-group"; each member is on the one hand a Third for all the others, constituting them as the group they are, and on the other at the same time an element of the group constituted by all the other members as reciprocal Thirds.

I should note here that the succession of stages is not as simple or as sequential in Sartre's own text as I am making it here. In the *Critique* this development occupies some 600 pages, and the process is far from linear.

The institution

The statutory group is an organization but not yet an institution – it has structure but not standing in a larger context. We might say that the development so far applies to self-contained social groups, which are not necessarily thought of as rivals, or as claiming dominance with respect to other groups, or as having histories other than internal ones in a relatively local context. But as has been clear from the beginning – given that Sartre' s examples of the group in fusion and the sworn group are drawn from the French revolutionary period – group formation has a potentially political role. The revolutionaries of 1789 were up against an entrenched institution and had as their aim the overthrow of that institution and its replacement by another. "Politics" so-called may be evident even in the petty squabbles among members of small local groups of limited scope, but this does not give them institutional standing. At the other end of the scale the state itself has the structure of an extended, ramified and inclusive statutory group, which is essentially institutional. The transition from statutory group to institution is not obviously marked by a discrete step – in this case (as indeed in the whole development of the theory) the group structure is idealized and does not always map neatly on to actual historical situations. What is "political" about the state is its claim to dominate and administer the polis. Just as in "state-of-nature" theories of the emergence of moral communities, Sartre's group theory would not hold that any actual state has come into being by an ascent from singular existential subjects via the various stages of group formation outlined above (Sartre 1976a: 635ff.); indeed the emergence of revolutionary groups depends on the prior existence of a fully formed state against which to engage in a dialectical confrontation, a state that is the result of historical processes bearing no resemblance to such an ascent. And yet Sartre's analysis would remind us that the institution reached by this point in the development still consists of individual subjects whose relations to one another exhibit just the features of the interpersonal praxis envisaged in his theory.

The return of seriality and the dialectic of history

Remembering that the group, even in its institutionally developed form, consists of individuals not wholly defined by their membership in it, prepares us for the next stage of the argument. For the institution, which evolves over time into an ossified form of statutory group, carries within it the seeds of its own dissolution. The political or administrative leadership becomes remote from the rank and file, whose members awaken one day to the realization that they are not in fact true elements of the group, but stand in a serial relationship to its leaders. They organize into a new group in fusion within the institutional structure, and by the now familiar development into sworn group and then statutory group emerge as a force capable of challenging the leadership. This for Sartre is, *mutatis mutandis*, the pattern of history, the dialectic of power. Movements, parties, governments, states, alliances – with time individuals and groups follow cycles in which revolutionary groups displace sitting governments, if only to become oppressors in their turn, and in their turn to be overturned by new revolutionary groups.

The weakness in this account, as Sartre very well realizes, is that it confines the revolutionary process to a relatively narrow domain, which is intelligible and even (dialectically) rational, but ignores lateral effects arising in other domains. The pattern evolves predictably over time until it is disrupted by an incursion from without. In a striking passage in the *Critique* there is a vivid account of a football game, which exhibits a pattern of praxis that is at once competition and cooperation between the members of the team, and leads to an elegant and satisfactory outcome – but then Sartre in a footnote reminds us that in a real football match everything is complicated by the presence of the opposing team (Sartre 1976a: 473, n. 35). There are forces at work in history that do not lend themselves easily to clarification by dialectical reason.

Can we hope, then, to come finally to the history we envisaged at the beginning as the culmination of the collective achievement of humanity, having followed a rational trajectory from existential awareness to world unity? There turn out to be two serious obstacles to this project. If history is to be the history of humanity, then there must be an intelligible entity designated by "humanity" as a whole for it to be the history of. By the end of his life Sartre had concluded that the history of one man – in his case Gustave Flaubert – worked out in the most painstaking detail, would still remain necessarily incomplete. The life of the existential subject, in its relations to its body, its proximate and remote Others, its work, its epoch, comprises riches enough to exhaust the industry of the most gifted historian. How then to do justice to the aggregate of mankind, how to bring it to any sort of focus as an object of world history? Sartre's eventual conclusion is that "Humanity is not" (Sartre 1993c: 403) – there is nothing unified or integral to constitute the subject of history. History is a series of brief sketches, each dealing with a broken-off chain of events whose governing principle is nothing more or less than the production of the human by the human, via local practice for limited ends.

The failure of totalization

To repeat, then – the first obstacle to a totalizing history on a world scale is the absence of a subject. The second is the absence of a historian. We saw how a Third is necessary to unify the couple as seen from the outside, and how a project of totalization is a possibility for every group. But who is to effect this totalization? A couple may of course have an internal history without a Third, and one might imagine this to be generalizable, although the degree of common feeling and understanding required would be entirely implausible for a group of any size. On a higher level of complexity – for example a conflict between two nations or classes – one could also imagine a historian emerging from within one side or the other, rather than taking the position of the Third (or in the case of large-scale historical developments the position of a totalizer). But such a historian would run the risk of partiality, or would – if able to maintain an impartial distance – become in effect an external totalizer after all. Sartre is aware of the difficulty of telling the story of the revolution from within, but in order to keep alive the idea of a universal history while avoiding the need for an external vantage-point he sometimes resorts to the concept of a "totalization without a totalizer". This conceit however runs into the problem that Kierkegaard so long ago commented on with respect to the Hegelian system: there was no room in the system for Hegel; totalization means being seen as a whole from someone's point of view.

This does not mean the failure of the group project. In this chapter we have followed a trajectory from the individual subject, via various group formations, to the recursive pattern of history – and the failure to reach unity or totality. This leaves the individual in the sovereign position from which he or she began. Sartre sometimes characterizes the historical forces that are at work in a given epoch as the objective spirit of the times, but he realizes that such an abstraction breaks the connection with the real agents of history: "the objective spirit ... exists in act only through the activity of men and, more precisely, through that of individuals" (Sartre 1993c: 41). The theory of groups was developed with an eye to a Marxist interpretation of history, but in the end even Marx gives way to an existentialist interpretation: "there are only human beings and the relations between human beings" (*ibid.*: 41).

Nevertheless the theory throws often-penetrating light on the nature of those relations, which is why it counts as one of the enduring elements of Sartre's philosophical legacy.

Further reading

Blenkinsop, S. 2012. "From Waiting for the Bus to Storming the Bastille: From Sartrean Seriality to the Relationships that Form Classroom Communities". *Educational Philosophy and Theory* 44(2) (March): 183–95.

Cannon, B. 2005. "Group Therapy as Revolutionary Praxis: A Sartrean View". In *Sartre Today: A Centenary Celebration*, A. van den Hoven & A. Leak (eds), 133–52. New York: Berghahn Books.

Caws, P. 1979. *Sartre*, especially chapters VII, X and XI. London: Routledge & Kegan Paul.

Rae, G. 2011. "Sartre, Group Formations, and Practical Freedom: The Other in the 'Critique of Dialectical Reason'". *Comparative and Continental Philosophy* 3(2) (November): 183–206.

SEVENTEEN

Sartre's second or dialectical ethics
Thomas C. Anderson

When Jean-Paul Sartre died in 1980, some in the French press called him the moral conscience of post-war France. In fact, in an interview he gave towards the end of his life, Sartre himself stated that he had always been a "moral philosopher" and also that he had attempted to write three different ethics in his lifetime. Of course, ethics was just one of his many interests. His exceptional talent led him to write plays, novels and short stories, works on psychology and political theory, ontology, philosophy of history, philosophy of art and philosophical biographies. Nevertheless, I believe that his interests in moral philosophy and moral values were at the centre of his life and constituted the underlying substructure (to use a Marxian term) of his life and works. One reason I say this is because almost from the beginning his ethics was humanistic in that he identified the goal of morality and the goal of human existence.

This chapter is primarily devoted to what Sartre himself designated as his second "realistic" ethics, thereby contrasting it with his first "idealistic" ethics. The latter was the one he promised at the end of *Being and Nothingness* and worked on for well over a decade. He eventually came to believe that this ethics, based on the ontological categories set forth in that early phenomenological ontology, was too far removed from the real world in which human beings existed. Although this chapter focuses on his second ethics, the fact is that in the writings of Sartre relatively few pages are devoted to it. Almost the only source we have is 165 pages of handwritten notes that were a lecture he gave in Rome in 1964. But even if we had more, it would still be very important that we understand a number of the basic concepts and ontological foundations of the first ethics in order to appreciate why he became so dissatisfied with it that he set it aside and attempted the second. As we shall see, there are significant and radical differences between these two moralities and they are rooted in the fundamentally different ontologies on which they are based.

Ontological foundations

From his earliest philosophical writings, Sartre sharply divided all reality into just two realms. This culminated in his distinction between being-for-itself and being-in-itself, set forth in detail in his major work of phenomenological ontology *Being and Nothingness* in 1943. Being-for-itself, human consciousness, is described as non-substantial and contentless ("total emptiness"; BN1: xxxii; BN2: 12). It is nothing but a web of all kinds of intentional conscious acts in relation to objects. It is "all activity, all spontaneity" (BN1: xxxv; BN2: 15), "self-determining", "self-activated", "cause of itself" and, therefore, free (BN1/BN2: introduction). Being-in-itself, on the other hand, is described as passive and inert. It is thoroughly identical with itself and filled with being. It is nothing but a full positivity of being, which contains no nonbeing and so "does not enter into any connection with what is not itself". It simply "is itself", "glued to itself" and so "isolated in its being". Thus being-for-itself and being-in-itself are "absolutely separated regions of being", Sartre asserts (BN1: xxxix; BN2: 19). One consequence of their separation is that being-for-itself is totally free from any influence of being-in-itself. Human consciousness is not affected by the being it is aware of; its relation to being is totally negative.

Sartre implies that his definitions of the characteristics of these two regions of being are the result of a phenomenological analysis, that is, are conclusions of careful reflection on and descriptions of the phenomena of consciousness and of its objects. I must confess that I consider that very implausible. But what is even more problematic in his analysis is that throughout *Being and Nothingness* he often without explanation simply equates being-for-itself, human consciousness, with human reality itself or "man" and freedom. Accordingly, when we turn to his most extensive treatment of freedom and its relation to other things (part 4), we find Sartre insisting not only on the total freedom of consciousness but also of human reality! He argues that consciousness/human reality is free because it can always transcend what is and grasp what is not, for example, non-existent goals or ideals. Every conscious act, he says, "is a projection of the for-itself towards what is not, and what is can in no way determine by itself what is not" (BN1: 435–6; BN2: 457). And he proceeds to identify this freedom with the freedom of human reality: my freedom "is very exactly the stuff of my being ... freedom is not a being; it is the *being* of man" (BN1: 439). He minimizes to the point of denial any limitations of human freedom referring to it as "absolute", "total", "infinite", and "without limits" (BN1: 435–41, 530–31, 549). "Man can not be sometimes slave and sometimes free", he asserts, "he is wholly and forever free or he is not free at all" (BN1: 441; BN2: 463).

Such a view of human reality and human freedom is for the later Sartre, the author of *Critique of Dialectical Reason* volume 1 (1960b, 1976a), far too "abstract" and "irreal" (his words). It is not the real freedom of concrete human beings who are thoroughly immersed in and conditioned by the natural and social worlds, which worlds inevitably restrict them to "a strictly limited field of possibilities". A major reason Sartre labels his second ethics "realistic" is because it accurately recognizes the dialectical character of human relations to the world. That is, there is mutual interaction and causation between humans and the world. This occurs because in the *Critique* and later works, human reality is described not simply as a free consciousness (or being-for-itself) separate from nature or the things of the world but as a completely material organism. Sartre characterizes his position in the *Critique* as a "monism of materiality" and a "realistic materialism" (Sartre 1976a: 29, 181). What distinguishes the human organism from all others, he says, is its consciousness, which, however, he no longer describes as non-substantial or pure spontaneous self-determining activity. Rather man is "wholly matter", he insists (*ibid.*: 180). We are made up of the very same physical atoms and molecules as any other material thing. Like any organism the human is a synthesis of parts that is threatened by all the things in the world which can dissolve or destroy it. Furthermore, the organism's maintenance and growth is thoroughly dependent on and dialectically conditioned by the material world and other material organisms to satisfy its many needs. Indeed, it is the organism's urge to satisfy its needs that initiates all of its actions on its environment.

Yet human consciousness is still considered by Sartre to be free because of its ability to go beyond or transcend every situation. It can in his words "negate", "deny", "wrench itself from" what is present in any given situation towards what is not – such as a not now existing goal or imaginary ideal (*ibid.*: 70–71, 83–8, 97, 422, 549). As we noted, however, human freedom is restricted by the natural and social milieu in which it exists, sometimes severely.

To conclude this section, let us note that since Sartre's early and his later ontologies have such fundamentally different conceptions of the nature of human reality and its relations to the world, it will not be surprising that Sartre's first and second moralities which are based on these respective ontologies will themselves differ significantly. As a first step toward grasping these differences, I turn next to consider what each ethics takes to be the ultimate foundation of human values and goals. After all every ethics, whatever its ontological base, is concerned with values (BN1: 626; BN2: 646).

The nature and source of values

In *Being and Nothingness* Sartre states unequivocally that the human being "is the being by whom values exist" and more precisely that "his freedom [is] ... the unique source of values" (BN1: 627; BN2: 647). He is equally clear on the devastating impact this position has on ethics. If human freedom makes values exist, then this "paralyses" and "relatives" ethics, for it means that no values exit objectively or apart from human freedom. Rather, whatever one freely chooses to value, whether love or hate, freedom or slavery, torture or kindness, will be of value. "My freedom is the sole foundation of values", he writes, and so "nothing, absolutely nothing justifies me in adopting this or that particular value, this or that particular scale of values" (BN1: 38; BN2: 62). I cannot appeal to any objective values to justify my actions for there are none and any morality which tries to set forth objective norms of human conduct is doomed from the start.

Sartre's argument for this position is as follows. Values are experienced as imperatives or norms. As such they are not being but are "beyond being"; they are not something that is but something which should be brought into being. As imperatives and norms, values are experienced not as something real but as requirements and demands to be made real. Since values are beyond what is, their reality can be due only to a being that is able to transcend what is and posit what is not. Such a being is, of course, human reality and values are precisely that towards which every human being surpasses what is.

As in the first ethics, Sartre in his second or dialectical ethics considers values to be imperatives or norms or obligations that we experience as requiring our adherence. They are not descriptions of facts but prescriptions for conduct (Sartre 1964b: 41, 65, 69, 72). In contrast to his first ethics, however, in his dialectical ethics Sartre insists that there is a "given", "assigned", even "imposed" (his words: *ibid.*: 67, 98, 145) character to moral values and goals. That is because he now believes that "the root of morality is in need" (*ibid.*: 100; see also 87–98). Needs, he explains, are not just a lack of something, they are felt exigencies, felt (at least obscurely) demands to be satisfied. Because we have various needs which demand their satisfaction, we experience certain objects (for example, food, health, knowledge and love) to be valuable and thus to be things we feel we should obtain. In other words, because we are specific kinds of organisms with specific needs, certain kinds of objects are necessary to satisfy these needs. Since we do not freely choose the needs we have, we cannot freely choose the kind of things that fulfil those needs. It is not up to an individual's free choice, for example, whether oxygen or knowledge or love fulfil his or her needs and are thereby of value for them. Thus, by making human needs rather than human freedom the source of moral values, Sartre's second dialectical ethics grants them a certain objectivity, that is, an independence from human freedom – for it can neither create nor remove their value. Oxygen and love have value for me whether I choose them to have it or not. And, again, because they are of value I experience them as something that should be attained.

The goal of ethics

The foregoing considerations naturally lead to a consideration of the primary value or ultimate goal Sartre posits for each of his two moralities. In this section we will also discuss the reasons (in other words, the justification) he offers in each ethics for proposing the respective goal he does.

The goal of Sartre's first ethics is freedom. He speaks of it as "the reign of human freedom" (Sartre 1988: 198), which is also the city of ends where each person treats the other as an end. This city is identified with a socialist, classless society "where freedom is valued as such and willed as such" (Sartre 1992: 418; 1988: 192). In one sense this is perfectly straightforward because, as we have seen, at this time Sartre often identified human reality with freedom. To propose freedom as our highest value is simply to propose human existence as our highest value. There is a serious problem with doing so, however, namely, Sartre's total subjectivism when it comes to values. If all values are human creations why not propose that humans value power or pleasure or, for that matter, world domination or destruction as their supreme goal/value? Why single out freedom?

Sartre's cryptic argument in his lecture *Existentialism and Humanism* involves an appeal to "strict consistency" (Sartre 1973: 51), both logical consistency and consistency with reality. Since human freedom is the only source of value in Sartre's universe, it is logical and consistent with the way things are that it be chosen as one's primary value. Once I realize that any value I confer on anything (such as my and others' lives, socialism, pleasure) comes from my freedom, the rational thing to do is to first and foremost value that freedom. It would be both logically inconsistent and inconsistent with the way things are not to do so. I must say that I believe Sartre's argument is a good one – but only if one first chooses to confer value on logical consistency and consistency with reality. Since in his early ontology, nothing possesses any intrinsic or objective value, there can be no logical or moral requirement for one to choose to value consistency. That choice simply cannot be justified without begging the question.

Even if one overlooks that problem, it remains very unclear what exactly it means to choose freedom as one's highest value and goal. Removing obstacles and limitations to freedom is one thing but what is liberated freedom for – for more freedom – for who or what? Surely not for just anyone and anything. Sartre clearly supports the oppressed and wretched of the earth, not their oppressors. But his justification for that preference remains unclear. Actually, this criticism is Sartre's own complaint that his first ethics was too abstract and irreal (idealistic).

The goal of the second, dialectical ethics is significantly more real and richer in content. Recall that in this ethics Sartre maintains that all values arise not from human freedom but from human needs. Given this connection it is not surprising that the ultimate value and goal of this ethics is not a vague freedom but human fulfilment, that is, the satisfaction of human needs, also called "human plenitude … the fully alive organism" and "integral man" (Sartre 1964b: 55, 95). Of course, human fulfilment does demand the attainment of freedom, our need for freedom is certainly one of our most fundamental needs, but a human organism has many other important needs. Sartre mentions our basic needs for protein, for vitamins, for life itself. He especially emphasizes our needs for knowledge, for culture, and for the love and valuation of others, as well as for a meaningful life (*ibid.*: 63, 66, 77, 81, 97–101, 132–5, 164). Because the goal of his dialectical ethics has far more content than the abstract freedom of his first ethics, it is, he suggests, able to be more specific about the type of acts or policies that are morally desirable – namely, those which promote the fulfilment of the varied needs of the human organism. Accordingly, in the second ethics Sartre states that he is attempting to set forth not an abstract morality but one that is also a praxis in the world, that is, a moral theory that can put forward both the ultimate value which human beings should seek (namely, human fulfilment) and also suggest, at least in general, what should be done to our particular capitalistic social, economic and political structures to achieve that end. Morality is something lived, he asserts, and at bottom it may be that morality and politics are one and the same.

In works after the Rome lecture, especially those after the French student and worker uprisings of 1968, Sartre argues for a society without hierarchies or classes, that is, one without power concentrated in an elite few. Instead of a ruling class, or state, he wants complete equality, a government by the people in the fullest sense. This will require the abolition of the division of labour, which, he believes, gives rise to narrow specialization and class distinctions. All people should have the right to participate in the economic, social and political governance of their country through "organs of decentralized power in work and in the entire social domain" (Sartre 1974c: 108). In the economic sphere these organs would involve collective ownership and management of the means of production, such as, the factories, mines, media, banks and other social-economic institutions. In the political sphere, Sartre advocates direct democracy, a society where the masses unite to express their wishes effectively. Even if a direct democracy takes a representative form, he wants a new system in which, for example, a representative elected by 5,000 people would be "nothing other than 5,000 persons; he must find the means for himself to be these 5,000 people" (*ibid.*: 307). Direct democracy would involve "popular" courts, that is, a judiciary chosen by the people, similar to those that arose in France in the late 1960s. At that time workers in factories and mines set up people's courts and publicly staged trials of their bosses and owners (Sartre participated in some of those courts).

Even in a direct democracy the implementation of policies may be the task of a smaller number of experts. But those experts must always be guided by the masses and return to them to make certain of their support. Even though he continues to refer to his ideal as socialism during this period, it is clearly a decentralized, debureaucratized and democratized version. And, the major advice Sartre offers to achieve this socialism is that one must join with the oppressed masses in their moral fight for liberation.

Finally, let me point out that what Sartre wants for his dialectical ethics, an ethics that is also a politics, would require detailed study of the socio-economic-political structures of the society in which we live – a gigantic task that would take the collaboration of many disciplines. That is the kind of thing he himself attempted to some degree in his analyses of French colonialism in Algiers, the Soviet Union and Stalinism in the twentieth century, French history in the nineteenth and twentieth centuries, the French Indochina and Vietnam wars, and the Czechoslovakian spring to mention just a few.

We still need to address the justification Sartre offers for proposing the fulfilment of human needs or integral man as the ultimate value and goal of his second ethics. The answer lies in the ontological structure, the needs, of the human organism: "Need posits man as his own end" (Sartre 1964b: 100), he writes. In the Rome lecture Sartre cryptically cites Marx who, he says, states that "need does not necessitate any justification" (*ibid.*: 98). The very fact that our needs demand to be satisfied makes their satisfaction our primary value and goal. We do not need to come up with reasons to justify seeking that goal which is required by our needs. Indeed, we are not free to decide what our ultimate end and primary value is. We are organisms with needs and so our ultimate end/value, human fulfilment, is "given", "assigned", even "imposed" on us, Sartre states (*ibid.*: 97–8). We do not need, nor can we find, any reason for valuing this goal other than the fact our needs require it. I believe this is what Sartre means when he cites another statement of Marx, "need is its own reason for its satisfaction" (*ibid.*: 97). It simply does not make sense to ask for reasons why we should choose human fulfilment as our ultimate value/goal. To demand such reasons is to seek what cannot be given, since there is no value/goal more fundamental than human fulfilment to which one could appeal to justify choosing it.

Human relations

One of the most important human needs that Sartre cites – especially in his last major work, *The Family Idiot* (Sartre 1971–2) – is for the affection and approval of other people. His early view of human relationships, he complained, was far too negative and too individualistic. In *Being and Nothingness* he minimized the power of human beings to affect each other and stressed instead the complete responsibility of each individual for his or her life. He also looked upon other people primarily as dangers to one's individual freedom and in conflict or potentially in conflict with me. "The essence of the relations between consciousnesses", he wrote, "is conflict". He also insisted that one can relate to another only as a free subject to an alienated object or vice versa: "one must either transcend [objectify] the other or allow oneself to be transcended [objectified] by him" (BN1: 429; BN2: 451).

I must hasten to add, however, that his early, posthumously published *Notebooks for an Ethics* (Sartre 1983b, 1992) shows clearly that Sartre moved very quickly beyond this negative position even in his first ethics. In *Notebooks,* which were written in the late 1940s, he stresses the importance of intersubjective relations of "authentic" love, friendship and generosity and makes it clear that the conflictual relations presented in *Being and Nothingness* were never meant to be taken as the only possible human relationships. In an explicit reference to that early work he asserts that one is able to transform the "hell" of human relations described there (Sartre 1992: 9, 20, 499) and that human beings can relate to each other primarily as subject to subject (*ibid.*: 418, 500). Furthermore, as we have already pointed out, Sartre's later work, the *Critique of Dialectical Reason* (and even the somewhat earlier *Saint Genet*) provide ample testimony to his recognition of the dialectic in history, in this case the tremendous impact human beings and their social structures have on each other. In fact, he admits that others through the social structures they build may limit the concrete freedom of many humans to almost zero – as in colonialization or slavery. Accordingly, Sartre repeatedly urges human beings to join together in groups in order to most effectively control the socio-economic-political systems they create so that they can be directed to the fulfilment of all, that is, the satisfaction of the needs of all.

Sartre's emphasis on human interdependency is used in another work of his first ethics, *Existentialism and Humanism*, to advance an argument that the freedom we should choose as our primary value is not just our own individual freedom but the freedom of all. "I am obliged to will the freedom of others at the same time as mine", he states. This is because, "In willing freedom, we discover that it depends entirely on the freedom of others and that the freedom of others depends on our own" (Sartre 1973: 51–2). In the practical order, it is obvious that both the range of options available to our free choice as well as our freedom to attain the goals we choose are heavily dependent on the choices and actions of others. Sartre focuses especially on the psychological interdependency of human beings. Only humans can confer value on my life. For me to obtain the fullest possible meaning and value for my life, then, I need other free subjects to freely confer positive value on me. Of course, each person can choose to value his/her life and that is important. Still that is value from only one freedom and, Sartre suggests, I both desire and can attain far more meaning if others also positively value me (Sartre 1992: 282–4, 499–500). Now if I positively value their freedom, instead of ignoring or oppressing it, it is more likely that they will reciprocate with a favourable evaluation of mine. Another suggestion (and it is only that) that Sartre offers is that I particularly want meaning and value given to me by those who *freely* choose to affirm me. Recognition from a vassal or slave is not worth nearly as much as authentic love freely bestowed. Thus I should will others' freedoms so that the value and meaning they freely give to me and my life will be favourable and will be from a source that I myself consider valuable.

I personally think these are solid arguments but I must point out that once again they require that one value logical consistency and consistency with reality, the reality that all value and meaning come from human freedoms. Simply put, Sartre's argument, even though he doesn't say so explicitly, appears to be that it is "inconsistent" for me to desire a fully meaningful life and at the same time not value the many freedoms which are the only sources of meaning and value for my life. But, to repeat my earlier objection, consistency itself possesses no intrinsic or objective value in the early Sartre's ontology. Furthermore, it still remains vague just what it means in the practical order to value the freedom of others. Surely I am not to value the freedom of everyone (including Hitler and Stalin) and support whatever goals they freely choose.

As for the second ethics, although neither in the Rome lecture nor any other later work does Sartre explicitly construct an argument to demonstrate that we should seek the fulfilment of others, not just of ourselves, the notion of human interdependency remains central to his thought. In his last major work, *The Family Idiot*, which he says contains "concrete morality", he emphasizes the needs human beings have for each other, in particular their needs for love.

If an infant is loved by his mother, Sartre generalizes from his study of Gustave Flaubert, he experiences himself to be of value and becomes valuable to himself. "The first interest he [the infant] attaches to his person is derived from the care whose object he is", Sartre writes; "If the mother loves him, in other words, he gradually discovers his being-an-object as his being-loved … [and] he becomes a *value* in his own eyes" (Sartre 1987: 129, n. 2).

Even a human being's awareness that he or she is a free agent capable of acting on the world to fulfil his or her needs is totally dependent on others, Sartre says. We also need the love of others to assure us that we have something worth doing, a mission in life, a reason for being: "Briefly, the love of the Other is the foundation and guarantee of the objectivity of the individual's value and his mission" (*ibid.*: 135). More than any other work of his, *The Family Idiot* describes in great detail the overwhelming need human beings have to be valued and loved by others and thus their complete dependence on each other to achieve human fulfilment. And in no other work did Sartre push human dependency and conditioning so deep, into infancy. In its own way his last major work demonstrates the need to liberate human beings from human relationships and structures that prevent them from becoming fully human – beginning in infancy. Towards the end of his study of Flaubert, Sartre refers to what he calls "true humanism" which he says involves human beings working together to "institute a new order that is proper to man". "True humanism", which is apparently the morality of the second ethics, "*should take these* [needs] *as its starting point* and never deviate from them" (Sartre 1991a: 263–4). Such humanism, he states, can only be built upon our mutual recognition of our common human needs and our common "right" to their satisfaction (Sartre 1987: 413).

Conclusion

I have tried to set forth the characteristics of Sartre's second (dialectical) ethics by contrasting it with his first attempt at ethics. I have argued that Sartre is correct in believing that the second ethics makes significant improvements over the first. Its goal – humans with needs fulfilled – contains far more content than the freedom of all of the first. Also, by rooting human values in human needs it provides them with a more objective character and so overcomes the radically subjective nature that values have in the first. The second ethics also provides a much more solid justification for making human fulfilment its primary value and goal by rooting all values in human needs. The first ethics cannot ultimately justify making the freedom of all (or anything else) its primary value. Finally by its deep account of the human need for love, the second ethics offers a greater understanding of the thorough dependence of human beings on each other and, consequently, their need to seek the fulfilment of the needs of all.

In one of his last interviews, he expressed himself especially forcefully on this point. We must create a society, he states, "in which we can live for others and for ourselves", which requires that we "try to learn that one can only seek his being, his life, in living for others" (Anderson 1993: 172). "In that lies the truth", he adds, "there is no other" (*ibid.*).

Further reading

Anderson, T. C. 1993. *Sartre's Two Ethics: From Authenticity to Integral Humanity*. Chicago, IL: Open Court.
Catalano, J. S. (ed.) 1996. *Perspectives on a Sartrean Ethics*. Lanham, MD: Rowman & Littlefield.
Crittenden, P. 2009. *Sartre in Search of an Ethics*. Newcastle upon Tyne: Cambridge Scholars Publishing.
Stone, R. & E. Bowman 1991. "Sartre's Morality and History: A First Look at the Notes for the Unpublished 1965 Cornell Lectures". In *Sartre Alive*, R. Aronson & A. van den Hoven (eds), 53–82. Detroit, MI: Wayne State University Press.

EIGHTEEN

Hope and affirmation: an ethics of reciprocity

Marguerite La Caze

Jean-Paul Sartre's final ethics of the "we" (or reciprocity) remains controversial and less developed than his other ethics. Scholars have generally accepted the periodization of his ethics into three, as Sartre himself described them: the first ethics of authenticity, the second Marxist or dialectical ethics, and this final ethics, that considers the ontological basis of ethics, based primarily on the 1980 interviews in *Hope Now* (*L'Espoir maintenant*; Sartre 1991b, 1996). It has been suggested that *Hope Now* is not worth discussing as Sartre is expressing his interviewer Benny Lévy's ideas, not his own, and Simone de Beauvoir's distress at their content is well known. However, as Ronald Aronson argues in the introduction to *Hope Now*, we should take Sartre's contribution here seriously and compare it with his other works, in spite of Lévy's insistent questioning based on readings of Sartre's work that are not entirely accurate or charitable. I will focus on Sartre's responses in the interviews, rather than contributions of his interlocutor so that I can reconstruct the lines of his thought. Sartre's comments in these interviews are also consonant with that in other earlier interviews, such as that with Michel Sicard (Sartre & Sicard 1979) and Leo Fretz (Fretz 1980). This article aims to show both the continuity with Sartre's earlier ethics in his responses to Lévy and the potential of the original ideas of the final ethics. My interpretation is that Sartre draws ideas from his earlier ethics, introduces some new ideas, and makes some startling formulations in suggesting the form of an ethics of reciprocity. I will discuss first the basis of the ethics of reciprocity, then the concepts of fraternity and democracy, and finally, Sartre's account of hope and messianism.

The ethics of reciprocity

Reciprocity in *Hope Now* concerns each human being's link to the other, a link that was difficult to envisage in the apparently conflictual conception of human relations in *Being and Nothingness*, where Sartre began from the isolated individual subject. Sartre makes clear that the ethics he is conceiving is different from the spirit of seriousness, criticized in *Being and Nothingness*, which desires being one's own foundation or cause (Sartre 1996: 59). Sartre's ethics of reciprocity provides an alternative to bad faith and conflict between human beings, an alternative that Sartre gestured to and struggled to describe throughout his writings. That conflict arose from incompatible and paradoxical projects to become one's own foundation. Nevertheless, as early as the *Notebooks for an Ethics* (Sartre 1983b, 1992), written in 1947 to 1948, the concept of reciprocity was important because it indicates the recognition of the freedom in situation of the other (Sartre 1992: 285). When Sartre returns to reciprocity in *Hope Now*, he expresses a fuller idea of being together, incorporating the concept of need from his dialectical ethics, where "what I have is yours, what you have is mine; if I am in need, you give to me, and if you are in need I give to you" (Sartre 1996: 91). Reciprocity is the ideal of an ethics where no-one is in lack because of the ethical relation shared with all others and the scarcity of resources has been overcome.

The source of this ethical relation, Sartre argues in *Hope Now*, is an ethical imperative, demand or obligation in our actions. This is an idea familiar from his dialectical ethics, including work then unpublished, such as "Morale et histoire", also known as the Cornell lectures (Sartre 1996: 70; 2005b). Ethics begins from this imperative or requirement. The imperative is seen as an "inner constraint" of our consciousness in everything we do, a must that is an ethical must. The constraint comes from striving to achieve something that goes beyond our present reality. Nonetheless this constraint is not a determining one; we can choose to follow it or not. Sartre sees this imperative as ethical because it involves a sense that things can and should be different from what they are, which motivates us to act. Such a motivation is only the beginning of an ethics, to be sure, but it contains a concept of normativity that can be linked to the ethical, or to our relations with others. In "Morale et histoire" Sartre had linked an unconditional imperative to the norms inherent in every imperative to act; what he describes in *Hope Now* is a link between the imperative and a fundamental bond between consciousnesses.

According to Sartre, ethics is "a matter of one person's relationships to another" (Sartre 1996: 68). In that way, ethics is distinguished from a political or purely communal link that concerns how our relationships are organized or how we form groups. He ties our consciousness with the existence of the other to define the moral conscience. This is what he means by considering the ontological sources of ethics (Sartre & Sicard 1979: 15), a change in his thinking attributed to the indirect influence of Emmanuel Levinas's ethics. We are always in the presence of the other and Sartre lyrically evokes scenes of co-presence in spite of absence: "in the form of an object when I'm alone in my room, in the form of some reminder, a letter lying on the desk, a lamp that someone made, a painting that someone else painted" (Sartre 1996: 71). Our response to this presence, he argues, is ethical because it concerns our relationship with the other. Sartre concedes that this way of thinking is a shift from the relative independence of individuals in *Being and Nothingness* to a concern with the interdependence of human beings, although he had begun to hint at this interdependence even then. Nonetheless, making the primary focus the necessary and basic relation with the other entails a conception of ethics where rather than competing with the other I am fulfilling myself in being ethical. In doing so I have given up pretensions to absolute being, or the desire to be God or my own foundation, and recognized the importance of the other and their bond with me. This change in our projects is the idea of ethical conversion or transformation that Sartre first refers to in *Being and Nothingness* and discusses in more detail in *Notebooks for an Ethics*.

While ethics is distinguished from politics, ethics provides the basis for a revolutionary transformation of society instead of a political or economic theory such as Marxism. This idea is expressed as the discovery of the "true social ends" of ethics that would provide "a guiding principle for the left as it exists today" (*ibid.*: 60), that is, a left that is exhausted and demoralized. The ethical desire is what Sartre calls a desire for society, and not a society with a Marxist economy or the democracy of the French Fifth Republic (*ibid.*: 60). The relations of such a society would be characterized by trust, justice, and generosity, a generosity that cannot be the craze to destroy and possess of *Being and Nothingness* nor the alienated generosity of *Notebooks for an Ethics*. It is rather a pure generosity that is not appropriative or economic and involves a recognition of freedom that comes after the ethical conversion of the *Notebooks*. This ethical society would be one "without power" "because a new form of freedom is established, which is the freedom of reciprocal relations of persons in the form of a we" (Fretz 1980: 233). His claim here articulates the sharp distinction between an ethics concerned with class struggle and an ethics of reciprocity where each person helps the others.

In recognition of the difficulties in reaching the final ethics, Sartre suggests that compromises will be needed, where the context of action and intention is taken into account and we may have to choose different means to our ends (Sartre 1996: 80). This compromise is one way of incorporating the political, yet what he is working towards is an ethics and a situation in which such compromise would not be necessary. The ethical imperative, which is conceived as leading to a situation where all will be generous to others in need, is juxtaposed with our simultaneous struggle against scarcity where there is not enough for everyone. In this sense, we currently have to live the tension between ethics and competition and lack. Sartre also concedes that "violence in certain circumstances is both necessary and justified" although it is the opposite of fraternity, as he understands it here (*ibid.*: 79). In extreme situations, such as that of the colonized in Algeria, violence may be necessary to become an active citizen, even though that is still far from becoming genuinely or totally human. Being an active citizen is only a step along the way to becoming ethical. Here we can see how Sartre is moving away from his dialectical ethics to articulate a more positive picture of human relations than one solely based on scarcity. A clearer picture of the ethics of reciprocity is drawn through Sartre's discussion of the concepts of fraternity and democracy.

Fraternity and democracy

Fraternity in the ethics of reciprocity involves solidarity and dependence. It expresses the ontological connection between human beings that distinguishes the ethics of the we. In this account, unlike in the dialectical ethics, Sartre accepts an understanding of fraternity without terror or uniting against a common enemy. Furthermore, he argues that fraternity must be thought in relation to democracy, as a principle behind democracy. It can be theorized while remaining open about the nature of democracy, although he connects democracy to the idea of mutual freedom (Fretz 1980: 233). Strikingly, Sartre states that "democracy seems to be not only a form of government, or a way of granting power, but a life, a way of life. One lives democratically, and in my view, human beings should live in that way and no other" (Sartre 1996: 83). This focus on democracy continues his concern with radicalizing it as a concept, gives some content to the ethics of reciprocity, and prefigures Jacques Derrida's stress on the same concept and his openness about what democracy means. Earlier, in "Elections: A Trap for Fools" (Sartre 1977b), Sartre argued for direct democracy on the grounds that indirect democracy rendered voters powerless to effect political change.

An important idea Sartre raises in relation to democracy is that we are conditioned by others and so when we vote there is a fundamental relationship that underlies how we think about voting and the vote itself. This relation is one of belonging to a single family in some sense. In a surprising and rather masculinist turn, Sartre refers to an essential relationship of fraternity or unity of human beings, an original "relationship of being born of the same mother" (Sartre 1996: 87). He does not mean this claim literally or biologically but as a way of describing the relationship of fraternity that exists between human beings, an aspect of the human condition. He says it is a truth we feel that is described in myths of a single origin of humanity, such as that in Plato's *Republic*. Sartre distinguishes this idea from equality and also from a principle, contending that "It's the relationship in which the motivations for an act come from the affective realm, while the action itself is in the practical domain" (*ibid.*: 89). In addition to fraternity relating to a common origin, he argues that it concerns a common end.

Sartre modifies his claim that fraternity exists by saying that this feeling will not come about until what he calls humanity, or a truly ethical state, is achieved:

> At that moment it will be possible to say that men are all the products of a common origin, derived not from their father's seed or their mother's womb but from a total series of measures taken over thousands of years that finally result in humanity. Then there will be true fraternity. (*Ibid.*: 90)

Thus, fraternity begins from a feeling and origin, and then is linked to a future goal of total or integral humanity, a goal that is signalled by the ethical imperative. Humanity will be achieved when all our needs, both basic and material, and for meaningful communication and friendly relationships, are fulfilled. This idea of a fulfilled humanity is one Sartre was concerned with for decades, referring to it in the first editorial for *Les Temps modernes*. Given that fraternity and democracy are linked, democracy cannot be genuine without the conditions of fraternity being realized either. The gap between the present situation and an ethical future, a vital issue for understanding his vision of ethics, is one that Sartre theorizes through his uptake of Jewish messianism as a particular expression of hope. This focus on messianism is one of the most controversial features of the interviews with Benny Lévy, yet my judgement is that Sartre transforms the idea of messianism for his own ends and anticipates much contemporary interest in messianism as an articulation of a concept of history distinct from the Enlightenment notion of history as simply gradual progress.

Hope and affirmation

Sartre discusses the question of hope at the beginning of the interviews, stating he believes that hope is part of what it means to be human and inherent in the nature of action in that action "always aims at a future object from the present in which we conceive of the action and try to realize it" (Sartre 1996: 53). Hope concerns our attempt to reach an end, and any particular practical end is meaningful in connection to a transcendent or absolute goal (*ibid.*: 56). This view is one that we can see in Sartre's concept of the fundamental project through which all our smaller projects make sense in *Being and Nothingness*. The further point Sartre makes is that hope survives the non-achievement of our goals, so is not necessarily connected with success. We may fail and still hope, fail and still go on acting. As in Immanuel Kant's work, hope for Sartre is intimately linked with progress, with our gradual awareness through history of the importance of other human beings (*ibid.*: 61). As we become more aware of others, the proper nature of value and of what should be affirmed becomes clear to us. Also similarly to Kant, Sartre conceived of progress as something that could be happening without our being entirely aware of it through fragmentary, limited, positive achievements growing from the midst of our failures (*ibid.*: 66). This possibility is what inspires hope. The end he has in mind is transhistorical and is dependent on finding what is truly human and a way to be and live together as human beings. At present, we are in a kind of less than human state, yet there are elements that could lead towards a more human future. These elements are demonstrated by our best acts (*ibid.*: 69). Sartre does not spell out what he means by our best acts, yet they must be connected with the generosity, justice and trust he mentions elsewhere in the interviews. These are intimations of the future if not inevitable progress. Sartre's affirmation comes from the idea that our relationships with each other will improve and will be important even in that better future.

Nevertheless, unlike Kant, Sartre appears to reject any gradual progression into the future when he discusses what he finds interesting about Jewish messianism. For him, the idea of Jewish messianism is a way of thinking about the future that is not tied to simple progress from the current situation. It suggests a possibility of a different, ethical, future for Jewish people and non-Jewish people alike (*ibid*.: 106). This way of understanding messianism is one that is not tied to a specific religious faith; rather, he is taking the form of the idea of a different future that does not simply extend from our present. The future is surprising, not inevitable, and not predictable. In that future state, ethics will not be concerned with rules and prescriptions, but with the way people "form their thoughts, their feelings" (*ibid*.: 107). Sartre ends with the thought and feeling of hope for the future, a hope that he would like to ground. This image of hope frames his ethical thinking and appears to be what motivated him to continue his struggle to develop an ethics. Sartre died not long after these interviews and so his thoughts concerning the ethics of reciprocity, planned as a book on "power and freedom", remain to be developed by others.

Further reading

Anderson, T. C. 1993. *Sartre's Two Ethics: From Authenticity to Integral Humanity*. Chicago, IL: Open Court.
Crittenden, P. 2009. *Sartre in Search of an Ethics*. Newcastle upon Tyne: Cambridge Scholars Publishing.

NINETEEN

Sartre's legacy
Steven Churchill and Jack Reynolds

Shaping and contesting Sartre's legacy

The shaping of Sartre's legacy began while he was still alive. In part, this was due to a concerted effort from Sartre himself, and from Simone de Beauvoir along with others in his inner circle, to pre-empt posthumous evaluations, both positive and negative. In an extended interview with Pierre Vicary and de Beauvoir that was broadcast in early 1975 on ABC radio in Australia, Sartre was asked by Vicary: "How do you want to be remembered? What would you like your epitaph to be? How do you want people to remember the name Jean-Paul Sartre?". Sartre responded in the following terms:

> I would like them to remember [my novel] *Nausea*, [my plays] *No Exit* and *The Devil and the Good Lord*, and then my two philosophical works, more particularly the second one, *Critique of Dialectical Reason*. Then my essay on Genet, *Saint Genet*, which I wrote quite a long time ago. If these are remembered, that would be quite an achievement, and I don't ask for more. As a man, if a certain Jean-Paul Sartre is remembered, I would like people to remember the milieu or historical situation in which I lived, how I lived in it, in terms of all the aspirations which I tried to gather up within myself. This is how I would like to be remembered.
> (Charlesworth 1975: 154)

One may take issue with Sartre's selection of the literary and philosophical works that he chose in this case to define his legacy; while few

Sartre scholars would dispute the quality of the works cited here by Sartre, some might wonder why he chose these works as definitive of his career and not others.

Yet it is the second part of Sartre's answer that is far more telling. Sartre explicitly asked that if he was to be remembered, he should first be *situated* within a particular historical, social and political context, and be understood as having pursued the possibilities open to him, through concrete action *in situ*. This suggests that Sartre regarded his philosophical legacy as consisting primarily in a philosophy of existence driven by his conceptions of human freedom and of self-creation, and grounded in a concrete situation, to be understood and interpreted at the level of lived experience. Arguably, these themes persisted in one form or another throughout Sartre's philosophical trajectory, although, of course, one may nevertheless distinguish between these ideas as they appear in Sartre's earlier existentialist works, and his later politically driven (and sometimes explicitly Marxist) works.

Given that Sartre gave this interview late in life, we may further infer from his request to be situated in a particular historico-political context, that Sartre hoped his legacy would be understood in explicitly dialectical terms; after all, it was just such a dialectical methodology (combined with insights from psychoanalysis and sociology) that came to define his later thought. Just as Sartre had sought to enmesh his biographical portraits of great French writers (for example, Gustave Flaubert, Charles Baudelaire and Jean Genet) in the broad sweep of history, so too may Sartre be understood here as requesting that the study of his legacy be historically enmeshed in this way.

As for the specific aspirations Sartre tried to "gather up within himself", to use his phrase, we may infer that Sartre hoped his legacy would be defined in terms of his aspirations for a world free of hierarchies and class distinctions, his aspirations for a world unencumbered by self-deception or "bad faith", and so on.

Of course, Sartre understood that in order to concretely situate his philosophical, political and literary legacy, he would have to project a certain *personal* image for posterity, as well. Sartre wanted those who encountered him to take away the message that he was serene, but nevertheless active, in the face of declining health and the looming spectre of death; he was almost totally blind by the time he turned seventy in 1975, after suffering haemorrhages behind his left eye, having been blind in his right eye since three years of age. This meant Sartre could no longer read or write as he had previously, such that he was effectively *forced* to rest from these activities, a state of mind that went entirely against his ferocious work ethic; he also had considerable difficulty walking, even over short distances, and suffered from high blood pressure and heart problems, as well as from the debilitating effects of several strokes. These health woes in later years were primarily caused by Sartre's decades of heavy smoking and drinking, a diet high in saturated fat, and his extreme overuse of Corydrane tablets; these tablets were a once legally available mixture of aspirin and amphetamine (banned as toxic in 1971), which Sartre used both to ward off drowsiness, and to increase the speed of his writing rhythm. The impression that Sartre wanted to give, though, was that the loss of his occupation as a writer, and of his health more generally, did not trouble him too much. In an interview to mark his seventieth birthday in 1975, Sartre had this to say: "I should feel very defeated, but for some unknown reason I feel quite good: I am never sad, nor do I have any moments of melancholy in thinking of what I have lost" (Sartre 1977a).

Certainly, this image of contentedness that was presented to the public by Sartre and his inner circle had some truth to it; Sartre continued to work industriously on various projects right up until his final hospitalization in March of 1980, particularly on a planned book entitled *Power and Freedom*, which he had been formulating for some years. Sartre hoped this book would arise out of taped dialogues between himself and his young secretary, a former Maoist militant turned Talmud scholar by the name of Benny Lévy (also known as Pierre Victor), since he could no longer write such a book on his own. Sartre had far-reaching ambitions for this ultimately never-completed work, describing it as the potential *summa* of all of his prior attempts at an ethics, and at a theory of political engagement. Sartre also continued to participate directly in political affairs until the end of his life, appearing at various rallies with other prominent French intellectuals, including Michel Foucault; Sartre also readily gave his support (both moral and financial) to various groups and causes, with one of his final political interventions being to support a boycott of the Moscow Olympic Games, set to take place over July and August of 1980. Aside from his philosophical and political work, Sartre continued to enjoy the company of others and he took holidays to picturesque locations. All of this suggests that for a good deal of this time, at least, life remained tolerable, and even pleasant, for Sartre. In short, one is left with the impression of a man seeking to make the best of a deteriorating situation, seeking to maximize his possibilities as they began to diminish in ways that were simply beyond his control; arguably, this is the very definition of an existentialist response to the "force of circumstance".

Despite the veracity of much of Sartre's stoic self-image in his final years, however, there was also a good deal of concealment, and even outright deception involved in sustaining this image. Simone de Beauvoir recounts in her memoir of her final decade with Sartre, entitled *The Farewell Ceremony* (alternatively titled *Adieux: A Farewell to Sartre*), that Sartre would frequently lapse into depression, agitation, and even anger at the thought of the loss of his health and his occupation as a writer (de Beauvoir 1988). This picture of Sartre appears at odds with his statements in interviews such as those we have just now considered. In fact, de Beauvoir writes that Sartre would often refer to himself as a "living corpse" (*ibid.*: 74), and that when he moved to a large new apartment with a view of the Eiffel Tower in the mid-1970s, he referred to it as "this dead man's house" (*ibid.*: 73). Adding to Sartre's distress in his final days was the reaction to the release in March 1980 of excerpts of his taped dialogues with Benny Lévy, under the title *Hope Now*. Although Sartre himself was pleased with the excerpts as they were published, those in Sartre's inner circle (and de Beauvoir in particular) were not at all impressed. In *Hope Now*, the views Lévy attributes to Sartre often appear at odds with views that he held throughout his career. For instance, Lévy has Sartre agreeing with the view that Sartre's conceptualization of existential despair was simply a "fashionable" view that he followed because others around him were interested in similar themes, especially readers of Kierkegaard (Sartre 1996: 55). Towards the conclusion of these excerpts, Lévy attributes to Sartre a complete re-orientation in his philosophical perspective, guided by a newfound appreciation for messianic notions. At one point in the dialogue, Lévy exclaims "you are beginning all over again at the age of seventy-five" (*ibid.*: 108). In *The Farewell Ceremony*, de Beauvoir was scathing of Lévy's involvement with Sartre, accusing him of having effectively "abducted" the Sartre she had known and loved, and more generally of having harassed Sartre, forcing him to accept Lévy's ideas as his own (de Beauvoir 1988: 119). For Lévy's part, he continued to insist throughout his remaining years (he died in late 2003) that he never bullied Sartre into accepting a particular position, and that any new developments in Sartre's thought expressed in *Hope Now* were entirely his own. Just as Sartre had shifted from his early existentialism to concrete political engagement, so too, Lévy argued, Sartre had shifted late in life to yet another way of thinking (Cohen-Solal 1987: 519).

However, de Beauvoir simply never accepted Lévy's version of events. So strongly did she object to the views attributed to Sartre by Lévy that, according to Sartre's adopted daughter Arlette Elkaïm-Sartre, de Beauvoir broke down screaming and crying at Sartre in his apartment over his collaboration with Lévy, even throwing the manuscript of the dialogues across the room (*ibid.*: 514). Elkaïm-Sartre recalls that Sartre was visibly shaken by this incident, declaring that he did not understand de Beauvoir; he is also said to have remarked to Elkaïm-Sartre that de Beauvoir – along with other Sartreans – were treating him "like a dead man who has the gall to appear in public" (*ibid.*: 516). For the first time in their lives, Sartre and de Beauvoir were in an apparently severe rupture. So stressful was this episode for Sartre that he spoke with increasing urgency of his next planned vacation over Easter of 1980 to Belle-Île, a French island off the coast of Brittany; presumably, Sartre hoped that the conflict would ultimately "blow over", so to speak. Of course, Sartre never made it to Belle-Île, and the controversy he was engulfed in followed him to the intensive care unit at Broussais Hospital, where he would ultimately die in April 1980. He repeatedly asked his visitors in hospital for news of the reception of *Hope Now*, seeking positive feedback on the text in contrast to the views of de Beauvoir and others (*ibid.*: 519).

In fairness to de Beauvoir, it is not hard to see why Sartre's collaboration with Lévy may have caused her such distress. By undertaking the taping of these dialogues with Lévy, Sartre was wilfully operating outside of the "truth" about his life and works that he and de Beauvoir (along with others) had worked hard over many decades to create. If these divergent views now being attributed to Sartre by Lévy were to gain widespread notoriety, or even acceptance, then the perspective on Sartre and his thought put forward by de Beauvoir in her memoirs, her biographies and so on would no doubt be placed under pressure.

As well as the "professional" motives de Beauvoir may have had in seeking to protect her investment in helping to shape Sartre's image (as well as her own), there is the personal aspect of this conflict to be considered. Previously, when Sartre had sought to put forward his views on his life and works for posterity, he had typically involved de Beauvoir in one way or another. For example, in 1974, Sartre had taped a long series of interviews with her, excerpts from which de Beauvoir pointedly included as an addendum to *The Farewell Ceremony*, as if to say that *these* interviews, and not those recorded by Lévy, reflected Sartre's "real" voice, his true convictions and intentions. Sartre's choice of Lévy as his final interlocutor, though, effectively left de Beauvoir shut out of this final phase in Sartre's life. Moreover, since Sartre and de Beauvoir had always pledged total transparency to one another regarding their relations with others, it must have come as a considerable shock to de Beauvoir to find views so utterly *foreign* to the enduring image of Sartre she had in mind attributed to him in his dialogues with Lévy. Of course, de Beauvoir records in *The Farewell Ceremony* that Sartre expressed love and affection towards her on his deathbed in hospital, and there seems no reason to doubt her version of events in this regard (de Beauvoir 1988: 123). Yet it is not clear that Sartre and de Beauvoir ever truly reconciled over their opposing views regarding Sartre's relationship with Lévy; certainly, de Beauvoir never spoke to Lévy again.

In any case, the distinction at issue between Sartre's "public" image as presented in interviews and through other media, and the "private" image of him as presented through the accounts of those closest to him, demonstrates that Sartre's efforts (and those of his inner-circle) to position him in a particular light both professionally and personally, were never a matter of seamless consensus-building; rather, there was a constant tension between the "public" and "private" images of Sartre, and in the case of the Lévy affair, these tensions were exposed and strained in ways that threatened the very sense of identity of all those involved. Sartre's legacy, then, was not merely collaboratively shaped, but actively *contested* by both Sartre himself and those closest to him. Indeed, Sartre's legacy is still being contested in various ways; he has been variously described as the moral conscience of his age, a supporter of murder and tyranny under Communist regimes, a womanizer, a fighter, a coward, and countless other things besides. For this reason, it is crucial that Sartre's legacy not be regarded as an evaluation of his life and deeds set in stone for all time, but rather as a "live" proposition, that continues to develop in new, and often unexpected directions.

The reaction against Sartre's legacy

The contest over Sartre's legacy, however, meant little (if anything) to the generation of philosophers that succeeded Sartre as the defining "voices" of French philosophy. Rather, the primary concern for Michel Foucault, Jacques Derrida, Jean-François Lyotard and others, in relation to Sartre, was to demonstrate conclusively that they were *not* like Sartre.

Foucault, for example, gave eloquent (if devastating) expression to a negative view of Sartre and his intellectual legacy, the basic contention of which was no doubt held in common with many intellectuals of Foucault's generation, and indeed those of subsequent generations. Foucault characterized the *Critique of Dialectical Reason* (1960b, 1960c), the work that Sartre treasured the most of all his philosophical treatises, in the following terms: "The *Critique of Dialectical Reason* is the magnificent and pathetic attempt of a man of the nineteenth century to think the twentieth century" (Foucault 2001: 541–2).

By attacking the Hegelian–Marxist project underpinning Sartre's *Critique of Dialectical Reason*, Foucault was not simply criticizing a particular work of Sartre's, considered in isolation. Rather, Foucault was attacking the *Critique* as representative of a particular *type* of philosophical work, written by a particular *type* of intellectual – a type which Foucault wanted to confine forever to the nineteenth century. The "type" that Foucault had in mind was that of the "universal intellectual": that is, an intellectual who critiques society and human affairs with recourse to transcendent or otherwise ahistorical principles, such as "freedom", "justice", "authenticity", and so on. For Foucault, any philosophical enterprise underpinned by such transcendental or otherwise ahistorical concepts was fatally undermined by a lack of analysis of the *localized* forces (relations of power, knowledge, etc.) involved in constituting concepts like "freedom", "justice" and "authenticity" as they appear in a particular historical context. In short, Sartre represented an outmoded conception of the intellectual on Foucault's account, who, like a builder trying to create modern housing using old-fashioned tools and materials, could never hope to create a framework capable of addressing the present epoch, let alone the intellectual's place within it.

Derrida, meanwhile, mentioned Sartre only sparingly, particularly in his earlier writings, with "The Ends of Man" (Derrida 1969) and *Glas* (Derrida 1986, first published in 1974) serving as notable examples. Despite the relative scarcity of direct references to Sartre, the negativity of Derrida's polemic against Sartre was no less apparent. In "The Ends of Man", for instance, Derrida criticized Sartre's claim that nothing human is strange to him, because all subjectivities are expressions of freedom; Derrida argued that Sartre had simply substituted one presupposed universal (namely "humanity") for another (namely "free subjectivities") (Derrida 1969: 34–5).

Another criticism of Sartre's methodology that is certainly evoked by Derrida's claim regarding the presupposition of universals, is that by positioning human subjectivity as central to his philosophy, Sartre had *constructed* the very object of his inquiry, by undertaking to investigate it; every account of the subject already constitutes its construction, on this view, meaning that the only productive way to proceed is to rigorously *deconstruct* subjectivity, along with all other such universal presuppositions. In *Glas*, Derrida's intertwined study of Hegel and Genet, Derrida dismissed Sartre's phenomenology as a "misontology", a perspective that allowed Sartre only superficial access to Genet's writing; Derrida instead championed his deconstructionist perspective as allowing for a genuine *immersion* in Genet's texts (Derrida 1986: 28b).

Derrida also discussed Sartre's influence on him in several interviews. In an extended interview in 1983 with Catherine David, for example,

Derrida acknowledged that Sartre had "played a major role" for him in his early philosophical development; however, he then immediately followed this acknowledgement with the assertion that he had since judged Sartre to have been a "nefarious and catastrophic" influence (Derrida 1995: 122). Pressed by David to elaborate, Derrida posed the following question:

> What must a society such as ours be if a man [that is Sartre], who in his own way, rejected or misunderstood so many theoretical and literary events of his time – let's say, to go quickly, psychoanalysis, Marxism, structuralism, Joyce, Artaud, Bataille, Blanchot – who accumulated and disseminated incredible misreadings of Heidegger and sometimes of Husserl, could come to dominate the cultural scene to the point of becoming a great popular figure?
> (*Ibid.*)

Derrida's contention was that Sartre, a man who had made so many mistakes, in his view, had attained the status of a cultural phenomenon in France – a status that could not be explained in terms of genuine philosophical or literary ability (notwithstanding that Derrida does praise *Nausea*, in passing, in a footnote in "Ends of Man": Derrida 1969: 35).

In other words, a deconstruction of Sartre's enduring cultural popularity *in spite* of his intellectual mediocrity (from Derrida's perspective) was of far more interest to Derrida than Sartre's works themselves. These were strong words indeed from Derrida, such that David felt moved to ask him: "So you see in Sartre the perfect example of what an intellectual should not be …?"(Derrida 1995: 123). At this point, Derrida resisted going down Foucault's path of explicitly characterizing Sartre as a negative model of all that was wrong with a certain generation or "type" of public intellectual; "I didn't say that", he replied (*ibid.*).

Nevertheless, it seems clear from his earlier remarks that Derrida viewed Sartre as a vexing, indeed, *bemusing* example of popularity (or perhaps more accurately, notoriety) without substance, and therefore as a negative reflection on a tendency in French cultural life to embrace such superficiality. Derrida's own early investment in Sartre is detailed at length in Edward Baring's (2011) *The Young Derrida and French Philosophy*, and Christina Howells also argues that Derrida's mature work also retains some surprising proximities with dimensions of Sartre's thought (Howells 1991), perhaps suggesting something like an anxiety of influence on Derrida's behalf.

Whereas Foucault had dismissed Sartre as outmoded, and Derrida had regarded him as symptomatic of a culture of rewarding intellectual superficiality, Lyotard turned to irony in critiquing Sartre. In "A Success of Sartre's", Lyotard largely devoted himself to what he regarded as having been Sartre's failures (Lyotard 1986). The titular "success" at issue for Lyotard was Sartre's belated acknowledgement of the role of language in his multi-volume biography of Flaubert, *The Family Idiot* (1971–2). According to Lyotard, Sartre realized in the course of formulating this work, that human subjects (or "transcendences", in Sartre's earlier existentialist terminology) do *not* simply originate meaning and then communicate it transparently with others. Rather, on this view, language has the power to constitute meanings, and to condition subjects in various ways (Lyotard 1986: xx). Although Sartre had by no means explicitly endorsed a structuralist, or indeed, post-structuralist perspective according to Lyotard, he had in fact arrived at a position closely related to these perspectives. On Lyotard's account, Sartre had recognized the "thickness" of words in an ontological sense, and therefore, their power over the subject (*ibid.*: xxii). In other words, Sartre's one real success, in Lyotard's view, was realizing that his existentialist perspective had been *wrong*.

So then, it may seem that Sartre's only significance for subsequent generations of French philosophers was to act as a kind of springboard, as it were, propelling them in new directions. Yet, this view ignores a very important aspect of many post-Sartrean philosophers' intellectual development, alluded to by Derrida in the interview with Catherine David; that is, the fact that many of these philosophers who would later seek to consign Sartre to irrelevance had, at one time or another, been card-carrying Sartreans themselves.

Another prominent example of this journey from Sartrean to Sartre-critic, is Gilles Deleuze. In the 1964 essay "He Was My Master", published in the wake of Sartre's refusal of the Nobel Prize for literature, Deleuze declares that Sartre was his "master" up until Sartre's turn toward a Kantian-inspired humanism in the 1940s (Deleuze 2004: 77). Deleuze writes approvingly of Sartre's *Being and Nothingness*, particularly with regard to the emphasis on conflict and violence in human relations that pervades this work. Deleuze also praises Sartre's earlier work *The Transcendence of the Ego* (1936–7, 1957a), asserting that Sartre's critique of Husserl's conception of the ego as transcendental yields a "pure immanence" of the transcendental field (Deleuze 2004: 102). Deleuze began to move away from Sartre, though, when Sartre attempted to reconcile his existentialist perspective with a humanist ethics of respect for the Other's freedom, a respect which Sartre had previously denounced in *Being and Nothingness*, as an empty platitude. In sum, Deleuze regarded Sartre's earlier existentialism as tough and uncompromising, while regarding Sartre's humanistic existentialism as an insipid attempt to compromise with those who decried Sartre as an "immoralist". Deleuze regarded Sartre as having needlessly re-animated the Kantian "Kingdom of Ends", to the detriment of his renowned radicalism.

Given that Deleuze was by no means alone in his trajectory in relation to Sartre, it would seem reasonable to reassess claims that Sartre's influence on subsequent generations was purely negative; the ways in which subsequent generations of philosophers have been *positively* influenced by Sartre's philosophy, ought to be taken more fully into account.

Returning to Sartre

In considering Sartre's positive influence on philosophy today, we might begin by acknowledging that central elements of Sartre's existential phenomenology in *Being and Nothingness*, *The Transcendence of the Ego* and elsewhere have been an important indirect influence on various interdisciplinary fields concerned with embodied agency and the perception of others. That is because Sartre's early work on the emotions and his chapter on the body in *Being and Nothingness* were a profound influence upon Maurice Merleau-Ponty's own philosophy of the body, which, for a variety of reasons, has become increasingly embraced in regard to debates concerning, for example, embodied and enactive cognition (see Varela *et al.* 1991), as well as J. J. Gibson's work on affordances (Gibson 1977); a negative evaluation of the prospects for projects in artificial intelligence realizing their aims and ambitions on an information-processing or computational model of the mind (see Dreyfus 1997); the extent to which our access to the minds of others (and to particular mental states, like anger) is predominantly inferential or perceptual in nature (Gallagher 2006; Overgaard 2012). In these regards (which are far from exhausting the contemporary interest) it is Merleau-Ponty who has been the phenomenological philosopher whose thought has received the most attention. But not only were many of Merleau-Ponty's insights developed contemporaneously with Sartre in relations of reciprocal influence, but Sartre also offers new resources for all of these debates that have not yet been as influential as they might soon become. While for a long time phenomenological work on embodied agency that affirmed the direct perception of others without intermediary appeared to many Anglo-American philosophers as an outmoded continental reinvention of Rylean-style behaviourism, the kind of anti-representational view proffered differently by Sartre and Merleau-Ponty is now back on the agenda in philosophical psychology and philosophy of mind, as well as associated sciences. Indebted to aspects of Gestalt psychology, their phenomenological accounts of hodological space, embodied motility and agency, the priority of the pre-reflective cogito, the primacy of perception, and so on, have played a significant role in transforming many of the intellectualist, empiricist and Cartesian biases that were dominant for a long time in these fields. Without being able to detail all of the contributions that Sartre's philosophy has already made to such fields, in what follows, the focus will be on the contribution that his theories of intersubjectivity are poised to make, given that developmental psychology and some of the cognitive sciences are under some internal pressure to find and develop new theoretical models.

Of course, it is true that Sartre's work on intersubjectivity is often the subject of premature dismissal. The hyperbolic dimension of his writings on the look of the Other and the pessimism of his later chapter on concrete relations with others, which is essentially a restatement of the "master-slave" stage of Hegel's struggle for recognition without the possibility of its sublation, are frequently treated as if they were nothing but the product of a certain sort of mind – a kind of adolescent paranoia or hysteria about the Other. To some extent this was apparent even in the earliest assessments of *Being and Nothingness*, including a review published by Herbert Marcuse (1948) and in Merleau-Ponty's chapter on other minds in *Phenomenology of Perception* (Merleau-Ponty [1945] 1962). What this has meant, however, is that the significance of Sartre's work on intersubjectivity, both within phenomenological circles and more broadly in regard to philosophy of mind and social cognition, has tended to be downplayed. Not only has Sartre's work been important within the phenomenological tradition, especially in highlighting issues with Husserl and Heidegger's treatments of intersubjectivity (Heidegger himself agreed with Sartre's criticisms of his treatment of *Mitsein* – see Zahavi 2001, fn 7), but even today it promises to make some important contributions in regard to contemporary interdisciplinary work on intersubjectivity. Building on the insights of Hegel, Husserl and Heidegger, Sartre proposes a set of necessary and sufficient conditions for any theory of the other, which are far from trivial. If correct, they would appear to be not only an *obstacle dissipating* solution to the epistemic problem of other minds, rather than an *obstacle overcoming* solution (see Cassam 2007: 2; Overgaard 2012), but also offer some important new insights for contemporary approaches to issues concerning social cognition.

In *Being and Nothingness*, Sartre suggests that various philosophical positions have been shipwrecked, often unawares, on the "reef of solipsism". His own obstacle dissipating solution to the problem of other minds consists, first and foremost, in his evocative descriptions of being subject to the look of another and the manner in which in such an experience we become a "transcendence transcended". On his famous description, we are asked to imagine that we are peeping through a keyhole, pre-reflectively immersed and absorbed in the captivating scene on the other side of the door. Maybe we would be nervous engaging in such activities for a little, given the socio-cultural associations of being a "Peeping Tom", but after a period of time we would be given over to the scene with self-reflection and self-awareness limited to merely the minimal (tacit or non-thetic) understanding that we are not what we are perceiving. Suddenly, though, we hear footsteps, and we have an involuntary apprehension of ourselves as an object in the eyes of another; a "pre-moral" experience of shame; a shudder of recognition that we are the object that the other sees, without room for any sort of inferential theorizing or cognizing. This ontological shift, Sartre says, has another person as its condition, notwithstanding whether or not one is in error on a particular occasion of such an experience (for example, the floor creaks, but there is no-one actually literally present). Our identity is hence experienced as transcending our own self-knowledge, or, to put it differently, one form of self-knowledge depends in a quasi-Hegelian manner on the recognition of the other. While many other phenomenological accounts emphasize empathy or direct perception of mental states (for example, Scheler and Merleau-Ponty), Sartre thus adds something significant to these accounts that seem to focus on our experience of the other person as an object (albeit of a special kind) rather than as a subject. Dan Zahavi suggests that Sartre's approach is distinctive in that:

> The other is exactly the being for whom I can appear as an object. Thus, rather than focussing upon the other as a specific object of empathy, Sartre argues that foreign subjectivity is revealed to me through my awareness of myself qua being-an-object for another. It is when I experience my own objectivity (for and before a foreign subject), that I have experiential evidence for the presence of an other-as-subject. (Zahavi 2001: 158)

In common with other phenomenologists like Merleau-Ponty and Scheler, Sartre also maintains that it is a mistake to view our relations with the other as one characterized by a radical separation that we can bridge with inferential reasoning. Any argument by analogy, either to establish the existence of others in general, or particular mental states, is problematic, begging the question and having insufficient warrant (could Mother Teresa, say, argue by analogy to the mental states of Adolf Hitler?). Does this suggest, then, that Sartre must be a quite radical sceptic about our relations with others? Can we merely deduce the structure of being-for-other from the first-personal experience of shame with little else to go on in our interactions with others? Does Sartre's philosophy leave us haunted by the unknowable other, leaving us with a kind of agnosticism about the other, as Merleau-Ponty says in *The Visible and the Invisible* (Merleau-Ponty [1964] 1968: 79), reprising themes from *Phenomenology of Perception*.

This, however, is not an entirely fair reading of Sartre's philosophy. Notwithstanding the sense in which for Sartre we are perennially "transcended" by the other who eludes our cognitive grasp in important respects, Sartre is actually not a sceptic about our knowledge of other's mental states *tout court*. We can, in fact, viscerally perceive bad faith, on his account. It is nothing other than its expression. This should not surprise us unduly, given that Sartre maintains that the body is a synthetic totality of life and action (BN1: 346; BN2: 370). While bad faith is admittedly a complex form of behaviour, there are other simpler situations in which direct embodied perception is also argued by him to be sufficient for understanding the emotions of others. Indeed, he adds a comment of clear resonance to Merleau-Ponty's own work and that of other phenomenologists who emphasize bodily expressivity and direct perception of others:

> Of course there is a psychic cryptography; certain phenomena are "hidden". But this certainly does not mean that the meanings refer to something "beyond the body" ... These frowns, this redness, this stammering, this slight trembling of the hands, these downcast looks which seem at once timid and threatening – these do not express anger; they are the anger. But this point must be clearly understood. In itself a clenched fist is nothing and means nothing. But we also never perceive a clenched fist. We perceive a man who in a certain situation clenches his fist. This meaningful act considered in connection with the past and with possibles and understood in terms of the synthetic totality "body in situation" is the anger. It refers to nothing other than to actions in the world (to strike, to insult, etc.). (BN1: 346; BN2: 370)

Basically, Sartre maintains there is direct perceptual access to others in emotions like anger, albeit of a different nature to our access to our own anger. Inferential models of our knowledge of others obscure this apparent descriptive fact (it seems that we don't infer, theorize, simulate, etc., when we see the raised and tense fist of an opposing supporter at a football game) and they also make various epistemic assumptions if they purport to show what a justification for our knowledge of others ought to consist in. After all, they tend to assume without argument that all mental states are necessarily hidden and inaccessible, and thus buy into a Cartesian perspective that both Sartre and Merleau-Ponty differently challenge. Moreover, any such inferential and theoretical considerations can only give us the other as a probability or a hypothesis as Sartre suggests, and thus seem peculiarly unable to deal with the apparent epistemic certainty we have in witnessing a given form of anger in context.

Now, it might be thought that any such direct perception view fits uneasily with other aspects of Sartre's work. After all, it is Sartre for whom the perspective of the other eludes and frustrates us in our concrete relations with them, whether that be in regard to love, desire, or anything else. But perhaps there is no incompatibility here. For Sartre, our relations with other people are not conflictual because we are stuck with hypothesizing about others, inferring what it is they are up to in an intellectualist's horror scenario that appears closely related to the actual experience of autism. While the other is given to us directly in their embodiment, for Sartre, their constitutive freedom also means that when we seize on this, or attempt to pin it down as a basis for our own self-knowledge, it is inevitably the other as they were rather than currently are that we grasp. We may even frame some of Sartre's insights in this respect in a more positive way; there is dynamic interaction, a structural coupling, in which self and other solicit each other in a free and unfolding expression that cannot be anticipated or predicted. What we are, and what the other is, is not what we (or they) will be. As he puts it, "The body-for-others is the magic object par excellence. Thus the Other's body is always a 'body more than body' because the Other is given to me totally and without intermediary in the perpetual surpassing of its facticity" (BN1: 351; BN2: 374). Whether this sort of position about the body-for-others should attract the sort of negative valence that Sartre gives it, admittedly quite often, is a question worth asking, but it is arguable that Sartre's necessary and sufficient conditions for a theory of intersubjectivity do not directly entail such a view (indeed, his abandoned *Notebooks for an Ethics* were one notable attempt to show this; Sartre 1983b, 1992).

While phenomenology alone may not be sufficient for a theory of inter-subjectivity as Sartre seemed to maintain, since other resources of a more empirical nature demand to be considered (for example, findings of developmental psychology, cognitive science, etc.), one of the reasons why Sartre's view promises to help contribute to contemporary debates is precisely because his work strongly challenges many of the basic presuppositions of the philosophical and psychological literature regarding social understanding that has dominated since the 1980s. Without summarizing the various psychological results concerning false-belief tests here, it suffices to say that the two dominant approaches in this field and within analytic philosophy – theory theory and simulation theory – remain mentalistic approaches to social cognition that emphasize the importance of mind-reading, as opposed to what we might call body-reading, notwithstanding the behaviourist connotations of such a term. Shaun Gallagher suggests that theory theory and simulation theory, and hybrid versions of them, have four basic assumptions:

1. Hidden minds
… Since we cannot directly perceive the other's beliefs, desires, feelings, or intentions, we need some extra-perceptual cognitive process (inference or simulation) to understand their mental states.
2. Mindreading as default
These mindreading processes constitute our primary, pervasive, or default way of understanding others.
3. Observational stance
Our normal everyday stance towards the other person is a third personal, observational stance. We observe their behaviours in order to explain and predict their actions.
4. Methodological individualism
Our understanding of others depends primarily on cognitive capabilities or mechanisms located in an individual subject.
(Gallagher 2012: 194)

As would be apparent, Sartre's necessary and sufficient criteria for an adequate theory of intersubjectivity contest all of these views. Moreover, pressure has also come on these commitments from within the relevant sciences themselves, perhaps especially in developmental psychology, given the capacity of early neonates to interact and understand intentions, emotions and so on prior to the acquisition of language and the passing of the false-belief test at the age of four or five.

Nonetheless, the standard approach has been to create hybrid versions of these two dominant perspectives, thus remaining largely guided by the above four basic assumptions. Much more needs to be said about this, but we hope to have done enough in this short discussion to suggest that there are important resources within the phenomenological tradition, and in Sartre's work in particular, for motivating more radical revisions within contemporary work on social cognition, helping to induce something like a paradigm shift in which the theoretical contributions of existential phenomenology has an important role to play.

Of course, the jury is still out in regard to just how fertile such a theoretical pairing might be. It would depend on the dialectical relationship between the given philosophical theory and what is revealed by new empirical investigations that have been shorn of some (arguably) faulty assumptions with which they have laboured. Yet there is at least some evidence that, in regard to embodiment and intersubjectivity, Sartre's early work may well be proved to have been right at the wrong time (which is what Sartre said of Cornelius Castoriadis on certain political questions). Perhaps now, however, it is also the right time for a return to Sartre on these and other issues.

Further reading

Boulé, J.-P. 2005. *Sartre, Self-Formation and Masculinities*. New York: Berghahn Books.

Fox, N. F. 2003. *The New Sartre: Explorations in Postmodernism*. New York: Continuum.

Leak, A. 2006. *Jean-Paul Sartre*. London: Reaktion Books.

McBride, W. L. 1997. *Sartre's Life, Times, and Vision du Monde*. New York: Garland Publishing.

Mirvish, A. & A. van den Hoven (eds) 2010. *New Perspectives on Sartre*. Newcastle upon Tyne: Cambridge Scholars Publishing.

Reynolds, J. & A. Woodward 2011. "Existentialism and Poststructuralism: Some Unfashionable Observations". In *The Continuum Companion to Existentialism*, F. Joseph, J. Reynolds & A. Woodward (eds), 260–81. London: Continuum.

Bibliography

Anderson, T. C. 1993. *Sartre's Two Ethics: From Authenticity to Integral Humanity*. Chicago, IL: Open Court.
Ayer, A. J. 1945. "Novelist–Philosophers v. Jean-Paul Sartre". *Horizon* (July): 12–25.
Ayer, A. J. (ed.) 1959. *Logical Positivism*. New York: Free Press.
Baring, E. 2011. *The Young Derrida and French Philosophy, 1945–68*. Cambridge: Cambridge University Press.
Barnes, H. E. 1959. *Humanistic Existentialism: The Literature of Possibility*. Lincoln, NE: University of Nebraska Press.
Barnes, H. E. 1981. *Sartre and Flaubert*. Chicago, IL: University of Chicago Press.
Barnes, H. E. 1991. "The Role of the Ego in Reciprocity". In *Sartre Alive*, R. Aronson & A. van den Hoven (eds), 151–9. Detroit, MI: Wayne State University Press.
Barnes, H. E. 1992. "Sartre's Ontology". In *The Cambridge Companion to Sartre*, C. Howells (ed.), 13–38. Cambridge: Cambridge University Press.
Barnett, L. & G. Madison (eds) 2011. *Existential Therapy: Legacy, Vibrancy and Dialogue*. London: Routledge.
Baruzi, J. 1931. *Saint Jean de la Croix et le problème de l'expérience mystique*. Paris: Alean.
Bealer, G. 1998. "Intuition and the Autonomy of Philosophy". In *Rethinking Intuition: The Psychology of Intuition and Its Role in Philosophical Inquiry*, M. DePaul & W. Ramsey (eds), 201–39. Lanham, MD: Rowman & Littlefield.
Beebee, B., S. Knoblauch, J. Rustin & D. Sorter 2005. *Forms of Intersubjectivity in Infant Research and Adult Treatment*. New York: Other Press.
Bell, D. 1990. *Husserl*. London: Routledge.
Bergson, H. 1992. *The Creative Mind*. New York: Citadel.
Blenkinsop, S. 2012. "From Waiting for the Bus to Storming the Bastille: From Sartrean Seriality to the Relationships that Form Classroom Communities". *Educational Philosophy and Theory* 44(2) (March): 183–95.
Bollas, C. 1987. *The Shadow of the Object: Psychoanalysis of the Unthought Known*. New York: Columbia University Press.
Boulé, J.-P. 2005. *Sartre, Self-Formation and Masculinities*. New York: Berghahn Books.

Brann, E. 1991. *The World of the Imagination: Sum and Substance*. Lanham, MD: Rowman & Littlefield.
Bromberg, P. 2001. *Standing in the Spaces: Essays on Clinical Process Process Trauma and Dissociation*. London: Routledge.
Bromberg, P. 2006. *Awakening the Dreamer: Clinical Journeys*. London: Analytic Press.
Bromberg, P. 2011. *The Shadow of the Tsunami and the Growth of the Relational Brain*. London: Routledge.
Brombert, V. H. 1961. *The Intellectual Hero: Studies in the French Novel 1880–1955*. London: Faber & Faber.
Busch, T. W. 1990. *The Power of Consciousness and the Force of Circumstances in Sartre's Philosophy*. Bloomington, IN: Indiana University Press.
Camus, A. 1951. *L'homme révolté*. Paris: Gallimard.
Camus, A. 1954. *The Rebel: An Essay on Man in Revolt*, A. Bower (trans.). New York: Alfred A. Knopf.
Cannon, B. 1991. *Sartre and Psychoanalysis: An Existentialist Challenge to Clinical Metatheory*. Lawrence, KS: University Press of Kansas.
Cannon, B. 2005. "Group Therapy as Revolutionary Praxis: A Sartrean View". In *Sartre Today: A Centenary Celebration*, A. van den Hoven & A. Leak (eds), 133–52. New York: Berghahn Books.
Cannon, B. 2009. "Nothingness as the Ground for Change". *Existential Analysis* (July): 192–210.
Cannon, B. 2011. "Applied Existential Psychotherapy: An Experiential Psychodynamic Approach". In *Existential Therapy: Legacy, Vibrancy and Dialogue*, L. Barnett & G. Madison (eds), 97–109. London: Routledge.
Cannon, B. Forthcoming. "Authenticity, the Spirit of Play and the Practice of Psychotherapy". *Review of Existential Psychology and Psychiatry*.
Carnap, R. [1932] 1959. "The Elimination of Metaphysics Through Logical Analysis of Language", A. Pap (trans.). In *Logical Positivism*, A. J. Ayer (ed.), 60–81. New York: Free Press.
Cassam, Q. 2007. *The Possibility of Knowledge*. Oxford: Oxford University Press.
Catalano, J. S. 1974. *A Commentary on Jean-Paul Sartre's Being and Nothingness*. Chicago, IL: University of Chicago Press.
Catalano, J. S. 1996a. *Good Faith and Other Essays: Perspectives on a Sartrean Ethics*. Lanham, MD: Rowman & Littlefield.
Catalano, J. S. (ed.) 1996b. *Perspectives on a Sartrean Ethics*. Lanham, MD: Rowman & Littlefield.
Catalano, J. S. 2010. *Reading Sartre*. Cambridge: Cambridge University Press.
Caws, P. 1979. *Sartre*. London: Routledge & Kegan Paul.
Charlesworth, M. 1975. *The Existentialists and Jean-Paul Sartre*. London: George Prior.
Cohen-Solal, A. 1987. *Sartre: A Life*, A. Cancogni (trans.). New York: Pantheon.
Cohen-Solal, A. 2005. *Jean-Paul Sartre: A Life*, A. Cancogni (trans.). New York: The New Press.
Contat, M. & Rybalka, M. 1981. "Chronologie". In *Œuvres romanesques*, J.-P. Sartre, xxxv–lxi. Paris: Gallimard.
Cox, G. 2009. *Sartre and Fiction*. London: Continuum.
Crittenden, P. 2009. *Sartre in Search of an Ethics*. Newcastle upon Tyne: Cambridge Scholars Publishing.
de Beauvoir, S. 1948. *The Ethics of Ambiguity*, B. Frechtman (trans.). Chicago, IL: Citadel.

de Beauvoir, S. 1954. *Les Mandarins*. Paris: Gallimard.
de Beauvoir, S. 1963. *Memoirs of a Dutiful Daughter*, J. Kirkup (trans.). London: Penguin.
de Beauvoir, S. 1983. *Prime of Life*, P. Green (trans.). London: Penguin.
de Beauvoir, S. 1987. *La Cérémonie des adieux suivie des entretiens avec Jean-Paul Sartre*. Paris: Gallimard.
de Beauvoir, S. 1988. *Adieux: A Farewell to Sartre*, P. O'Brian (trans.). London: Penguin.
de Beauvoir, S. 1989. *La Force de l'âge*. Paris: Gallimard.
de Beauvoir, S. 2001. *The Prime of Life*. Harmondsworth: Penguin.
de Beauvoir, S. 2005. *Philosophical Writings*, M. A. Simons (ed.). Chicago, IL: University of Illinois Press.
de Beauvoir, S. 2006. *Diary of a Philosophy Student, Vol I: 1926–27*. Urbana, IL: University of Illinois.
de Coorebyter, V. 2000. *Sartre face à la phénoménologie*. Brussels: OUSIA.
de Coorebyter, V. 2003. "Introduction". In *La Transcendance de l'Ego et autres textes phenomenologiques*, J.-P. Sartre, 7–76. Paris: Vrin.
Deleuze, G. 2004. *Desert Islands and Other Texts*, F. Guillame (trans.). New York: Semiotext(e).
Derrida, J. 1969. "The Ends of Man". *Philosophy and Phenomenological Research* 30(1): 31–57.
Derrida, J. 1986. *Glas*. Lincoln, NE: University of Nebraska Press.
Derrida, J. 1995. *Points: Interviews 1974–1994*. Palo Alto, CA: Stanford University Press.
Descartes, R. 1988. "Rules for the Direction of the Mind". In *The Philosophical Writings of Descartes*, vol. 1. Cambridge: Cambridge University Press.
Detmer, D. 2008. *Sartre Explained: From Bad Faith to Authenticity*. Peru, IL: Open Court.
Deutscher, M. 2003. "On Lacking Reason for Desire". In his *Genre and Void: Looking Back at Sartre and Beauvoir*, 89–109. Aldershot: Ashgate.
Dreyfus, H. 1997. *What Computers Still Can't Do: A Critique of Artificial Reason*. Cambridge, MA: MIT Press.
Fanon, F. 1963. *The Wretched of the Earth*. C. Farrington (trans.). New York: Grove Press.
Flajoliet, A. 2010. "Sartre's Phenomenological Anthropology between Psychoanalysis and 'Daseinanalysis'". *Sartre Studies International* 16(1): 40–59.
Flynn, T. 1994. *Sartre and Marxist Existentialism: The Test Case of Collective Responsibility*. Chicago, IL: University of Chicago Press.
Flynn, T. 1997. *Sartre, Foucault and Historical Reason, vol.1: Toward an Existentialist Theory of History*. Chicago, IL: University of Chicago Press.
Foucault, M. 2001. *Ditset écrits*, vol. 1. Paris: Gallimard.
Fox, N. F. 2003. *The New Sartre: Explorations in Postmodernism*. New York: Continuum.
Frank, M. 1991. *Selbstbewußtsein und Selbsterkenntnis*. Stuttgart: Reklam.
Fretz, L. 1980. "An Interview with Jean-Paul Sartre". In *Jean-Paul Sartre: Contemporary Approaches to his Philosophy*, H. Silverman & F. A. Elliston (eds), 221–39. London: Harvester.
Freud, S. [1895] 1953–74. *Studies on Hysteria*. Vol. 2 of *The Standard Edition of the Complete Psychological Works of Sigmund Freud*, 24 vols, J. Strachey (trans.). London: Hogarth Press.
Freud, S. [1905] 1953–74. "Fragment of an Analysis of a Case of Hysteria". In his

Three Essays on the Theory of Sexuality. Vol. 7 of *The Standard Edition of the Complete Psychological Works of Sigmund Freud*, 24 vols, J. Strachey (trans.). London: Hogarth Press.

Freud, S. [1916–17] 1953–74. *Introductory Lectures on Psychoanalysis*. Vols 15–16 of *The Standard Edition of the Complete Psychological Works of Sigmund Freud*, 24 vols, J. Strachey (trans.). London: Hogarth Press.

Freud, S. [1920] 1953–74. *Beyond the Pleasure Principle*. Vol. 18 of *The Standard Edition of the Complete Psychological Works of Sigmund Freud*, 24 vols, J. Strachey (trans.). London: Hogarth Press.

Freud, S. [1930] 1953–74. *The Future of an Illusion, Civilization and its Discontents and Other Works*. Vol. 21 of *The Standard Edition of the Complete Psychological Works of Sigmund Freud*, 24 vols, J. Strachey (trans.). London: Hogarth Press.

Freud, S. [1950] 1953–74. *A Project for a Scientific Psychology*. Vol. 1 of *The Standard Edition of the Complete Psychological Works of Sigmund Freud*, 24 vols, J. Strachey (trans.). London: Hogarth Press.

Frie, R. 1997. *Subjectivity and Intersubjectivity in Modern Philosophy and Psychoanalysis: A Study of Sartre, Binswanger, Lacan, and Habbermas*. Lanham, MD: Rowman & Littlefield.

Gallagher, S. 2006. *How the Body Shapes the Mind*. Oxford: Oxford University Press.

Gallagher, S. 2012. *Phenomenology*. New York: Palgrave Macmillan.

Gardner, S. 2006. "Sartre, Schelling, and Onto-theology". *Religious Studies* 42(3): 247–71.

Gardner, S. 2009. *Sartre's* Being and Nothingness: *A Reader's Guide*. London: Continuum.

Gerassi, J. 1989. *Jean-Paul Sartre: Hated Conscience of the Century*. Chicago, IL: University of Chicago Press.

Gerassi, J. 2009. *Talking with Sartre: Conversations and Debates*. New Haven, CT: Yale University Press.

Gibson, J. J. 1977. "The Theory of Affordances", In *Perceiving, Acting, and Knowing: Toward an Ecological Psychology*, R. Shaw & J. Bransford (eds), 67–82. Hillsdale, NJ: Lawrence Erlbaum.

Guignon, C. 2004. *On Being Authentic*. London: Routledge.

Hatzimoysis, A. 2011. *The Philosophy of Sartre*. Durham: Acumen.

Heidegger, M. [1929] 1978. "What Is Metaphysics?". In his *Basic Writings*, D. F. Krell (trans., ed.), 95–112. London: Routledge & Kegan Paul. Originally published in German as "Was ist Metaphysik?".

Heidegger, M. 1962. *Being and Time*, J. Macquarrie & E. Robinson (trans.). London: SCM Press.

Henrich, D. 1967. *Fichte's ursprüngliche Einsicht*. Frankfurt: Klostermann.

Howells, C. 1988. *The Necessity of Freedom*. Cambridge: Cambridge University Press.

Howells, C. 1991. *Derrida: Deconstruction from Phenomenology to Ethics*. Cambridge: Polity.

Husserl, E. 1980. *Ideas Pertaining to a Pure Phenomenology and to a Phenomenological Philosophy*, vol. 1, E. Klein & W. E. Pohl (trans.). The Hague: Martinus Nijhoff.

Husserl, E. 1983. *Ideas Pertaining to a Pure Phenomenology and to a Phenomenological Philosophy*, vol. I, F. Kersten (trans.). The Hague: Martinus Nijhoff.

Husserl, E. 1994. *Cartesian Meditations*, D. Cairns (trans.). The Hague: Martinus Nijhoff.

Husserl, E. 1995. *Cartesian Meditations: An Introduction to Phenomenology*, D. Cairns (trans.). Dordrecht: Kluwer.

Husserl, E. 2001a. *The Shorter Logical Investigations*, J. N. Findlay (trans.). London: Routledge.
Husserl, E. 2001b. *Analyses Concerning Passive and Active Synthesis*, A. J. Steinbock (trans.). Dordrecht: Kluwer.
Jeanson, F. 1980. *Sartre and the Problem of Morality*, R. Stone (trans.). Bloomington, IN: Indiana University Press. Originally published as *Le probleme moral et la pensee de Sartre* (Paris: Editions du Seuil, 1965).
Jones, E. [1953] 1961. *The Life and Work of Sigmund Freud*, L. Trilling & S. Marcus (eds). New York: Basic Books.
Jopling. D. A. 1997. "Sartre's Moral Psychology". In *The Cambridge Companion to Sartre*, C. Howells (ed.), 103–39. Cambridge: Cambridge University Press.
Judaken, J. 2006. *Jean-Paul Sartre and the Jewish Question: Anti-Semitism and the Politics of the French Intellectual*. Lincoln, NE: University of Nebraska Press.
Kant, I. 2003. *Critique of Pure Reason*, N. K. Smith (trans.). Basingstoke: Palgrave Macmillan.
Kaufman, W. 1975. *Existentialism from Dostoevsky to Sartre*. New York: New American Library.
Laing, R. D. [1959] 1979. *The Divided Self.* New York: Penguin.
Laing, R. D. & D. G. Cooper. [1964] 1971. *Reason and Violence*. New York: Vintage.
Larmore, C. 2011. *The Practices of the Self*, S. Bowman (trans.). Chicago, IL: University of Chicago Press.
Leak, A. 2006. *Jean-Paul Sartre*. London: Reaktion Books.
Leibniz, G. W. 1973. "Correspondence with Arnauld". In *Leibniz: Philosophical Writings*, G. H. R. Parkinson (ed.), 48–74. London: J. M. Dent & Sons.
Levinas, E. [1930] 1963. *La Théorie de l'intuition dans la phénoménologie de Husserl*. Paris: Vrin.
Lewis, D. 1983. *Philosophical Papers: Volume I*. New York: Oxford University Press.
Light, S. 1987. *Shuzo Kuki and Jean-Paul Sartre*. Urbana, IL: Southern Illinois University Press.
Lucretius 1940. "On the Nature of Things". In *Selections from Hellenistic Philosophy*, G. H. Clark (ed.), 8–48. New York: Appleton-Century-Crofts.
Lyotard, J.-F. 1986. "A Success of Sartre's". In *The Politics of Prose: Essay on Sartre*, D. Hollier, xi–xxiii. Minneapolis, MN: University of Minnesota Press.
Manser, A. 1961. "Sartre and 'le Néant'". *Philosophy* 36(137): 177–87.
Manser, A. 1981. *Sartre: A Philosophic Study*. Oxford: Greenwood Press.
Marcuse, H. 1948. "Existentialism", *Philosophy and Phenomenological Research* 8(3): 309–36.
McBride, W. L. 1991. *Sartre's Political Theory*. Bloomington, IN: Indiana University Press.
McBride, W. L. 1997. *Sartre's Life, Times, and Vision du Monde*. New York: Garland Publishing.
McCulloch, G. 1994. *Using Sartre*. London: Routledge.
Merleau-Ponty, M. [1945] 1962. *Phenomenology of Perception*, C. Smith (trans). London: Routledge.
Merleau-Ponty, M. [1947] 1969. *Humanism and Terror: An Essay on the Communist Problem*, J. O'Neill (trans.). Boston, MA: Beacon Press.
Merleau-Ponty, M. [1964] 1968. *The Visible and the Invisible*, A. Lingis (trans.). Evanston, IL: Northwestern University Press.
Mirvish, A. & A. van den Hoven (eds) 2010. *New Perspectives on Sartre*. Newcastle upon Tyne: Cambridge Scholars Publishing.

Mitchell, S. A. 2000. *Relationality: From Attachment to Intersubjectivity*. New York: Psychology Press.
Moran, D. 2000. *Introduction to Phenomenology*. London: Routledge.
Morris, K. 2008. *Sartre*. Oxford: Blackwell.
Mouillie, J.-M. (ed.) 2001. *Sartre et la phénoménologie*. Paris: ENS.
Murdoch, I. 1968. *Sartre: Romantic Rationalist*. London: Fontana.
Nietzsche, F. 1993. *The Birth of Tragedy*, S. Whiteside (trans.). London: Penguin.
Nietzsche, F. 2001. *The Gay Science*, B. Williams (trans.). Cambridge: Cambridge University Press.
Noudelmann, F. & P. Gilles (eds) 2004. *Dictionnaire Sartre*. Paris: Honoré Champion.
O'Donohoe, B. 2005. *Sartre's Theatre: Acts for Life*. Bern: Peter Lang.
Overgaard, S. 2007. *Wittgenstein and Other Minds*. New York: Routledge.
Overgaard, S. 2012. "Other People". *Oxford Handbook of Contemporary Phenomenology*, D. Zahavi (ed.), 460–79. Oxford: Oxford University Press.
Priest, S. 2000. *The Subject in Question: Sartre's Critique of Husserl in The Transcendence of the Ego*. New York: Routledge.
Rae, G. 2011. "Sartre, Group Formations, and Practical Freedom: The Other in the 'Critique of Dialectical Reason'". *Comparative and Continental Philosophy* 3(2) (November): 183–206.
Reddy, V. 2008. *How Infants Know Minds*. Cambridge, MA: Harvard University Press.
Reisman, D. 2007. *Sartre's Phenomenology*. London: Continuum.
Reynolds, J. & A. Woodward 2011. "Existentialism and Poststructuralism: Some Unfashionable Observations". In *The Continuum Companion to Existentialism*, F. Joseph, J. Reynolds & A. Woodward (eds), 260–81. London: Continuum.
Richmond, S. 2007. "Sartre and Bergson: A Disagreement about Nothingness". *International Journal of Philosophical Studies* 15(1): 77–95.
Ricoeur, P. 1981. "Sartre and Ryle on the Imagination". In *The Philosophy of Jean-Paul Sartre*, P. A. Schilpp (ed.), 167–78. LaSalle, IL: Open Court.
Roeckelein, J. 2004. *Imagery in Psychology: A Reference Guide*. Westport, CT: Praeger.
Rolls, A. & E. Rechniewski (eds) 2006. *Nausea: Text, Context, Intertext*. Amsterdam: Rodopi.
Rybalka, M. 2000. "Une vie pour la philosophie: entretien avec Jean-Paul Sartre". *Magazine littéraire* 384: 40–46.
Sartre, J.-P. 1936. *L'Imagination*. Paris: Alcan.
Sartre, J.-P. 1936–7. "La Transcendance de l'ego". *Recherches Philosophiques* 6: 85–123.
Sartre, J.-P. 1938. *La Nausée*. Paris: Gallimard.
Sartre, J.-P. 1939a. *Esquisse d'une théorie des emotions*. Paris: Hermann.
Sartre, J.-P. 1939b. "Une Idée fondamentale de la phénoménologie de Husserl: l'intentionnalité". *Nouvelle Revue Française* 304: 129–31.
Sartre, J.-P. 1939c. *Le Mur*. Paris: Gallimard.
Sartre, J.-P. 1940. *L'Imaginaire: psychologie phénoménologique de l'imagination*. Paris: Gallimard.
Sartre, J.-P. 1943a. *L'Être et le néant: essai d'ontologie phénoménologique*. "Tel" edition. Paris: Gallimard.
Sartre, J.-P. 1943b. *Les Mouches*. Paris: Gallimard.
Sartre, J.-P. 1945a. *L'Âge de raison*. Vol. 1 of the Roads to Freedom series. Paris: Gallimard.
Sartre, J.-P. 1945b. *Huis clos*. Paris: Gallimard.

Sartre, J.-P. 1945c. *Le Sursis*. Vol. 2 of the Roads to Freedom series. Paris: Gallimard.
Sartre, J.-P. 1946a. *Réflexions sur la question juive*. Paris: Morihien.
Sartre, J.-P. 1946b. *L'Existentialisme est un humanisme*. Paris: Nagel.
Sartre, J.-P. 1946c. "Matérialisme et révolution". *Les Temps modernes* (June).
Sartre, J.-P. 1946d. *Explication de L'étranger*. Paris: Aux dépens du Palimugre.
Sartre, J.-P. 1946e. *Morts sans sépulture*. Lausanne: Marguerat.
Sartre, J.-P. 1946f. *La Putain respectueuse*. Paris: Nagel.
Sartre, J.-P. 1947a. *Situations, I. Essais critiques*. Paris: Gallimard.
Sartre, J.-P. 1947b. *Baudelaire*, M. Leiris (intro.). Paris: Gallimard.
Sartre, J.-P. 1947c. *L'Homme et les choses*. Paris: Seghers.
Sartre, J.-P. 1947d. *Les Jeux sont faits*. Paris: Nagel.
Sartre, J.-P. 1947e. *The Age of Reason*, E. Sutton (trans.). New York: Vintage. Translated from Sartre 1945a.
Sartre, J.-P. 1947f. *The Reprieve*, E. Sutton (trans.). New York: Vintage. Translated from Sartre 1945c.
Sartre, J.-P. 1948a. *Situations, II: qu'est-ce que la littérature?* Paris: Gallimard.
Sartre, J.-P. 1948b. *Anti-Semite and Jew*, G. J. Becker (trans.). New York: Schocken. Translated from Sartre 1946a.
Sartre, J.-P. 1948c. "Conscience de soi et connaissance de soi". *Bulletin de la Société Française de philosophie* 42(3) (April–June): 49–91.
Sartre, J.-P. 1948d. *Les Mains sales*. Paris: Gallimard.
Sartre, J.-P. 1948e. *Visages; précédé de Portraits officiels*. Paris: Seghers.
Sartre, J.-P. 1949a. *La Mort dans l'âme*. Vol. 3 of the Roads to Freedom series. Paris: Gallimard.
Sartre, J.-P. 1949b. *Nourritures; suivi d'extraits de La Nausée*. Paris: Damase.
Sartre, J.-P. 1949c. *Situations, III*. Paris: Gallimard.
Sartre, J.-P. 1950a. *What Is Literature?* B. Frechtman (trans.). London: Methuen. Translated from Sartre 1948a.
Sartre, J.-P. 1950b. *Iron in the Soul*, G. Hopkins (trans.). London: Hamish Hamilton. Translated from Sartre 1949a.
Sartre, J.-P. 1951. *Le Diable et le Bon Dieu*. Paris: Gallimard.
Sartre, J.-P. 1952. *Saint Genet, comédien et martyr*. Paris: Gallimard.
Sartre, J.-P. 1954. *Kean*. Paris: Gallimard.
Sartre, J.-P. 1955. *No Exit*, S. Gilbert (trans.). In *No Exit and Three Other Plays*. New York: Vintage. Translated from Sartre 1945b.
Sartre, J.-P. 1957a. *The Transcendence of the Ego*, R. Kirkpatrick & F. Williams (trans.). New York: Farrar, Strauss, & Giroux. Translated from Sartre 1936–7.
Sartre, J.-P. 1957b. *The Transcendence of the Ego*, F. Williams & R. Kirkpatrick (trans.). New York: Noonday. Translated from Sartre 1936–7.
Sartre, J.-P. 1957c. *Questions de methode*. Paris: Gallimard.
Sartre, J.-P. 1958a. *Being and Nothingness: An Essay in Phenomenological Ontology*, H. E. Barnes (trans.). London: Methuen. Translated from Sartre 1943a.
Sartre, J.-P. 1958b. *Search for a Method*, H. Barnes (trans.). New York: Random House. Translated from Sartre 1957c.
Sartre, J.-P. 1960a. *Transcendence of the Ego: An Existentialist Theory of Consciousness*, R. Kirkpatrick & F. Williams (trans.). New York: Hill & Wang. Translated from Sartre 1936–7.
Sartre, J.-P. 1960b. *Critique de la raison dialectique, vol. 1: Théorie des ensembles pratiques*. Paris: Gallimard.
Sartre, J.-P. 1960c. *Critique of Dialectical Reason*, vol. 1, J. Ree (ed.), A. Sheridan-Smith (trans.). London: Verso/NLB. Translated from Sartre 1960b.

Sartre, J.-P. 1960d. *Les Séquestrés d'Altona*. Paris: Gallimard.
Sartre, J.-P. 1961. "Merleau-Ponty vivant". *Les Temps modernes* 184–5 (May): 304–76.
Sartre, J.-P. 1962a. "Materialism and Revolution". In his *Literary and Philosophical Essays*, A. Michelson (trans.). New York: Collier Books. Translated from Sartre 1946c.
Sartre, J.-P. 1962b. *Bariona, ou le Fils du tonnerre*. Paris: Anjou-Copies.
Sartre, J.-P. 1963. *Saint Genet: Actor and Martyr*, B. Frechtman (trans.). New York: George Braziller. Translated from Sartre 1952.
Sartre, J.-P. 1964a. *Saint Genet: Actor and Martyr*, B. Frechtman (trans.). New York: Mentor. Translated from Sartre 1952.
Sartre, J.-P. 1964b. Lecture at the Gramsci Institute, Rome, May. Available in the archives of Raynor Memorial Library at Marquette University, Milwaukee, WI.
Sartre, J.-P. 1964c. *Les Mots*. Paris: Gallimard.
Sartre, J.-P. 1964d. *Situations, IV: portraits*. Paris: Gallimard.
Sartre, J.-P. 1964e. *Situations, V: colonialisme et néo-colonialisme*. Paris: Gallimard.
Sartre, J.-P. 1964f. *Situations, VI: problèmes du marxisme*. Paris: Gallimard.
Sartre, J.-P. 1965a. *Nausea*, R. Baldick (trans.). Harmondsworth: Penguin. Translated from Sartre 1938.
Sartre, J.-P. 1965b. *Anti-Semite and Jew*, G. J. Becker (trans.). New York: Schocken Books. Translated from Sartre 1946a.
Sartre, J.-P. 1965c. *Situations, VII: problèmes du marxisme, II*. Paris: Gallimard.
Sartre, J.-P. 1965d. *Les Troyennes*. Paris: Gallimard.
Sartre, J.-P. 1966. *The Psychology of Imagination*, B. Frechtman (trans.). New York: Washington Square Press. Translated from Sartre 1940.
Sartre, J.-P. 1967. "Consciousness of Self and Knowledge of Self". In *Readings in Existential Phenomenology*, N. Lawrence & D. O'Connor (eds), 113–42. New York: Prentice Hall. Translated from Sartre 1948c.
Sartre, J.-P. 1968. *Search for a Method*, H. E. Barnes (trans.). New York: Vintage Books. Translated from Sartre 1957c.
Sartre, J.-P. 1969a. *The Wall (Intimacy) and Other Stories*, L. Alexander (trans.). New York: New Directions.
Sartre, J.-P. 1969b. *Les Communistes ont peur de la révolution*. Paris: Didier.
Sartre, J.-P. 1970. "Intentionality: A Fundamental Idea of Husserl's Phenomenology", J. Fell (trans.). *Journal of the British Society for Phenomenology* 1(2): 4–5. Translated from Sartre 1939b.
Sartre, J.-P. 1971–2. *L'Idiot de la famille: Gustave Flaubert de 1821–1857*, 3 vols. Paris: Gallimard.
Sartre, J.-P. 1972a. *Imagination: A Psychological Critique*. Detroit, MI: University of Michigan Press. Translated from Sartre 1936.
Sartre, J.-P. 1972b. *Situations, VIII: autour de 68*. Paris: Gallimard.
Sartre, J.-P. 1972c. *Situations, IX: mélanges*. Paris: Gallimard.
Sartre, J.-P. 1972d. *Plaidoyer pour les intellectuels*. Paris: Gallimard.
Sartre, J.-P. 1973. *Existentialism and Humanism*, P. Mairet (trans.). London: Methuen. Translated from Sartre 1946b.
Sartre, J.-P. 1974a. *Writings of Jean-Paul Sartre, vol. 1: A Bibliographical Life*, M. Contat & M. Rybalka (eds), R. McCleary (trans.). Evanston, IL: Northwestern University Press.
Sartre, J.-P. 1974b. "The Itinerary of a Thought". In *Between Existentialism and Marxism*, J. Mathews (trans.). New York: William Morrow & Co. Translated from Sartre 1972b, c.
Sartre, J.-P. 1974c. *On a raison de se révolter, discussions*. Paris: Gallimard.

Sartre, J.-P. 1975. *The Emotions: Outline of a Theory*, B. Frechtman (trans.). New York: Philosophical Library. Translated from Sartre 1939a.
Sartre, J.-P. 1976a. *Critique of Dialectical Reason*, vol. 1, A. Sheridan-Smith (trans.). London: New Left Board. Translated from Sartre 1960b.
Sartre, J.-P. 1976b. *Situations, X: politique et autobiographie*. Paris: Gallimard.
Sartre, J.-P. 1977a. "Self-Portrait at Seventy". In *Life/Situations: Essays Written and Spoken*, P. Auster & L. Davis (trans.). New York: Pantheon Books. Translated from Sartre 1976b.
Sartre, J.-P. 1977b. "Elections: A Trap for Fools". In *Life/Situations: Essays Written and Spoken*, P. Auster & L. Davis (trans.). New York: Pantheon Books.
Sartre, J.-P. 1978. *Sartre by Himself*. New York: Urizen. Book of interviews conducted in 1972 for documentary film of same name (dir. A. Astruc & M. Contat, released 1976; see www.imdb.com/title/tt0142822).
Sartre, J.-P. 1979. *Between Existentialism and Marxism*, J. Mathews (trans.). New York: Morrow Quill Paperbacks. Translated from Sartre 1972b, c.
Sartre, J.-P. 1981a. *Œuvres romanesques*. Bibliothèque de la Pléiade. Paris: Gallimard. Comprises Sartre 1938, 1939c, 1945a, 1945c, 1949a and incomplete fictional work.
Sartre, J.-P. 1981b. "Interview with Sartre". In *The Philosophy of Jean-Paul Sartre*, P. Schillpp (ed.). LaSalle, IL: Open Court.
Sartre, J.-P. 1981c. *The Family Idiot*, vol. 1, C. Cosman (trans.). Chicago, IL: University of Chicago Press. Translated from Sartre 1971–2.
Sartre, J.-P. 1983a. *Lettres au Castor*, S. de Beauvoir (ed.). Paris: Gallimard.
Sartre, J.-P. 1983b. *Cahiers pour une morale*. Paris: Gallimard.
Sartre, J.-P. 1983c. *Les Carnets de la drôle de guerre: novembre 1939–mars 1940*. Paris: Gallimard.
Sartre, J.-P. 1984. *Le Scénario Freud*. Paris: Gallimard.
Sartre, J.-P. 1985a. *War Diaries*. New York: Pantheon Books.
Sartre, J.-P. 1985b. *Critique de la raison dialectique*, vol. 2: *L'intelligibilité de l'histoire*, A. Elkaïm-Sartre (ed.). Paris: Gallimard.
Sartre, J.-P. 1986a. *The Freud Scenario*, J.-B. Pontalis (ed.), Q. Hoare (trans.). Chicago, IL: University of Chicago Press. Translated from Sartre 1984.
Sartre, J.-P. 1986b. *The Age of Reason*, E. Sutton (trans.). Harmondsworth: Penguin. Translated from Sartre 1945a.
Sartre, J.-P. 1986c. *Mallarmé: la Lucidité et sa face d'ombre*, A. Elkaïm-Sartre (ed.). Paris: Gallimard.
Sartre, J.-P. 1987. *The Family Idiot*, vol. 2, C. Cosman (trans.). Chicago, IL: University of Chicago Press. Translated from Sartre 1971–2.
Sartre, J.-P. 1988. *What Is Literature? and Other Essays*, B. Frechtman (trans.). Cambridge, MA: Harvard University Press. Title essay translated from Sartre 1948a.
Sartre, J.-P. 1989a. *The Family Idiot*, vol. 3, C. Cosman (trans.). Chicago, IL: University of Chicago Press. Translated from Sartre 1971–2.
Sartre, J.-P. 1989b. *Vérité et existence*, A. Elkaïm-Sartre (ed.). Paris: Gallimard.
Sartre, J.-P. 1990. *Écrits de jeunesse* [*Writings of Youth*], M. Contat & M. Rybalka (eds). Paris: Gallimard.
Sartre, J.-P. 1991a. *The Family Idiot*, vol. 4, C. Cosman (trans.). Chicago, IL: University of Chicago Press. Translated from Sartre 1971–2.
Sartre, J.-P. 1991b. *L'Espoir maintenant: les entretiens de 1980*. Lagrasse: Verdier.
Sartre, J.-P. 1992. *Notebooks for an Ethics*, D. Pellauer (trans.). Chicago, IL: University of Chicago Press. Translated from Sartre 1983b.
Sartre, J.-P. 1993a. *Existentialism and Humanism*, P. Mairet (trans.). London: Methuen. Translated from Sartre 1946b.

Sartre, J.-P. 1993b. *Quiet Moments in a War: The Letters of Jean-Paul Sartre to Simone de Beauvoir, 1940–63*. New York: Simon & Schuster.

Sartre, J.-P. 1993c. *The Family Idiot: Gustave Flaubert, 1821–1857*, vol. 5, C. Cosman (trans.). Chicago, IL: University of Chicago Press. Translated from Sartre 1971–2.

Sartre, J.-P. 1994. "Kean, or Disorder and Genius", K. Black (trans.). In his *Three Plays: Kean, Nekrassov, The Trojan Women*. London: Penguin. Translated from Sartre 1954.

Sartre, J.-P. 1995. *Truth and Existence*, A. van den Hoven (trans.). Chicago, IL: University of Chicago Press. Translated from Sartre 1989b.

Sartre, J.-P. 1996. *Hope Now: The 1980 Interviews*, B. Lévy (interviewer), A. van den Hoven (trans.). Chicago, IL: University of Chicago Press. Translated from Sartre 1991b.

Sartre, J.-P. 2000a. *Words*, I. Clephane (trans). London: Penguin. Translated from Sartre 1964c.

Sartre, J.-P. 2000b. *War Diaries: Notebooks from a Phoney War, 1939–1940*, Q. Hoare (trans.). London: Verso. Translated from Sartre 1983c.

Sartre, J.-P. 2001. "Existentialism is a Humanism". In *Jean-Paul Sartre: Basic Writings*, S. Priest (ed.). London: Routledge. Translated from Sartre 1946b.

Sartre, J.-P. 2002. *Sketch for a Theory of the Emotions*, P. Mairet (trans.), 2nd edn. London: Routledge. Translated from Sartre 1939a.

Sartre, J.-P. 2003. *Being and Nothingness: An Essay on Phenomenological Ontology*, H. E. Barnes (trans.). London: Routledge. Translated from Sartre 1943a.

Sartre, J.-P. 2004a. *The Imaginary: A Phenomenological Psychology of the Imagination*, J. Webber (trans.). London: Routledge. Translated from Sartre 1940.

Sartre, J.-P. 2004b. *Sketch for a Theory of the Emotions*, P. Mairet (trans.). London: Routledge. Translated from Sartre 1939a.

Sartre, J.-P. 2004c. *The Transcendence of the Ego: A Sketch for a Phenomenological Description*, A. Brown (trans.). London: Routledge. Translated from Sartre 1936–7.

Sartre, J.-P. 2005a. *Théâtre complet*. Bibliothèque de la Pléiade. Paris: Gallimard.

Sartre, J.-P. 2005b. "Morale et histoire". *Les temps modernes* 60(632–4): 268–414.

Sartre, J.-P. 2006. *Critique of Dialectical Reason*, vol. 2, Q. Hoare (trans.), F. Jameson (intro.). London: Verso.

Sartre, J.-P. 2007. *Nausea*, L. Alexander (trans.). New York: New Directions. Translated from Sartre 1938.

Sartre, J.-P. 2009. *The Last Chance: The Roads to Freedom IV*. New York: Continuum.

Sartre, J.-P., & M. Contat 1975. "Sartre at Seventy: An Interview", P. Auster & L. Davis (trans.). *The New York Review of Books* (7 August).

Sartre, J.-P. & M. Sicard 1979. "Entretien: L'écriture et la publication". *Obliques* 18–19: 9–29.

Sartre Studies International 2012. "A Symposium on Sartre's Theater". *Sartre Studies International* 18(2): 49–126.

Schafer, R. 1976. *A New Language for Psychoanalysis*. New Haven, CT: Yale University Press.

Schore, A. N. 2011. *The Science of the Art of Psychotherapy*. New York: W. W. Norton.

Sepp, H. R. & L. E. Embree (eds) 2010. *Handbook of Phenomenological Aesthetics*. Dordrecht: Springer.

Sontoni, R. E. 1995. *Bad Faith, Good Faith and Authenticity in Sartre's Early Philosophy*. Philadelphia, PA: Temple University Press.

Stawarska, B. 2001. "Pictorial Representation or Subjective Scenario? Sartre on Imagination". *Sartre Studies International* 7(2): 87–111.
Stawarska, B. 2005. "Defining Imagination: Sartre between Husserl and Janet". *Phenomenology and the Cognitive Sciences* 4(2): 133–53.
Stern, D. B. 2003. *Unformulated Experience: From Dissociation to Imagination in Psychoanalysis*. New York: Routledge.
Stern, D. N. 1985. *The Interpersonal World of the Infant*. New York: Basic Books.
Stern, D. N. 2004. *The Present Moment in Psychotherapy and Everyday Life*. New York: W. W. Norton.
Stolorow, R. D. 2011. *World, Affectivity, Trauma: Heidegger and Post-Cartesian Psychoanalysis*. London: Routledge.
Stolorow, R. D. & G. E. Atwood 1992. *Contexts of Being. The Intersubjective Foundations of Psychological Life*. Hillsdale, NJ: Analytic Press.
Stone, R. & E. Bowman 1991. "Sartre's Morality and History: A First Look at the Notes for the Unpublished 1965 Cornell Lectures". In *Sartre Alive*, R. Aronson & A. van den Hoven (eds), 53–82. Detroit, MI: Wayne State University Press.
Strawson, G. Forthcoming. "Self-intimation, Phosphorescence, *Svaprakāśa*, Conscience (de) Conscience".
Taylor, C. 1976. "Responsibility for Self". In *The Identities of Persons*, A. O. Rorty (ed.), 281–99. Berkeley, CA: University of California Press.
Theunissen, M. 1984. *The Other: Studies in the Social Ontology of Husserl, Heidegger, Sartre, and Buber*, C. Macann (trans.). Cambridge, MA: MIT Press.
Thompson, M. G. 1994a. *The Ethic of Honesty: The Fundamental Rule of Psychoanalysis*. Amsterdam: Rodopi.
Thompson, M. G. 1994b. *The Truth about Freud's Technique: The Encounter with the Real*. New York: New York University Press.
Van Inwagen, P. 1997, "Materialism and the Psychological-Continuity Account of Personal Identity". *Philosophical Perspectives* 11: 305–19.
Varela, F., E. Thompson & E. Rosch 1991. *The Embodied Mind: Cognitive Science and Human Experience*. Cambridge, MA: MIT Press.
Wahl, J. 1932. *Vers le concret: études d'histoire de la philosophie contemporaine: William James, Whitehead, Gabriel Marcel*. Paris: Vrin.
Webber, J. 2009. *The Existentialism of Jean-Paul Sartre*. London: Routledge.
Webber, J. (ed.) 2011. *Reading Sartre: On Phenomenology and Existentialism*. London: Routledge.
Webber, J. Forthcoming. "Sartre on Knowing Our Own Motivations". In *Prereflective Consciousness: Early Sartre in the Context of Contemporary Philosophy of Mind*, S. Miguens, C. Bravo Morando & G. Preyer (eds).
Winnicott, D. W. [1971] 1985. *Playing and Reality*. London: Tavistock Publications.
Zahavi, D. 2001. "Beyond Empathy: Phenomenological Approaches to Intersubjectivity". *Journal of Consciousness Studies* 8(5–7): 151–67.
Zahavi, D. 2002. "Intersubjectivity in Sartre's Being and Nothingness". *Alter* 10: 265–81.
Zheng, Y. 2005. *Ontology and Ethics in Sartre's Early Philosophy*. Oxford: Lexington Books.

Index

absence 27–8, 34, 59–60, 193, 208
  Pierre in the café 95–9, 103, 147
absurdity 9, 48, 50, 52, 66–8
artificial intelligence 222
Althusser, Louis 182
anguish 15, 35, 61, 68, 70, 101–3, 119–20, 125, 128, 153, 156–7, 166–7
authenticity/inauthenticity 3, 6, 10–11, 47, 119, 129–30, 131–42, 168–70, 205, 206, 212, 219
Aron, Raymond 14–16, 46, 55, 175

bad faith 1, 3, 7, 10–11, 29, 35, 42, 46, 56, 69, 76–7, 85–8, 102, 115–16, 118–30, 131–2, 134–5, 137, 139–40, 163, 167–72, 207, 214, 225
Baruzi, Jean 15
being-for-itself 164, 167, 169, 184–5, 196–7
being-in-itself 12, 100, 152, 159, 161, 184–5, 196
being-for-others 110, 115, 168
being-in-the-world 18, 148, 155–6
Being and Nothingness (Sartre) 1–3, 9, 21–2, 32–43, 46, 70, 76, 87, 93–105, 106, 129, 131–42, 143, 145, 149, 152, 164–70, 174–7, 190, 195–203, 207–8, 211, 221–4

Being and Time (Heidegger) 95
Bergson, Henri 1, 10, 16, 24–5, 96–7, 103, 105, 145
Binswanger, Ludwig 91
body 10, 27, 77–8, 80, 84, 90–91, 108, 143, 155, 158, 184–5, 188–9, 192, 222, 225–7
Buber, Martin 117

Camus, Albert 178
Critique of Dialectical Reason (Sartre) 2–3, 7, 9, 83, 180, 187, 194, 197, 203, 213, 218, 234, 236–7, 239
cinema 16, 24, 74
cognitive science 223, 227
cogito 19–20, 35, 37–42, 57, 166, 223
concrete reality 14, 23, 60, 62, 84–5, 95, 112, 114–16, 159–61, 168, 170–71, 197, 203–4, 214, 216, 223, 226
consciousness 6–7, 10, 12, 16–31, 32–43, 54–64, 78–81, 93–105, 118–29, 143–50, 152–61, 165–7, 196–7
  pre-reflective/reflective 19, 22, 29, 34–42, 58–9, 82, 85–91, 99, 120, 126, 128, 133–8, 166, 223–4
  transcendental 12, 21–2
contingency 5, 16, 22, 44–64, 66

Dasein 81, 109, 112
death 22, 49, 53, 57, 68, 74, 78, 120, 128, 214
de Beauvoir, Simone 2, 5–6, 8, 14–15, 28, 45–8, 53, 94, 142, 162, 174–5, 177, 182, 206, 213, 216–18
Deleuze, Gilles 221–2
Derrida, Jacques 209, 218–21
Descartes, René 24–5, 35, 57–8, 80, 145–6, 166
desire 40–41, 45, 56, 61, 79, 81, 83, 86–7, 115, 133, 135, 138, 140, 153–4, 158–62, 169, 185, 203–4, 207–8, 226–7
dialectic 3, 18, 20–21, 30, 114, 143, 171, 186–7, 191–4, 195–205, 206–9, 214, 228
dogmatism 18, 145, 176, 180
Dostoevsky, Fyodor 65, 160
Dreyfus, Hubert 222

ego 32–8, 40, 44, 55–64, 78–81, 86, 105, 110, 121, 166, 170 *see also* transcendental ego, *Transcendence of the Ego*
egological 17, 23
eidetic phenomenology 20, 25, 28, 30, 167
embodiment 107–8, 111, 184, 186, 222–3, 225–6, 228 *see also* body
emotions 3, 28, 29, 32, 35, 81, 154, 174, 185, 222, 225–7
  Sketch for a Theory of the Emotions (Sartre) 2, 6, 16, 28, 35, 76, 137
epoché 19, 23, 29, 34, 57, 61
ethics 2–4, 6, 43, 57, 62, 129, 131, 134, 141–2, 160–61, 175, 195, 205, 206–12, 215, 221, 226
existential psychoanalysis 3, 6, 9, 76–91, 118, 128, 158–161, 169

facticity 10, 42, 87, 122–5, 128–9, 153, 155, 157, 168–9, 188, 226
faith 39, 166–7 *see also* bad faith, religion
Fanon, Frantz 180
fear 50, 119–20, 137, 153, 185
freedom 10–11, 27–30, 46, 87–9, 93–4, 99–104, 114–15, 118–28, 135, 152–62, 164–72, 196–205, 207–9
Foucault, Michel 172, 215, 218–21
Freud, Sigmund 24, 74, 76–82, 85–7, 89–91, 159, 180
future 10, 30, 82–4, 88, 120–21, 124–5, 157, 159–60, 167, 171–2, 175, 178, 186–7, 210–12

gender 187
Gerassi, Fernando 14–15, 173–4
God 49–50, 60, 74, 83, 146, 156, 160–61, 208
guilt 70–71, 129, 170

Hegel, G. W. F. 10, 39, 94, 106, 114, 193, 218–19, 223–4
Heidegger, Martin 10, 15, 17, 27–8, 31, 40, 54, 81, 91, 94–5, 98, 101, 106, 108–12, 114–115, 117, 153, 220, 223
humanism 68, 177, 204–5, 221
  Existentialism and Humanism (Sartre) 1, 3, 8, 131, 141, 199, 203
Husserl, Edmund 5, 10, 12–31, 33–5, 43, 54–8, 61–2, 64, 80–81, 95–6, 105, 106–12, 117, 144–5, 148, 163, 165, 220–21, 223
hyle 17, 25, 30

idealism 13–14, 23, 25, 30, 34, 45, 62–4, 73, 149
Ideen (Husserl) 12–28
image 16, 24–8, 31, 33, 93, 100, 108–9, 111–12, 147
imaginary 25–8, 69, 105, 133, 167, 197
  The Imaginary (Sartre) 2, 7, 76, 93–4, 99–100, 103, 105
imagination 3, 7, 12, 16–17, 22, 24–9, 32–3, 84, 93–4, 99–100, 122, 150, 174, 186
  The Imagination (Sartre) 2, 16, 24, 33, 76
intentionality 17, 19–22, 25–8, 33, 44, 55, 62–4, 80, 82, 85, 105, 149
intentional consciousness 18, 20, 30, 166
intersubjectivity 106–7, 116–17, 223, 226–8

INDEX

Jaspers, Karl 24

Kant, Immanuel 6, 10, 19, 24, 30, 34, 99, 211, 221, 222
Kantianism 19, 21
Kierkegaard, Søren 193, 216
Kuki, Shuzo 15

Laing, R. D. 77, 86, 90–91
Levinas, Emmanuel 14–15, 208
lived experience 15, 85, 91, 145, 161, 214
literature 3, 5–7, 9, 15, 44–5, 110, 157, 163, 175–6, 221
Les Temps Modernes 2, 165, 175–80, 210
look, the 3–4, 70–71, 85–6, 90, 106–17, 123, 168, 185–7, 223–4
love 21, 29, 78, 114–15, 158–9, 169, 185, 198–205, 226
Lyotard, Jean-François 218, 221

Marcuse, Herbert 223
Marx, Karl 3, 6–7, 17, 46, 171, 176, 179–80, 182–3, 193, 195, 202, 206, 208, 214, 218, 220
master–slave dialectic 114, 203, 223
Merleau-Ponty, Maurice 4, 31, 175, 177, 222–6
morality 49, 162, 172, 176, 195, 198–201, 204–5
mortality 10

nausea 44, 50–52, 63–5, 67
Nausea (Sartre) 1, 3, 5–6, 8–9, 22, 50, 53, 55, 58, 61, 63–4, 66–9, 173, 213, 220
Nazism 174
negation 42, 93, 96, 103, 119, 121, 131, 150, 153, 164
Nietzsche, Friedrich 46–50, 52–3, 64
nihilation 39–43, 97, 155
nihilism 74
nothingness 10–11, 17–18, 27, 39–42, 81, 85–6, 88, 92, 93–105, 153, 155, 167

objectivity 165, 168, 190, 199, 204, 224
oppression 142, 172, 183, 188, 192, 200–201, 203

Other, the 4, 19, 21, 23, 71, 85, 90, 106, 108–17, 168–9, 184–94, 199, 202, 204, 207–9, 221, 223–7

past 30, 68, 70–72, 82–3, 85, 87–8, 120, 123–8, 135, 137, 153–5, 157–8, 172, 225
perception 19–20, 24–8, 33–4, 81, 96, 108, 123–4, 222–6
phenomenology 3, 5–6, 12–31, 34, 40–41, 54–5, 57, 61–2, 64, 80–81, 90–91, 94, 117, 130, 143, 163, 219, 222–3, 225, 227–8
Plato 49, 144, 210
politics 3, 8, 12, 23, 31, 44–7, 50, 57, 61–2, 64, 69–70, 73, 128, 163, 165, 167, 170, 172, 173–83, 191–2, 195, 200–201, 203, 208–10, 214–16, 228
psychoanalysis 3, 6, 9, 76–92, 118, 128, 158–62, 169, 180, 214, 220
psychology 3, 6, 9, 23, 28–9, 31, 74, 77, 80, 96, 135, 159, 162, 195, 223, 227

realism 18, 34, 45–6, 49, 54, 64
rebellion 18, 23, 178
reciprocity 4, 91, 206–12
religion/religious experience 15, 136, 138, 212
representation 13, 17, 22–3, 26, 33–4, 42, 58, 103, 166, 223
responsibility 10, 35, 42, 46, 52, 69, 71, 118, 128, 156, 162, 171, 175, 183, 202

Schopenhauer, Arthur 50
self 3, 9–10, 22–3, 29, 32–43, 56–8, 80–89, 120, 125–8, 132, 135, 141–2, 145, 149, 162, 163, 165–72, 196–7, 214–15, 224, 226, 228
self-awareness 128, 166–7, 169, 224
self-knowledge 41, 224
shame 52, 67, 85, 113, 185, 224–5
situation 10, 49, 62, 67, 83, 87, 143, 148, 153, 157, 160, 163–4, 169–72, 180, 184–7, 191, 197, 207, 209–10, 213–15, 225
structuralism 181, 220

subjectivity 19, 34, 60, 108, 114, 133, 164–5, 167–70, 185, 188, 219, 224

thrownness 109, 152, 189
time/temporality 10, 42, 83–4, 102–3, 120–21, 125, 145, 153, 157, 167, 169
transcendence 18, 20, 22, 25–6, 30, 34, 40, 55–6, 61, 110, 122–5, 129, 149, 168, 221, 224
Transcendence of the Ego (Sartre) 2, 32, 34–7, 39, 41, 43, 55–6, 58, 60–64, 76, 86, 165, 167, 221–2

transcendental ego 19, 22–3, 34–5, 56–61, 81
truth 32, 48, 53, 74, 85, 87, 89, 118–19, 122–3, 125, 127–9, 133, 136, 146, 160–61, 168, 205, 210, 217

unconscious 6, 16, 29, 76, 78–81, 84–7, 89–91, 128, 159, 166

violence 57, 71, 74, 209, 221

Wahl, Jean 14
war 10, 12, 44–5, 64, 66–8, 73–4, 163–5, 170, 173–8, 181, 187, 195